The Reluctant Money-Minder

KV-339-458

To the men in my life who taught me
to understand and to spend money, starting with my husband and ending with . . . ?

The Reluctant Money-Minder

By Sheila Black

Whittet/Windward

First published 1980

Text ©1980 by Sheila Black
Drawings ©1980 by Whittet Books Ltd

Whittet Books Ltd , The Oil Mills, Weybridge, Surrey

All rights reserved.

Design by Richard Adams

Diagrams by John Seabright

British Library Cataloguing in Publication Data

Black, Sheila P
    The reluctant money-minder.
    1. Finance, Personal - Handbooks, manuals, etc.
    I. Title
    332'.024   HG179
    ISBN 0-905483-16-2
    ISBN 0-905483-17-0 Pbk

This book is sold subject to the condition that it shall
not, by way of trade or otherwise, be lent, re-sold, hired
out, or otherwise disposed of without the publisher's
prior consent in any form of binding or cover other than
that in which it is published and without a similar condition including this condition being imposed on the
subsequent purchaser.

The publishers are grateful for the kind permission of
the Building Societies Association to reprint the table
on p. 67; and the kind permission of the Controller of
Her Britannic Majesty's Stationery Office to reprint the
tables on pp. 27, 28, 29, 100, 101, 102, 103, the tax
form on pp. 33-6 and the quotation on p. 98.

Printed in Great Britain by
Butler & Tanner Ltd, Frome and London

Page 7
Introduction

Introduction

You need this book because you cannot live without money any more than you can live without love, friendship and people.

You need this book because there are so few books on money but plenty on love, friendship and people.

You need this book because the books there are seem full of confusing financial jargon. Not a bad jargon because, once explained, the words and phrases become logical and easy to remember. But a jargon that is almost another language just the same.

I have tried to translate that language into our everyday English, and to make it more familiar than it probably is to you. Financial experts use the language far too readily, even larding their consumer leaflets and sales brochures with words that only financiers use. They may not be trying to blind us with their skill and science, but perhaps to invest themselves with a little authority, to prove they know more than we do. One of the world's most famous economists, who wrote pretty lucidly (for an economist), once said that using these strange words and phrases engenders trust; that the Holy Bible would carry less respect and authority if written in simple English.

So look upon this book as a kind of dictionary, but with longer explanations as well as a great many useful facts and some practical guidelines to personal financial management.

Some of the figures included will change. Obviously, I can use only the relevant figures as I write and money statistics change with changing circumstances; with Govern-ment changes in policy; with the popularity and strength (or weakness) of our own currency, the pound sterling; with new laws; with the gradual equalizing of opportunities for women; and with inflation, naturally, which erodes the money continually and creates a need for the regular raising of pension payments and other benefits, or with the lowering of taxation (which we all hope will go on, however infuriatingly inaccurate it makes some of the figures in this book).

You also need this book to give you confidence about your money. Confidence to handle your own money, but also confidence to discuss its handling and management with others, with the professionals or semi-professionals you meet as you buy your home, bank your salary or buy your insurance. You can get down to proper discussions if you understand their language and they soon understand that there is no point merely in dazzling you with their expertise.

I also hope that you need this book because it is not boring. Despite its being the essence of life, money can sound terribly boring; most people build up a mental barrier about it, refusing to understand what their intelligence is perfectly capable of grasping. I have tried to avoid too much that is incomprehensible. I cannot explain every-thing in detail or we should have to produce such a heavy, expensively produced book that you would never buy it, let alone read it. For that reason you must take some of the book on trust, and believe me that such-and-such happens because I say so.

I discovered, when doing my research, that there seem to be very few books about the history of money, or rather very few that we can afford to buy. So I have given a little of that which I find interesting and hope that you do too. I am sure you know of the Bank of England, but do you know what it does? You will at the end of the book.

Most of all, I think you need this book because money is one of those things about which you should never have to worry. It is an old cliché but a true one that you need to worry about money only if you have none.

That, alas is not true and more people worry about it when they have just a little more than they need. Enough money is lovely, but who ever has enough? The moment we do have enough, we immediately raise our standards of living or covetousness to make it inadequate, so that we once more feel broke.

Nothing wrong with that. But it is one thing to be broke when you have secured your home, your family's needs and your retirement future. Once you have done those things, you can be as broke as you like because it really does not matter. You will be carefree. And, if you have some spare money after doing those things and buying food and warmth, you can spend, spend, spend.

That is what money management is all about. Doing what you must to liberate your mind to enjoy what you have left over. Money can help to buy happiness. And, if it doesn't, wisdom about money certainly makes being miserable a darn sight more bearable.

Acknowledgements
My thanks to everyone who helped me, especially the spokesmen of the Inland Revenue, the Company Pensions Centre, the Department of Health and Social Security, insurance companies and their associations of brokers and others, the Unit Trust Association, the Stock Exchange, the Building Societies Association, the Bank of England, the Harlow Meyer foreign-exchange dealers and many, many others. Special thanks to Margaret Hutber who grew weary tramping the streets and riding the tubes and buses of London to collect weighty packages of documents and data, figures and facts in her holiday from college where she is now studying economics. To my mother for not interrupting me at work and to my grandchildren for ditto at half-term and in the holidays. To my bank manager for not sorrying about a pause in my earnings while I wrote this book. To the man who serviced my typewriter so fast. To the man in my life for understanding. But mostly to my publisher for her help, her long hard working hours and her patience. To all these, and to anyone I have inadvertently omitted, thank you very, very much.

Chapter One

Banks

Banking, as we shall discover in more detail in Chapter 10, naturally developed from the sheer inconvenience and danger of carrying coins or precious metals around. Not only was it nonsense to carry coins but also the multiplicity of coins became utterly confusing. According to John Kenneth Galbraith, one of the world's most famous and lucid economists, the merchants of Amsterdam had to deal, at the end of the sixteenth century, in literally hundreds of kinds of coins, some silver and some 'debased silver containing copper or other alloys to maintain the size or weight of the coin while lowering the value.

Their beginnings

In 1606, the Dutch Parliament published a manual for moneychangers which listed 341 silver and 505 gold coins, turned out by 14 private mints in that small country alone. To weigh out coins was an awful business and scales were not entirely to be trusted, since it is fairly easy to adjust them to give false readings. So the City of Amsterdam helped, by guaranteeing its funds, to set up a bank which took in foreign coins, debased coins, worn coins and such; the payer-in then had credit with the bank at a kind of official valuation rate, with a deduction of only the bare expenses of handling. Credit thus became as valuable as the actual ownership of coins, and institutions like banks soon sprouted in other Dutch cities, especially in trading cities like Delft and Rotterdam. The merchants trusted the banks until 1672, when the army of Louis XIV threatened

Amsterdam; then the merchants dashed to draw out their coins which had – they assumed – lain so long unused and untouched in the vaults while they all traded in pieces of paper like cheques. The fear that their coins might not be there suddenly spread; the relief that followed the discovery that the bank was as honest as everyone had supposed led to an eternal trust in banking. But, by the late eighteenth century, dramas lay in store for Amsterdam, when the Dutch East India Company began to lose ships and money while at war in Britain. Loans made to the company were not being repaid to the bank and merchants were in trouble. The bank finally closed down in 1819, more than 200 years after opening. But the system, already spreading to England, remained.

Banking probably originally began in Italy with the great Medici family, and the banking houses of Venice and Genoa (two trading ports, and you must have noticed how money follows traders) were becoming famous wherever traders travelled. The banks came and went during the thirteenth, fourteenth and fifteenth centuries, for there were many failures as the bankers put up the money for trade and ships liable to disaster. Gradually the banking system moved inland, especially along the fertile Po river valley where agriculture and manufacturing settlements began, and therefore through the plain of Lombardy. The practice spread to London, so that the street on which moneylending (as distinct from modern banking) began was called Lombard Street as it still is today.

The combination of the Dutch deposit system and the Italian lending system led to relatively sophisticated banking in Britain, which has learned much from the failures of its forerunners abroad. Banking spread through the old and new worlds rapidly, fostered by some bad and many wise and good people. Crashes became fewer and laws stricter so that people were protected against their own rashness and gambling instincts. Just as the Bank of England (see Chapter 10) emerged as the guardian of the nation's money supply, so did reputable banks with government blessing worldwide. The Bank of England's own history, chequered by wars, government intervention and stiff demands for more cash (for wars or for peace), as well as by the natural vicissitudes of trade, became the history of other central banks, and the Bank of England has exported more know-how about how to keep countries and their currencies stable, about how to manage money, more than any other entire industry in this country.

Our high street banks, the 'Big Four' and some others, were born, as were their systems and methods, of a blend of commercial banking from Italy, central and national banking from Britain and 'paper' banking from the Americans. It was a very long time before private individuals used banks for their private means. Even now, many people stick to depositing their money in the Post Office, a Trustee Savings Bank, a building society or some organization other than the Big Four (National Westminster, Midland, Lloyds and Barclays). Of the Big Four, National Westminster (Natwest) has about 3,600 branches with Barclays close behind at about 3,200. Midland has 2,700 and Lloyds 2,300. The numbers fluctuate a little from time to time. These latter banks are called 'clearing banks', the Big Four are most familiar but there are altogether eight of them in England and Wales; the others being Williams and Glyn's (actually a subsidiary of National Westminster) with some 300 branches; Coutts (also a subsidiary of Natwest and the Queen's personal banker);

the Trustee Savings Banks; and the Co-operative Bank (of the Co-operative Wholesale Society). Fifty-five people out of every hundred use these banks. Scotland runs its own system with Bank of Scotland, Clydesdale Bank and the Royal Bank of Scotland which, as we shall see in Chapter 10, still prints its own banknotes.

A clearing bank

These have mutually co-operative clearing services so that money circulates between them all freely and it is possible to pay money into any one of the eight banks for transfer to any of the others, just as it is possible to draw money from any bank as long as a bank card from one of the other banks confirms the drawer's credit-worthiness.

A clearing bank must — like one of the Big Four — keep in stock any money it might need to meet customers' immediate demands for withdrawals — huge sums require a little notice but few of us ever need such sums without warning. A bank must also by law hold a good fund of 'reserves' in Treasury bills (paper bonds issued by the Government, which must honour them in cash if necessary, though they may have varying redemption dates). And it must keep something like 60 per cent of its funds in cash available to customers as loans, overdrafts or such. This proportion of the reserves may vary from time to time under Bank of England edict and control; if the Bank of England thinks money is available to us all to spend too freely, thus upsetting its economic policies to limit spending, then it may reduce the proportion. The idea of curbing our spending is to prevent us buying too much more than we make within our shores, thus increasing the value of imports, and destroying our balance of payments (on the one hand, our income from exports, and, on the other, our expenditure on imports). This, in a nutshell, is Britain's notorious balance of payments problem. When the Bank of England imposes restrictions on the amount of money banks may lend, she is 'tightening her corset'. Banks will then be sticky about overdrafts and loans for certain periods, suddenly beginning to advertise such facilities again when the money supply is allowed to run more freely.

Banks are also investors (mainly in safe Government stocks and shares). The investment experts are not necessarily at your nearest bank but at headquarters or the 'centre'.

Clearing banks (and other banks too) deal as much with traders and businesses as with private customers. The banks take deposits of money, which are reclaimable on demand; more money and more trade are 'created' by lending from the depositors to those who need temporary finance over and above what they have put into the bank. They then use the money to trade at a profit (we all hope) and put more money back into the bank, and so on. When they lend large sums of money, the banks generally lend it 'against security'; if anything goes wrong, they have a claim on the security, such as buildings or shares, whether they be held by a company or an individual.

There are various types of lending and borrowing — such as short- or long-term — but most of us need be concerned only with personal loans, home improvement loans or overdrafts. In Britain, most clearing bank lending tends to be short-term, unlike the longer-term lending of European banks.

Banks, which started mainly as guardians and lenders, are now providers of many, many professional services. Initially, they needed the professionals to handle their own legal, investment and other affairs as well as to be trustees of their depositors' money in life and death. Gradually, it made sense to 'sell' such professional services to their depositors. Obviously, not every service is available at every branch, many of which are simple depositing and withdrawing branches, but they are so widely available as to be near at hand for almost everyone.

The Banks can administer the estates of the dead, look after tax affairs, and plan your income or estate so that you save as much tax as you possibly can. Many a bank will look after your personal tax affairs and help to make wills. One Barclays bank manager in West London told me that he has more trouble — and his clients land themselves in more expense — over badly made wills than almost anything else. There was one horrific case where a mother had, by making her will foolishly or at the wrong time, actually left all her money to her step-children while her own children got none of it, something she had clearly never intended. There is provision for the law to be umpire if someone left out of a will contests it on the grounds that it was not what the deceased intended. But such litigation is costly and long drawn out and it is really everyone's duty to make a proper will if he or she loves his or her chosen heirs. The confusion can be terrible.

Banks will also buy and sell stocks and shares for you, and keep the certificates safely. Many of them have direct links with unit trust companies and can handle the buying and selling of these too, not always only in their own unit trusts. They can help with most investment services, in fact.

Their travel services extend beyond merely arranging for foreign currency or getting travellers' cheques and they can arrange many insurances.

They have savings schemes, student accounts, all sorts of services. If you examine the booklets tucked into those pockets near the counters or doorways, you will be surprised at what a bank can handle for you. It may be that you will need to make a special appointment and that the expert you want to see comes to your branch on a Thursday morning or Friday afternoon.

My own opinion used to be, and still largely is, that you should choose your bank manager very carefully and that, having chosen him, you should stay with him if possible even when he moves, as long as he doesn't move too far away. One can cash cheques anywhere, so the actual closeness of your particular bank to your home is not very important. Things have changed a lot and modern bank managers are generally a better, more understanding race with much knowledge of their clients as well as their jobs. So my opinion has largely changed. It is your relationship with the bank that counts. Your doings (and mis-doings) are on record and no amount of friendship with the manager can change that, so it is important to keep the record straight. That means that you confide in the bank at all times, telling them why you want to overdraw and for how long, whether or not you are in financial trouble or likely to be, whether you plan to sell and buy a house, and so on. It is not always necessary to bother the manager, whose deputies will probably be *au fait* with your file and be able to help or advise. But honesty is very important.

I am often asked if it is cheaper to use a bank's professional services on tax, wills, estates and such than to use other professional services. It is not but then it is very rarely costlier either and it is usually a great deal more convenient. On the other hand, I do not think one always gets such a personal service as one does from a chosen lawyer or accountant. That varies from branch to branch, manager to manager and client to client. Some of the latter are just damned irritating, and any bank manager would be forgiven for showing them the door. Banks will tell you exactly what the fees are for various jobs and deduct the sum from your bank account when the work is done. One advantage is that they do know all your financial affairs, and the best part of your financial history, so that can save a fair amount of time since you would have to explain it to a solicitor or accountant. The real point about money is that one should shop around for the services connected with it, not just settle on the bank or the advertiser whose name catches your eye. I do believe one should borrow from the banks. Indeed, it is best to put all one's borrowing into one lump, from one

source (apart from the mortgage on your home, that is) and to make arrangements for repayment in a way that suits you.

Bank charges

Never forget that bank charges, which are partly composed of handling charges, can add up like crazy if you write masses of cheques and it is cheaper as well as simpler to have all your affairs if possible under one account, though there are special circumstances calling for more than one account (such as a joint account, a savings or investment account, etc.). In fact, so much can cheque transactions add up that it often makes sense to draw fairly large cash sums and to pay for a lot of small items in cash. Those repeated cheques for a few pounds here and there to one person or firm are just plain and expensive nonsense.

You can always keep charges down – to nil in fact – by keeping your current account (the one you use for paying and drawing out your more or less daily or weekly needs) in credit. Each bank states an amount at which charges are not made: all the banks are at pretty much the same level. A truly sophisticated financier might try to tell you that the charges and interest on being in debit are small compared with what you might be making on the money on the Stock Exchange. Such arguments can be sound but they take no account of how much can be lost on the Stock Exchange by the unwary and unknowing.

When times are bad and you need to borrow – or even if they are good and you want a loan – it will also be much easier if all your affairs are in one place. Do not start writing cheques which you have not the money to cover in the hope the bank will meet them. Just at first, they may not 'bounce' the cheque (which means they refuse to meet it, and send it back to you marked 'Refer to Drawer': it is 'bounced' back to you). They will write or telephone and try to talk to you about it. Do have that talk, because they do want to help.

Luckily for the banks, seven out of ten people never get into the red (red ink was for debits and black for credits when accounts were done in pen and ink by hand).

Borrowing from banks

Personal loans

These may well be the simplest way for you to borrow money – not always the cheapest, but certainly the one most likely to be readily available if you have a bank account, and, let's fact it, you probably need the money without undue delay if you have decided you need to borrow at all. Mostly, loans start at £50 and go up in multiples of £10 so that you can take exactly what you need: don't take a penny more, because you have to pay interest on the loan. Do not be tempted to think you are borrowing easily and can take just that little more than you need. The bank will almost certainly want to know what the loan is for and may advise you what you can manage from what it knows about you. Listen to that advice. On the other hand, don't take too little and watch your current account running into the red because that kind of 'red' may cost you even more in interest than the personal loan. Interest rates for personal loans vary according to the Bank of England's minimum lending rate (MLR).

MLR is just what it says: the minimum lending rate available anywhere. MLR used to be called the Bank Rate but that was thought misleading because it implied that you could actually get that rate on bank overdrafts, which was never the case. The rate on which you borrow at the bank, on whatever type of loan, will be above MLR – how much above depends on your record, your assets, the time you need the loan and a good many other things including whether or not the loan is secured by assets that the bank can realize if you were to default (the bank having a hold over such assets). You will probably, however, pay 3 per cent above MLR.

With a personal loan, the interest rate is fixed right at the beginning of the loan and remains constant throughout until you have fully repaid. All the interest is added to the capital sum and then divided up into monthly repayments; you are therefore not paying interest on a reducing sum, but on the same capital sum throughout. Some medium-term loans do give you the benefit of a reducing sum. It will cost more than most overdrafts, but you may not be given an overdraft. Since interest rates vary from time to time, and your loan is fixed, you may benefit as they rise or 'lose' a little as they fall; for the term of your personal loan, you will probably find you neither gain nor lose by paying the constant rate rate fixed at the start, because interest rates go up as well as down.

Every schedule of repayments is bound by law to give you the 'true' rate of interest over a year. These true rates vary according to the period over which the loan is made and the true annual rate is slightly higher for the whole of the first year than for a short six-month loan. The rate is at its highest between 18 months and 24 months, after which there is a gradual fall. The reason is that the bank is little out of pocket, as it were, on the really short loan and yet wishes to encourage customers. On the longer loan, the bank has time to invest its money so as to get a better chance of a good return or profit on it and can afford to lend at slightly lower rates. The medium-term loan is the more difficult one for them being neither one thing nor the other and therefore carrying a number of unpredictables about it. As I said, personal loans are never cheap but often the only kind you can get easily.

If you are fit and well and under 60 or 61, the bank will probably give you free life cover during the loan period so whatever is outstanding on the loan is fully paid off at death, leaving your heirs out of trouble. If unhealthy and over 61, you could still arrange some insurance, but you would obviously have to pay the premiums. This can be done through the bank or your normal insurer.

Everyone will want to know your reason for borrowing, whether it be for a new sofa or a holiday. They won't disapprove so be truthful about it. If the loan is for the home, to improve it or to add to it or some such thing, the loan may well be eligible for tax relief (see Chapter 3). If in doubt, ask the bank in any case for a certificate of interest paid and you and your accountant or your local tax office can sort out its eligibility. Business loans may also qualify for relief.

Anyone over 18 may apply for a loan, and the whole thing is normally arranged pretty quickly and informally. The banks have minor variations among themselves but they run mostly in parallel with each other on the terms and agreements. In some cases, there are government rules about how much you may borrow and for how long and these change periodically, often being announced by the Chancellor in his major annual Budget, but sometimes in between. The bank will know, of course.

Overdrafts

These may well be the cheapest way to borrow because the interest is calculated on a daily basis, and you can thus take advantage of falls in MLR. The interest charged is usually a few percentage points above MLR. and it can vary according to your credit rating at the bank. You are charged always on what you owe at any given time. It is not as easy to get an overdraft as a personal loan. However, since tax relief is never available on personal overdrafts, but is available on certain loans (for home improvements, etc.), the loans in such cases may not be more expensive.

Though private customers provide the bulk of the bank's deposits, they get no more than about one-sixth of the money available for lending. That is not as unfair as you might think, since the business of the bank is not to take risks with its money; in fact it tries to make money out of its money,

which is why it lends to enterprises that will make profits (everyone hopes). Private customers find it less easy to get overdrafts than businesses and they usually pay higher interest rates. But the money is there, in varying supply according to the country's economic health and wealth, so do apply.

An overdraft can really be a long-term loan, but you must ask for one. Your bank manager will give you a date by which he would like it cleared, usually six months. Then, if the debt is still outstanding by the agreed time, he will want to know more about you and he may agree to 'roll the credit' and to extend the term of the overdraft. If you are wise, you will contact him any time you are about to 'go into the red' because it creates a good impression and shows you are aware of your responsibilities. Then, after the next six months, contact him again. Be trustworthy as well as creditworthy.

Also be sensible. While a personal loan for a car or a holiday may be acceptable practice, an overdraft is not. If you have someone to guarantee the overdraft, it may help, but remember the guarantor has to pay up if you fail to do so. They don't grow on trees. If you have shares, an endowment-life policy or some such thing, those also count as assets or security against which you might get an overdraft.

Home improvement loans

These are like personal loans, geared to home improvements. Loans start at £500 and go on up to £10,000 over any period from one to five years though some banks might look at seven years under certain circumstances. The total interest and the loan are added together and the whole is repaid in equal monthly instalments over the agreed period. There will be an arrangement fee at the outset which is usually 1 per cent of the sum borrowed and this covers the legal and other costs of making the agreement. A personal insurance policy to cover the loan is essential and can be arranged independently or through the bank.

The interest rate is fixed at the start and this can vary from one borrower to another depending on his assets and securities. If the loan be covered by shares, an insurance policy, a trust that will revert to you, something of that kind, then interest rates might be a little lower than for the borrower who has nothing but his credit rating, particularly if this isn't very good. On the whole, these are relatively inexpensive loans, especially as the interest is properly subject to tax relief (which needs a re-check with the Inland Revenue).

Home loans

These loans for buying homes, or for topping up loans from other sources, such as the standard building society mortgages, are a relatively new departure for banks. There are few leaflets about because they can be such individual loans, tailored to each borrower, so talk to your bank manager or his deputies about them. Generally speaking, they are advanced to clients of the bank for anything up to ten years on the basis either of monthly repayments or lump sum repayments at stated or haphazard intervals. They should also qualify for tax relief (see Chapter 3) on the interest and should be worth consideration by high taxpayers. The problem of whether to borrow cheaply (because of the tax relief) on the home or to pay off the mortgage (when one has the money) is a complicated arithmetical problem and I advise anyone who does not fully understand it to get expert advice. For some, it might pay to have a home loan of some kind, to take the tax relief and to invest any spare money. The income from the investment may well not be enough to cover the out-payments if the investment surcharge is paid (see Chapter 2): but, if one's unearned income is small, the investment surcharge will not 'bite', and the whole thing looks different. It is not possible to lay down rules or tables since each individual case differs so. But in later life or when there is some expectation of a financial wind-

fall, bank loans for the home might be a good idea. They are more flexible, repayable with lump sums as pension sums are paid or endowments mature, and the low overheads are probably very welcome, as may be the shorter borrowing term.

Secured loans

These loans are, as the name suggests, fully secured by giving the bank first 'charge' on an asset. That means that, if the loan is not repaid, the asset is sold to pay the debt; the bank has first priority over the sum realized for the sale and may take its debt out before you can get the use of the rest of the money. The asset may be your home, your insurance policies, your stocks and shares. The arrangement is much as above for the home loans, though sums may be limited to about £5,000 maximum. In the case of your house, you may be able to agree with the bank that it has a second mortgage after the building society or whoever holds the first mortgage. This would be possible in the event of the value of your home far exceeding the value of the first mortgage. Not a cheap way of borrowing but, again, useful to some. Read the proposal carefully. You may notice that the interest rate seems exceptionally cheap. But look more carefully and you will notice that the 'effective' rate is actually higher. The explanation is that you pay the same interest each year for two years, although the sum borrowed is reducing all the time. You are not paying interest on the reducing sum, you agree instead to certain fixed sums of interest. There is nothing wrong with such an agreement and it is much more convenient for most borrowers, to say nothing of the lenders, to have these known, predictable fixed-sum agreements. Of course rates are not always as above and may vary as you take out your loan, but it will probably cost more than a building society loan. You repay in equal monthly instalments (hence the way they work out interest to keep all the payments equal over two, three or however many years you borrow). There would be an initial administrative and legal charge when you arrange the loan, not usually a large one.

Budget accounts

These are accounts with the bank, through which you can borrow. They are a very good idea for those who just cannot manage money and for the always broke. And here a word of my philosophy. I do not condemn those who can't manage money. I condemn only those who will do nothing about their mismanagement. Banking today is so sophisticated as to make help easy. With a budget account, you sit down and work out all the essential bills you are likely to face in any given year. Add something for contingencies. Include rates, fuel bills, holidays, clothes, everything. Then divide the total by twelve or thirteen, and arrange with the bank (most of them will do it) to transfer a regular sum every month or every four weeks to a budget account from your current account. As the bills arrive, write a cheque for them from your budget account, as long as no bill actually exceeds one quarter of the total commitment. Sometimes you will be in credit, sometimes in debt with the bank.

Naturally, the bank charges for handling your money in this way, usually about £10 for the first £200 and £1 per £50 or part of £50 thereafter. At certain times, you may be slightly overdrawn but, because the bank knows the account will be in credit again soon, with the next monthly instalment, and the overdraft is purely temporary, there will be no interest or any other charge for it.

Apart from helping the feckless to manage money, a budget account can actually save money. For example, one could buy a season ticket or the annual road fund tax licence, both of which are cheaper bought annually than monthly or quarterly. This kind of account is only useful to those with regular incomes so that some freelancers should not be encouraged (and might be refused such an account). The scheme has different names according to the bank but all are pretty much the same.

Credit cards

If you think you are not a borrower, but you use a credit card, think again. This is fast becoming the commonest form of borrowing through Access, Barclaycard, Diners, American Express and the many, many credit cards operated by shops and stores for credit buying of their own merchandise. The stores mostly use one of the leading credit card firms like Barclaycare (Barclaycard), an American bank or two and others. Some stores actually run their own credit systems.

Interest rates vary but are mostly anything between about 2 per cent and up to 3 per cent a month. Note that — per month — so multiply by 12 for the total annual commitment. Not that it works quite like that because, by law, you must pay off something of your debt every month to try to lower it, so that the outstanding amount varies from one month to the next. You pay interest only on what is outstanding and not the original debt you incurred. Not a cheap way of borrowing by any means but quick, convenient and free of questions after the first application form and all its questions have been answered and your credit checked.

Credit cards are not popular with everyone and there are many who still think that borrowing or buying 'on tick' is disgraceful; and so it is if the card-holder/borrower exceeds what he can afford — that is the disgrace, not the borrowing. My own advice to all is to decide on and to set your own credit limit, regardless of what the banks allow. (For, although credit cards seem bottomless pits of money, they only allow you to owe a certain amount on them; if you overstep, they will refuse to pay out on your behalf.) Go as far as to write to them and say that you wish your limit to be even more limited and you will probably sleep better at night. We can all resist almost anything but temptation, as Oscar Wilde put it, so we are often weak about our credit cards. Be wise and enjoy them. They can save money, you know. The furniture or the builder or the washing machine may all cost you several pounds more in two or three months. To buy now with a credit card rather than pay the higher price can be very sound finance.

The credit limit obviously varies and the bank's right to refuse a card is absolute. Students may get cards with a limit of about £50 and others may well be held down to £200 or £250 — the national average is around those figures. Few people get more than £500 credit.

You pay nothing for the card, since the bank is making money on the interest charges. With other credit cards, as distinct from bank cards, you pay an annual subscription (American Express, Diners, etc.). Now that Barclay and Access cards are becoming more acceptable abroad as well as in so many outlets here in Britain, there seems to me little point in having anything other than Barclaycard although credit may well be more extended on the private cards. Department store account cards are subject to the same laws as bank credit cards and you have to pay a monthly minimum. Better than the old days when some thoughtless customers, often the very rich ones, let their accounts run into hundreds of pounds of unpaid bills which led to higher prices for everyone and so to penalization of the good payers.

Discount cards

You may have one of these because you are a director or a friend of the organization, a special shareholder, an employee of the civil service or even of the store or shops where you work. Discount cards mean that you pay cash but get an agreed discount. There is a national concern called Countdown which issues such cards on payment of an annual subscription. The idea is that credit cards actually cost a company money since they pay a service fee to the credit card company; so they are willing to give discounts for cash down. Some say it is worth asking for discounts for cash anyway. I haven't done it, but hear stories from those who successfully have. Discount cards are not issued by banks but should be mentioned in the context of credit cards.

Keep all cards safe and make a note of their numbers. Telephone the card operator with your number as soon as you lose one (or even think you have lost it). Have the card stopped and a new one issued so that your card cannot be used for any longer than the short period before you report it and it goes on the black list. Confirm by letter. If you find your card, cut it up into useless pieces and tell your card operator what you have done. A credit card is money. Guard it carefully.

Your credit rating

Any time you fill in an application for a loan, for hire purchase, for credit cards, for a mortgage or an account with a store, your credit rating is likely to be checked (though the bank may well rely on its own knowledge of you). It is worth noting that your credit rating, which is on file, can be altered if you redress some of the wrongs of the past. Do not resent what is on record about you but, if you find yourself being refused loans or credit cards, etc., do find out. There are specific credit reference companies which keep records and they must by law open their books to you as far as your own personal entry is concerned.

Ask the firm that checks your credit for a specific application for the name of the company which vets their would-be clients. You ask for this information under Section 157 of the Consumer Credit Act of 1974 and the answer must be sent to you within 28 days. You may then visit or write to the credit-vetting concern and see your file on payment of a fee (currently 25p).

Should the file show you in an unfair light, you might be able to have the credit rating changed. For example, it may show an uncleared debt which you have since paid off. Prove how you have righted your wrongs and the record can be put straight, but do not try to lie or your record gets worse and worse. If the credit-vetting company disputes or refuses, take the whole matter up with the Office of Fair Trading. You may not need this service, but few people seem either to know about it or to use it so I thought it worth bringing to your attention.

Bank accounts

Drawing money out

People used mostly to draw money only from the branches where they had their accounts, except by special arrangement at other banks. Cheque cards have changed all that, enabling bank account owners to cash their cheques at any bank in any town, to pay by cheque at shops and railways stations and generally to be sure of being able to pay their way. The card sets an upper limit on each person — usually £50 per day for adults with an average banking record but less for some and for students. The limit may vary as inflation attacks it, so that the upper limit (only £30 when cards were started) might rise still further.

Students, by the way, will need the guarantee of a parent or guardian to get a card at all. May I plead that parents and guardians should never give such guarantees too readily. It is difficult and seems rather mean to curb the young, but they can be their own worst enemies. Better perhaps to start with Post Office accounts, which can be opened anywhere and which allow money to be withdrawn from anywhere — but only if the book shows a credit. There are often special terms for students at banks, including no bank charges. But there should be some supervision of the young while they learn.

Anyone can draw from his or her own bank without a card; though, unless known to the cashier, it might be easier to use the card which saves the wasted time of the man or woman having to go to the back of the bank to look up your name and financial state. At Barclays, the Barclaycard credit card counts as a bank cheque card.

As banks become more electronic, there are other plastic cards that allow withdrawals from machines at any hour. As yet, these machines are not at all banks but they are becoming increasingly available and they allow withdrawals of anything from £10 to £200 according to your credit rating and the type of card as well as the type of machine. Such service tills are usually of the keyboard kind and you can even get a statement of your current account at some. Very useful when banks are crowded. It is, alas, only too easy to get money out. What we need is to find the magic formula for easy paying-in or, rather, for earning the easy money to pay in. By the way, you can always pay money into someone else's account (as long as you know the branch and bank), though, obviously, you cannot draw from other accounts without special 'Pay bearer' cheques.

When you write your cheque and draw out the money, the cheque goes to London or head office for clearance. Banks have long been centralized and the credits and debits computerized, which speeds up everything. You get your credits more quickly but your debits are also more or less instantaneous by computer. At one time, it took several days, even when the posts were reliable. If you have made a cheque out to someone else (the payee), the cheque goes from his bank to the London clearance. The cleared cheque returns to your bank and your account is then debited and the new total of balance or overdraft immediately recorded on your statement. It takes about three days for a cheque paid into another bank to reach yours. It is at that stage that the 'bouncing', if any, occurs: your bank, seeing your account descending too horribly into the red, will call a halt and refuse to pay out on your behalf.

Stopping a cheque

Should you write a cheque twice, change

your mind about a payment, fail to like the goods you bought with a cheque or something of the sort, you can stop a cheque at any stage on its journey to your bank. (But beware: if you merely change your mind, the payee can sue you.) Telephone, then write a letter confirming the stop. Give the payee's name and the cheque number and date as well as your own name and account number. If the cheque has been met, you are too late and have to find other ways of getting your money back. Incidentally, cheques written under guarantee of a banker's cheque card cannot be stopped. Worth remembering if you are an inveterate mind-changer.

Joint accounts

I don't like them. While I do advocate that everyone has a bank account rather than stashes their cash beneath the bed, I also believe in separate acounts, even for the closest of loving turtledoves. Some banks like joint accounts where children are involved, but that is rather different; and the point there is probably that it involves two signatures so that the parent or guardian can countersign the cheques and so make sure the child is learning the proper ways of handling money.

Why should a married couple have a joint account, especially when she might be deemed to be the 'agent' rather than the principal and so will not be able to draw on the account when he dies until after the will is proved? Then again there are dangers. One partner may not tell the other what he or she has drawn out, either from fear or forgetfulness. Such unpredictability can push the account into the red.

I really do think adults ought to handle their affairs separately without getting jealous. If they must have a joint housekeeping acount into which both pay then make sure it really is joint and not his, with her as agent or vice versa. Open it together, confirming that both have equal rights. But it is much, much better for each to have a separate account. Anything either contributes to the other can go into it and he or she should meet the responsibilities of paying whatever it is intended to pay for. Suppose divorce hits: I know of one couple personally where he walked off with the £4,000 in their joint account. True, she finally won her half back, but with difficulty and after a long time. NO joint accounts, that's my advice.

Deposit accounts

When you put your money on deposit you agree to give notice before withdrawing it of seven days, a month, three months, or whatever. The normal description is to say the money is on seven-day call or three-month call and that you will not 'call' or draw the money except at such seven days' or three months' notice. Interest on such deposit is automatically transferred to your account at a percentage below MLR (often 2 per cent but it varies with the term of deposit among other things). You have to declare to the taxman any interest you get as the next chapter on tax will tell you. Such interest counts as unearned income, obviously enough, because you do not actually work for it.

Standing orders and direct debits

These are useful ways of tranferring money from bank to bank to meet regular payments without using cheques and having to remember to draw money, post it on by cheque or cash and maybe default on an important payment like the mortgage or an insurance premium. The joy is that you can order such payments and then relax, always provided you make sure that your funds are there to cover such outgoings. In fact, that is the one slight danger of such payments, that some bank customers forget about them when working out how much available spending money they have each month. Direct debits are agreements where the payee applies to your bank directly for money from your account; you sign a form assigning him this right, and he can therefore vary the sum without giving you notice.

I prefer the standing order and have usually insisted upon it even when asked to transfer by direct debit. It has the advantage that you always know where you are but is naturally inconvenient if the payments vary in amount at all, such as payments geared to interest rates. Watch direct debits, however, and check carefully, because I have twice known the same debit to be made twice by one firm, actually a Government department. Always check bank statements anyway. Computers can make mistakes too. A chore, I know, but so is being short of money. I find the easiest way is to fill in the counterfoils of cheques and paying-in-slips or books, so that you can check at leisure and know roughly where you are when the statements come in. It is much easier to keep a running check, or to monitor short periods, than to struggle through the bank statements and cheque stubs over a longer period.

There are other banks, apart from the clearing banks, but they are gradually becoming more and more alike.

Trustee Savings Banks

Originally exactly what the name implies, with limited banking services, these have become real clearing banks with similar services, but not yet quite so many, as the Big Four. They have access to the clearing systems, lowish bank charges but no overdrafts, though they do extend personal loans of various kinds. They have their own unit trusts, like the Big Four, save-as-you-earn schemes and they sell Government stocks 'over the counter'.

National giro

A Government institution that offers some of the services of banks to people who have no bank accounts. Works closely with the Post Office. Deposit your money with any of the country's 21,000 Post Offices and you can draw from them amounts of up to

£30 every other day (remembering that Post Offices are open only five and a half days a week).

You can transfer funds by National Giro to anyone who has a National Giro account, and your telephone, fuel and other bills will have a special form on them for this particular transaction. Postal transactions are free of postage and the Post Office will provide you with a free envelope. Standing orders are free, statements are free and there are personal loan schemes arranged through one of Britain's leading finance houses, Mercantile Credit; you can get details from any of their branches. Since giro is not wholly understood by many and not therefore acceptable in many shops and other places, it is awkward to have only a giro account, although it may also be cheaper for those with little money. Some shops will not accept giro cheques.

National savings banks

Simply another extension of the Government's banking services, like National Giro. They used to be called Post Office Savings Banks and sometimes still are, wrongly. These accounts are purely savings accounts and come in two kinds. The ordinary savings account allows you a maximum deposit of £10,000 in one or more National Savings Banks. You have no cheques but can use warrant forms from any Post Office. You can draw up to £50 in any one day but you may draw more than £30 only twice in any week without your bank book being taken away to the centre for your balance to be checked. Interest rates on such savings accounts are low, as you would expect if you are allowed to draw money on demand.

Investment accounts at National Savings Banks attract greater interest and you can deposit up to £50,000. Interest must be returned for tax, of course (the first £70 is tax-free). I am a great believer in opening such accounts for children (they can actually use them when they are seven) and trying to teach them the value of banking and of saving, of managing money while they are really young.

Merchant banks

You are very unlikely to have any dealings with merchant banks except, indirectly, through some insurance or unit trust schemes. Very few have current account clients, although they are opening a few branch offices. They are mainly of interest to those starting their own businesses or acquiring others, needing business help and loans, arranging foreign exchange and gold or silver transactions, leasing equipment and so on. Vital to British trade, they derive from the old lenders to trading merchants and are still the traders' banks. You will often see their names in stories of takeover bids and the defence of such bids, but they will rarely enter your lives or mine.

Fringe banks

United Dominions Trust, better known for personal loans and hire purchase, comes readily to mind as one of those that, along with many, many others, nearly went crashing in 1974-5, but was baled out by the Bank of England's lifeboat (see Chapter 10). Some of the interest rates and terms fringe banks offer look attractive, but be careful. As described in Chapter 10, they come directly under the jurisdiction of the Bank of England now so you will be able to check very surely. Unless you know what you are at, stick to the Big Four or the other clearing banks.

Finance houses

These offer mainly hire purchase; originally started to help people and companies buy their goods and equipment in easy instalments, they evolved the kind of hire purchase we all know today. All the finance houses are strictly under government control just as the clearing banks are. Indeed, their money comes mainly from banks and other financial institutions. They themselves advance personal loans and some take deposits from savers. These offer deposit interest that can be very attractive. As a rule, one can pay in fairly small sums, though most special accounts look for a minimum of £1,000. They are trouble-free since they assess current interest rates and adjust their interest accordingly. Interest is payable twice yearly. Rates are normally competitive. The names are familiar, such as United Dominions Trust, Mercantile Credit, Lombard or such; in order to lend, they need to borrow.

Apart from managing the hire-purchase agreements of most stores, shops, manufacturers and others who offer their goods in this way, the finance houses will advance personal loans, whether secured or not, and they are generally most sympathetic about loans for home improvements.

Use only one with a good reputation — your own bank may have links with a finance house or be able to recommend one. If in doubt, don't deal, is the best advice I can give. Read the small print very carefully, insist on getting a clear table of what your payments are over what period and be quite, quite sure of what you are in for this year, next year and sometime. Hire-purchase and personal loans from finance houses can no longer be referred to as 'never-never' schemes because there must now legally be a limit on the term of repayment, unlike the bad old days when you might have found yourself on a treadmill of debt.

Hire-purchase rates vary from one company to another so look for a true annual rate (which they are bound in law to give you) very close to the bank's rate for personal loans — H.P. will always cost more so bear that in mind. You must, with a hire-purchase transaction, put down some kind of deposit by law and you may borrow for up to 2½ years on most goods or 2 years only on a car.

You do not own your purchase until it is fully paid off, and the lender has the right to seize it and sell it to recover his debt if you persistently miss the payments. But the law says he must first take you to court for the money. Your financial standing will be checked after the lender gets your application form. If you fall on bad times and cannot meet the payments, ask the finance house to extend the period or to allow smaller payments or something. Work it out with them, because they are pretty human. Never get more than £100 in arrears because that way you will have to pay the lender's legal costs in recovering the money in England and Wales (Scotland has its own laws in this and many other respects).

The credit price is not to be confused with the purchase price: it is the total of the money owing plus all interest on it plus administrative or legal costs. After you have paid one-third of the total credit price, then the lenders must get a court order to 'seize' the goods to sell in order to recover their losses. In fact, they try to find other ways of settling the matter and will try to talk to you or to negotiate before going to such extremes. If you ever do get into arrears or other trouble over such loans, come clean with the lending company and try to make some arrangement that you can stick to until the debt is paid off.

Should you find that you just cannot cope at all with the payments and feel you have to return the goods, you must legally pay any instalments missed between your last payment and the time you return the merchandise. If you have paid off less than half the credit price — once again I stress that phrase 'credit price' as being larger than the actual purchase price of the article — then you must make up the difference between what you have paid and that half.

If you have failed to look after the goods, or damaged them in any way, you are bound to pay compensation to the lender or get the goods put into mint condition yourself.

Doorstep loans are illegal, so turn away anyone who tries to offer them unless you have specifically asked them to call on you in writing. And please read advertisements carefully because you may think you are simply filling in a form answering the advertisement and asking for more details, only to find you have also signed your name to a written request for a salesman's call.

There are still people getting themselves into hot water when they really are being more and more protected by government, so if ever in any doubt at all, do go to the nearest Citizens Advice Bureau, consumer service or your own bank. Never pay or sign anything about which you are unsure, that you do not fully understand. I cannot repeat that often enough. Advice is still cheaper, even when it has to be paid for, than a bad mistake.

You may use a credit broker who, like the members of the C.M.B. (see Chapter 3) may not charge you more than £1 until he fixes you up with the loan you seek and even then you have six months to think about the loan offer. Some may seek a deposit, returnable in law unless you take out the loan he arranged for you. That is legal but I would refuse it and go to someone else. Really, the sharks are easy to identify. So why do more people not do so?

Chapter Two

Taxes

When capital gains tax was first introduced in this country, there was much weeping and gnashing of teeth. The man who got my admiration was the one who wrote a letter to the *Financial Times* of which the gist was: 'Will anyone please tell me how I can become liable for this tax?' Right on, as they say down under. Always start with the premise that you are lucky to be earning or gaining enough to qualify for payment of taxes. Anyone who does not qualify is, in modern financial terms, fairly near the bread-line. Also be glad to live in a nation that is resonably full of taxpayers, especially of honest ones. Never join the brigade of 'It is just not worth getting a rise/promotion, etc., because it all goes in tax.' Even at its worst, and it has been awful, direct taxation has rarely reached 100 per cent and you always get some change out of extra earnings. Of course everyone is entitled to decide whether the small extra sum is worth the large extra effort and to decide that unpaid leisure might be preferable, but at least the Government leaves you something.

My own view is that it is also rather a waste of time, effort and peace to spend too much time on looking for legal tax loopholes, on playing the tax avoidance game to the limit. I remember a conversation once with Brian Epstein, the man who discovered, groomed and built up the fame and popularity of The Beatles famous pop group, talking about his office administration and the number of people who seemed to work fulltime on avoiding tax; on forming new companies and launching new enterprises; on holding funds abroad when they were needed in the U.K.; or any conceivable legal tax dodge they could dream up. He had counted up their combined salaries or fees, looked at their luxury offices and glamorous secretaries, studied their entertainment expenses (non-deductible, of course) and decided that it all seemed to add up to his firm spending a lot more than the gentlemen claimed they were saving him. 'Does it make sense? Can't I just pay the tax, keep the change and save the hassle?' He meant it, too, but it didn't work out like that for him. I don't blame his premature death on the tax avoiders but the stress and anxiety or his corporation life, to a man who was an individualist and entrepreneur, were undoubtedly contributory factors.

It bears repeating — and you will find I repeat it often — that money should help people to enjoy life and that it should never be allowed to harass, to intrude, to worry its owners. I am not suggesting sheer lunacy, or even that one should pay all one's demands blindly. Quite the opposite. I do not think one should pay tax demands without questioning the appropriate accountant or employer. It takes a devil of a long time to get rebates of overpayment, though they do come in the end, and one's bank account suffers in the meantime.

Accountants

But I do believe in the pay up and don't complain policy, as long as you are sure that you have claimed all the allowances to which you are entitled. There are plenty of advisers about, and getting tax problems sorted out is a lot easier than getting sound advice on almost any other aspect of personal finance. A good accountant is necessary if your earnings are complicated, coming from many sources or involving several different types of taxation. He is also necessary — or a good solicitor specializing in tax — when it comes to making wills, leaving money, giving money away, running a business, buying and selling land and a host of other things which bear tax liability.

Never be tempted by accountants who boast about what they can save for you. The Inland Revenue knows its contacts pretty well and certainly knows who it can trust after long experience. Take an accountant who enjoys good relations with the Revenue men, who will be the true and honest middleman, because he serves you best. I cannot say for sure, but I think most tax offices have their private black list, especially of accountants.

You will hardly need an accountant if you are on simple pay-as-you-earn (PAYE) earnings, where tax deductions are made at source. Your paycheck may look rather disappointing but at least those hefty bills that come through the letterboxes of the self-employed will not invade your home. Do query your code number (see p. 37) if the tax deductions look too high. The fault may be yours, and you may not be disclosing something that could help you, such as mortgage or insurance payments or premiums. Never be fearful of questions and never be fearful of the Revenue, Look them up in your local phone book under 'Inland Revenue', go to your appropriate office and ask them for help and explanation. They really are kind, human and often quite lucid. They are not out to grab, but to be fair, to take their dues and leave you yours.

There is a curious idea in many minds that you have to go to Bootle to sort out your tax queries because that is the office address on all your tax correspondence. That is not so; as tax offices and computers become more and more centralized, the

advisers in local areas become more and more helpful. Look up your telephone directory for your nearest branch and you will find one pretty close to you. In any case, you would be surprised at how much you can do by telephone. But please do have your papers by you when you telephone because you will need your reference number and do quote that number on all correspondence. It may be stating the obvious to say that the tax year or 'fiscal year', runs from April 6th to April 5th.

Keep your personal accounts as neatly as you can and carefully file all notes of mortgages and such things because they attract tax reliefs and some people do not claim such reliefs, foolishly, because they fail to keep proper records. If you are on wages or salary, with PAYE (pay-as-you-earn) deductions made by your employer at source, your personal accounts will be very simple. If you are self-employed, whether part-time or fulltime, it is a legal duty to keep accurate accounts. If you hate book-keeping, try to find a book-keeper. You would be amazed, in many areas, at how easy this is. Retired accountants, bank managers and others are often glad of a little freelance work to relieve their leisure as much as to earn a little extra money. Asking small local businesses or shops may be a way of tracking one down, but advertising in local papers often produces a willing book-keeper. My own happens to be my hairdresser's wife, a competent book-keeper who loves the work and looks after her husband's business as well as a few freelancers reluctant to handle the chore. Obviously, if you are methodical by nature or have a willing and competent spouse, lover or friend, you may not need to advertise.

Whatever you do, do not think of your accountant as a book-keeper and merely bundle all your bills into an envelope for him. He (or she) is a costly professional whose charges for simple book-keeping, charged by the time it takes for him or his employer company, will come to a goodly sum. You will naturally have to pay him less for simply auditing clear and well-kept accounts. Such charges are deductible, of course, as a business expense.

Incidentally, if you are for your main job on PAYE, but self-employed part-time, you must declare such earnings and include them on your tax return. Suppose you write short stories (but not enough to live on) or repair cars, then such earnings must be shown, and the proper account of the relevant costs, expenses and freelance income must go in with your simple tax return. Your code number will not be changed but you will have to pay tax twice yearly on the freelance 'profits'. You do not make two separate tax returns which, I am told, many people believe to be the case.

And now for our tax system, which is divided into two main classes: direct and indirect taxation.

Direct taxation

This is sub-divided again into four parts:

1. Unified income tax

Mostly payable through PAYE for those on salaries or wages. As stated, the employer is bound to deduct tax from all such payments according to the relevant code number of the employee, the code number being settled by the tax office for that district. The code takes into account your allowances and reliefs and it is the guide to the amount of tax to deduct, listed in printed tables which are issued to all employers. At the year end, you will get a form that tells you what tax you paid during the year on what income and adds how much was either underpaid or overpaid. Alas, you may find that you underpaid, but you are not asked for a lump sum to meet the difference; your code number can be adjusted to make small extra payments to meet the deficit through the year after the underpayment. PAYE payments and deductions are made weekly or monthly according to when you are normally paid.

The self-employed receive their fees 'gross', with no deductions. They pay their tax twice a year, in January and July, and get charged interest on any sums overdue. If they have failed to put in their annual accounts, on which their tax liability is assessed, they may be charged too much and it is up to them to appeal (or to get their accountants to do so) but the appeal must be backed with some reliable documentation and, preferably, their accounts. The self-employed, when paid, should put aside an estimated sum for tax which will become due or he/she might get into arrears that become difficult to pay.

2. Investment Income Tax

Which means tax on income that is unearned as opposed to the income for which you work, that you therefore earn. Unearned income may include dividends from shares, interest payable on invested capital (at the bank or a finance house of some kind), rent on a second property or part of your house, that kind of thing – anything for which you do not actually work. You are allowed to get up to £5,000 a year of unearned income without paying a higher percentage rate than on your earned income, but you pay a surcharge over and above the standard levels on more than that total.

3. Capital gains tax

Is the tax you pay on gains made by selling or giving away valuable belongings, shares, houses (other than your owner-occupied home), paintings and such.

4. Capital transfer tax

Is payable on gifts of money or property that is worth money. If you give away during your lifetime, you get taxed at a lower rate than on gifts made in your will, or after your death, and you are allowed to give up to a certain sum, plus some smaller sums, without declaring such gifts for tax.

There are other direct taxes but, since they mostly concern businesses, farmers, agriculturalists and property developers, I think it unnecessary, even time-wasting to go into them here. They do, in any case, need expert advice as and when they arise and most people affected by them have such professionals retained by their businesses.

So we come to

Indirect taxation

Which covers Value Added Tax, Customs and Excise duties (such as are built into the prices we pay for spirits, tobacco, wines, cigarettes, etc.), petrol tax, stamp duties on property purchases and share purchases, and so forth.

So much for the main taxes that we pay. Before paying them on our incomes, we are allowed to claim a number of allowances and reliefs.

Allowances

These are the sums you are permitted to earn before you start paying tax, the tax-free slice of your income. First, everyone gets a personal allowance. A single person's or an earnings wife's allowance is at the moment £1,165, the result of a substantial increase made in the June 1979 Budget, and it is widely expected that this and other allowances will rise fairly regularly in order to decrease the sum we pay in direct taxation while indirect taxes may well increase.

The married allowance is £1,815, and the husband gets the full allowance on his income, the wife only being allowed the single person's allowance (unless the couple choose to be separately taxed, of which more later). That may also change as the move towards equality accelerates. But I am afraid that, however much it does accelerate, there is no way of accelerating tax reforms to high speed because the Inland Revenue staff are already overworked, understaffed and way behind with the existing tax systems; the

implementation of new ones can be very complicated and time-consuming until, in about 1984, the computer can speed things up considerably. The poor old Revenue are constantly accused by liberationists of unfair sexist practices, when the truth is quite simply that they would love to keep abreast of the times but just cannot cope.

Additional personal allowance
(A.P.A.)
These are designed to be added to the personal allowances of single people with sole care of the child or children. The A.P.A. is £650 and, if you add that to the single person's allowance, you will notice that it brings single persons up to the same allowances level as a married man with wife. The A.P.A. goes to single parents or to husbands with disabled wives who cannot look after the children, provided that he has the continuing care of the children.

The old child allowance has now been phased out and superseded by bigger, tax-free cash allowances for each child, called 'child benefit' and drawn from the Post Office just as senior citizens' pensions are. The benefit changes with time, as do personal allowances, though one could hardly pretend that either keep abreast of inflation in recent years. There are also allowances for children or students too old for benefit who, because they are studying fulltime and still dependent on parents, would otherwise be too big a drain on their parents and might therefore be forced to give up studies. There are allowances for parents living overseas but with children in Britain and there are rights for step-children, about which too few people know so that the Inland Revenue comes in for some unfair criticism on this score. Changes concerning children and students are still in a rather fluid state and it is advisable always to ring up the local tax office which you should do about any section you don't understand on the form you get every spring for the return of your income and claims of allowances, reliefs, etc.

Tax payable

All earned income					
Single person				Married person where no wife's allowance	
On total income of	People under 65 years old		People over 65*	People under 65 years old*	People over 65*
	No dependants'	One parent family†			
£	£	£	£	£	£
1,200	8.75	—	—	—	—
1,400	58.75	—	—	—	—
1,600	108.75	—	15.00	—	—
1,800	158.75	—	65.00	—	—
2,000	213.00	46.25	115.00	46.25	
2,500	363.00	171.25	250.50	171.25	11.25
3,000	513.00	318.00	400.50	318.00	136.25
3,500	663.00	468.00	550.50	468.00	276.00
4,000	813.00	618.00	700.50	618.00	426.00
4,500	963.00	768.00	850.50	768.00	576.00
5,000	1,113.00	918.00	1,000.50	918.00	726.00
6,000	1,413.00	1,218.00	1,413.00	1,218.00	1,218.00
7,000	1,713.00	1,518.00	1,713.00	1,518.00	1,518.00
8,000	2,013.00	1,818.00	2,013.00	1,818.00	1,818.00
9,000	2,313.00	2,118.00	2,313.00	2,118.00	2,118.00
10,000	2,613.00	2,418.00	2,613.00	2,418.00	2,418.00
15,000	4,588.25	4,295.75	4,588.25	4,295.75	4,295.75
20,000	7,030.00	6,705.00	7,030.00	6,705.00	6,705.00
25,000	9,721.75	9,364.25	9,721.75	9,364.25	9,364.25
50,000	24,663.50	24,273.50	24,663.50	24,273.50	24,273.50
100,000	54,663.50	54,273.50	54,663.50	54,273.50	54,273.50

*The tax shown takes no account of any allowances other than the lowest personal allowance that everyone gets, plus the A.P.A. (Additional Personal Allowance) or Age Allowances in the relevant places.
†A single person with school age or student child gets the lower personal allowance plus the A.P.A.

Tax Payable

On total Income of	All unearned (investment or property)					
	Single person			Married person	
	People under 65 years of age		People over 65*	People under 65 years of age*	People over 65*
	No dependants*	One parent family†			
£	£	£	£	£	£
1,200	8.75	—	—	—	—
1,400	58.75	—	—	—	—
1,600	108.75	—	15.00	—	—
1,800	158.75	—	65.00	—	—
2,000	213.00	46.25	115.00	46.25	—
2,500	363.00	171.25	250.00	171.25	11.25
3,000	513.00	318.00	400.50	318.00	136.25
3,500	663.00	468,00	550.50	468.00	276.00
4,000	813.00	618.00	700.50	618.00	426.00
4,500	963.00	768.00	850.50	768.00	576.00
5,000	1,113.00	918.00	1,000.50	918.00	726.00
6,000	1,563.00	1,368.00	1,563.00	1,368.00	1,368.00
7,000	2,013.00	1,818.00	2,013.00	1,818.00	1,818.00
8,000	2,463.00	2,268.00	2,463.00	2,268.00	2,268.00
9,000	2,913.00	2,718.00	2,913.00	2,718.00	2,718.00
10,000	3,363.00	3,168.00	3,363.00	3,168.00	3,168.00
15,000	6,088.25	5,795.75	6,088.25	5,795.75	5,795.75
20,000	9,280.00	8,955.00	9,280.00	8,955.00	8,955.00
25,000	12,721.75	12,364.25	12,721.75	12,364.25	12,364.25
50,000	31,413.50	31,023.50	31,043.50	31,023.50	31,023.50
100,000	68,913.50	68,523.50	68,913.50	68,523.50	68,523.50

* The tax shown takes no account of any allowances other than the lowest personal allowance that everyone gets, plus the A.P.A. (Additional Personal Allowance) or Age Allowance in the relevant places.
† A single person with school age or student child gets the lower personal allowance plus the A.P.A.

Allowances for the elderly/infirm

There are also allowances for supporting elderly relatives and, in the case of married couples, these can include in-laws on the same basis as one's own parents. The cost of support must be in excess of £75 a year to qualify for tax relief, and that seems little enough these days. The relative need not be either inform or totally incapable but can merely be widowed or divorced, maybe living with son or daughter in a state of depression or simply for company and comfort. The relative's income must not

What you can earn without paying tax

	PAYE code ending in letter	£ £
Single or wife's earnings allowance	L	1,165
Married allowance or single allowance plus additional personal allowance (A.P.A.)*	H	1,815 (or £1,165 + £65 A.P.A.
Full single age allowance	P	1,540
Full married age allowance	V	2,455
Age allowance income limit		5,000

* The A.P.A. is the allowance given to certain people who have single-handed responsibility for children. The single allowance and the A.P.A. together are equivalent in amount to the married allowance.

be more than the basic National Insurance retirement pension for a single person; or, if it is, your tax allowance is reduced by £1 for every £1 over and above that level, which is fair enough and does not put the poor at a disadvantage against richer people receiving allowances since the latter must sacrifice tax benefits.

This brings us to one possible pitfall. If a husband and wife choose to be assessed and taxed separately (see later in this chapter), each may claim only for his or her relative and not the in-laws. You are however allowed to share the cost of elderly relative support with another member of the family, such as brother or sister.

The elderly may also claim tax relief for the maintenance of a son or daughter living in to care for the old or infirm, though a married man is not able to claim such relief unless his wife is also old and infirm or in some way unable to care for him. Presumably, the same would be true, if it

isn't already, of a wife's claim unless the Revenue persist in the idea that women do the looking-after and that men are incapable of it. Legislation is gradually equalizing the drawbacks as well as the benefits of being either male or female. It may be better business to claim a housekeeper's allowance for the son or daughter because the permitted maximum is £100 (as compared with £55 only for a member of the family). Such housekeeper allowances are legally payable to relatives (excluding wives) but, since there are moves to iron out this slight oddity, the two rates may become the same before long. Blind people get bigger allowances than those with other disabilities. None of it is very generous but government is pledged to do more for the unfortunate. The trouble is that far too little was ever done in the past and catching up is both expensive and time-consuming.

Age has a tax advantage called the 'age allowance', added to the basic personal allowances of anyone, male or female, over 65 years old. Thus the tax-free earnings of a 65-plus person are now £1,540 (instead of the £1,165 of younger single people). A married couple over 65 gets £2,455 (as compared with £1,815). There is, however, a limit of £5,000 and, should you earn more than that in old age, your allowances are reduced by £2 of age allowance for every £3 of income in excess of £5,000 until the normal levels are reached for single person's allowance (£1,165) or married allowance (£1,815).

For example, take someone over 65 earning £5,600 in a year. That being £600 above the permitted £5,000, he/she will lose in age allowance

$$\frac{£600}{3} \times 2 = £400$$

Thus he or she loses the entire age allowance of £375 and gets down to the normal person's level. If the earnings were £5,500 the sum would be

$$\frac{£550}{3} \times 2 = £366.66$$

In such a case, the age allowance lost would be not quite as much as the total allowance so that an age allowance of £8.34 would remain.

Wrongly, some people believe that pensions and annuities are not taxable. Of course they are — some think unfairly since they were often 'bought' out of taxed income and so pensioners might be paying twice on a portion of their pensions. However, most private pensions are bought out of tax-deductible contributions so there is really very little unfairness, the higher extra pensions only being possibly penalized in this way. War widows' pensions became exempt from any tax in the June 1979 Budget whether payable in U.K. or from a foreign country.

State pensions are also taxable if the total income comes to a taxable sum. Thus, on the annual tax return, one must include the senior citizens' pension (still called the old age pension here and there, though decreasingly so) along with other income from all sources. A word of warning to married men. Do not pass your wife's pension over to her without first deducting the tax that may be due on it because you may never get it back. Pensions are not subject to deductions at source and the male is still responsible for her dues as well as his.

Blind people are given an extra allowance of £180 per year — but if they receive the £75 disability allowance, this must be deducted.

Children

In the old days of special child allowances claimed by the parent(s) or guardian, a child's earnings rights were offset against such allowances. Now a child who earns money (in amounts exceeding the personal allowance), be it from newspaper deliveries, mushroom picking, modelling or running the occasional disco gigs, must make such returns (or have them made on their behalf).

He/she gets the full single person's allowance on earned income, like any adult, regardless of whether the child still lives at home and regardless of age. Even a baby who may model for TV will have a separate tax return and the single person's allowance.

Parents must return a child's investment income on their own annual return forms because any income derived from investments made by the child's parents is deemed to be part of the parent's unearned or investment income. This is essential to avoid loopholes because parents could get away with not paying the investment income surcharge that operates on unearned income of more than £5,000 per annum. A man with four children, if rich, could otherwise invest enough in the names of four children to yield him an extra £20,000 a year without paying the surcharge, besides his own £5,000.

Deeds of covenant

There may be tax advantages in giving money to a child by means of a legal deed or covenant, especially if the child is a minor and not your own. Say a grandfather gives his grandson, under covenant, £1,000 per annum. Grandfather, provided that he has adequate taxable income over and above the gift (which he ought to have), may deduct tax at 30 per cent and actually hand over only £700 cash. Grandson may then claim his personal allowance of £1,165 at the moment to the

to the £700 and the Inland Revenue will give him a 'refund' of £300. Thus Grandfather's £700 becomes £1,000.

That looks like magic and it is. But be warned. If the child is earning, there will be no chance of the £300 as he will already be claiming his personal allowance (if only a proportion of it, then the balance can be claimed against the covenanted gift).

There are no reliefs for higher rates of income tax in any covenant, whether between relatives or ex-spouses. Since present payments to ex-spouses now carry similar reliefs to those of covenants, few now pay alimony under such deeds.

There is no advantage for parents to give

by covenant while the son or daughter is under 18 and unmarried, since the child's payment will be looked upon as the parent's income and not eligible for personal allowances. Nor is there an advantage between husband and wife. Once the child is 18, then he can claim his personal allowance, and there may be a benefit in the parent giving him a deed of covenant if he is not earning (though in the case of students there can be pitfalls as regards grants, so consult your accountant).

Tax reliefs

Tax reliefs are not the same as allowances though their effect is the same — to reduce the amount of tax payable. Such reliefs are allowed on mortgage interest and insurance premiums — not on every pound of the premium unless you happen to be self-employed and buying one of the special self-employed annuities. As things stand, you still get a part of your endowment-life insurance premiums for tax relief (see Chapter 4) but these are not necessarily constant levels. Indeed, there is a Government plan being considered to stop tax reliefs on insurance premiums altogether but the change will not take place until the level of direct taxation has dropped to give us more spending money so that we can actually afford the premiums. To strike the balance between what the reliefs are worth and what extra money we keep after paying tax is to work out a very complicated equation so changes may be slow. At the moment, you get relief on 17½ per cent of premiums.

As it is, you now do not have to pay the full premium and then claim the tax relief on your annual return form as previously. You now pay reduced premiums — the insurance company will tell you what — and the life assurance companies reclaim in bulk, as it were, the tax relief on all the premiums they receive. More work for the companies, less for the Government. There is a limit above which premiums carry no

tax relief, that being that such premiums should not total more than one-sixth of your total income. This is one respect in which the annual return form will have changed from those you knew in the past.

Before and after standard rate tax

After the allowances and reliefs we get a small tranche of income at a low percentage rate of tax before reaching what is called standard rate tax. The 1979 Budget dropped the standard rate to 30 per cent (from 33 per cent). But, before it is payable, there is a tranche of £750 (above the tax-free allowances) taxable only at 25 per cent. Married couples get only one £750 band between them, not £750 each unless each is earning in which case each does qualify for it. Frequently, Mrs Thatcher's Government has reiterated its dedication to lowering direct taxation as and when possible, the 'as and when' being the capability of the Inland Revenue staff to cope with change. When standard

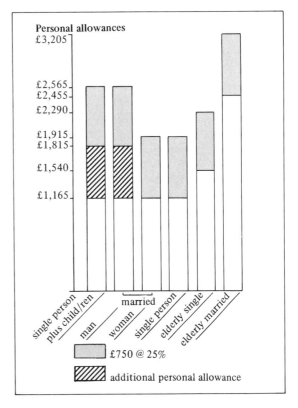

Personal allowances

- £750 @ 25%
- additional personal allowance

rate was dropped, there was also an increase in the level of earnings at which it was payable, before one got to the higher tax rates (from 40 per cent to a maximum of 60 per cent on earned income plus a surcharge of 15 per cent on unearned).

At the time of going to press, the tax levels are as follows on your 'taxable income' — which means your income *after* deducting your personal allowaces:

£1 - £750: tax is payable at 25 per cent
£750 - £10,000: tax is payable at 30 per cent
£10,000 - £12,000: tax is payable at 40 per cent
£12,000 - £15,000: tax is payable at 45 per cent
£15,000 - £20,000: tax is payable at 50 per cent
£20,000 - £25,000: tax is payable at 55 per cent
All income above £25,000 tax is payable at 60 per cent

Company cars

I have already underlined that it is one's legal duty to return all income from all sources, whether salaried or freelance or from partnerships and other business in which you might have an interest. I have not said that you are also supposed to enter fringe benefits like the company car. Some portion of the value of this benefit is allowed as a genuine business expense and some is regarded as personal and pleasure usage so that the value of the latter may be added to your income and regarded as 'extra income'. The relative values of the two sectors obviously vary from one case to another. If you claim a high business mileage, you or your accountant may be asked to prove it. If you are self-employed, there may be a case for keeping a diary of mileage, etc., but this is usually not necessary provided the claims are fair. Self-employed people rarely get a company car though some salesmen's contracts are to be self-employed, with the loan of a car. Employees' cars are usually sorted out by

the employer company which returns the car expenses every year to the Revenue. You must also return such benefits on your annual tax return form. Do not forget, if you have a company car, to check with your employer under what conditions you have it, what your business use is and so forth. Again, this kind of 'fringe benefit' is under the shadow of the Conservative Government's axe hatchet, due to be phased out as possible tax benefit when lower income tax frees more of our personal spending money. The same hatchet will possibly deal with such things as staff discounts for certain goods or services, even of the employers' own goods and services, season ticket loans and rented suits.

Golden handshakes

Golden handshakes carry some tax benefit; compensation for loss of office must be properly documented and the tax relief is not automatic but must be agreed with the Inland Revenue as such compensation — anything above £10,000 is taxable. Payments on retirement are at the moment 'ex gratia' payments and may carry more tax advantages than 'compensation' payments. There are expected to be some changes in this area soon. Nothing is automatic with the Inland Revenue, so do not expect it to be so, and always have written proof of how and why you received unusual payments of this kind.

How tax is deducted

PAYE (Schedule E)

I shall explain the schedules a little later but, for now, let's look at how your tax is taken from you. As I said, you get a code number which tells your employer how much to deduct in tax from your income. The numbers stand for the total of your permitted allowances without the final digit. If your allowances plus tax reliefs this is the form for most of us on PAYE; high earners and the self-employed have a different one. Always keep a copy. Don't worry if you make a mess of it — initial your corrections.

INCOME: Year ended 5 April 1979

Amount for year

the form is due for a change, and if this doesn't change, there will be some angry voices

fill this in if you're a hairdresser, waiter, taxi-driver, etc.

	See Note	Details	Self £	Wife £
EARNINGS		Own full-time employment. You need not enter details or pay relating to your own full-time employment but you must enter tips below.		
	1	Wife's employment — Employer's name and address / Works No. (if any)		
	2	All other earnings — Type of work		
		Name and address of anyone for whom work done		
	3	Tips and incidental receipts from ALL sources		
		If the duties of your employment were performed wholly or partly outside the United Kingdom tick "√" here ▶		

Expenses against earnings

	See Note	Details	Self £	Wife £
	4	If a fixed deduction applies tick "√" here ▶ [Self] [Wife]		
		Where no fixed deduction applies state nature and amounts of expenses		
	5	Fees or subscriptions to professional bodies — Name of professional body		
SOCIAL SECURITY PENSIONS AND BENEFITS	6	Retirement pension or Old Persons' pension. If wife's pension paid as a result of her own contributions tick "√" here to claim wife's earned income allowance ▶		
	7	Widow's and other benefits — Nature of benefit .... (See identity page of Order Book)		
OTHER PENSIONS	8	Pensions from former employer and other pensions (including war widow's pension) — Payer's name / Address		

ALL PENSIONS—FURTHER DETAILS

THESE DETAILS WILL HELP ME GIVE YOU THE RIGHT PAYE CODE

Please state here the current weekly/monthly/quarterly rate of each Social Security or other pension you receive	Nature of pension	Self	Wife	State "Weekly", "Monthly" or "Quarterly"
		£	£	
		£	£	
		£	£	

If you or your wife are likely to begin receiving a pension before 6 April 1980 please state:	
	Nature of pension ....
	Starting on (date) ....
	Rate of pension .... per week/month/quarter ....
	Payable to (self or wife) ....

page 2

this means 'how much'

in the new form there will probably be a space for you to enter details of life insurance (though tax relief will have already been deducted from your payments)

INCOME: Year ended 5 April 1979*(continued)*

could also include building society bonds

this will be a net amount as tax will have been deducted

this means the tax you had deducted

this will be the gross amount

this should include any part-time work

	See Note	Details		Amount for year	
				Self £	Wife £
INTEREST NOT TAXED BEFORE RECEIPT	9	National Savings Bank *including any exempt amount (see note 9)* Trustee Savings Bank — *Enter all the interest from each account* — Ordinary account ▶ / Investment account ▶ / Ordinary account ▶ / Investment account ▶			
	10	Other banks *Name of bank*			
	11	Other sources *(including Co-operative deposits and British Savings Bonds and other Government securities).* *Nature of source*			
INTEREST FROM BUILDING SOCIETIES	12	Name of Society *Enter all the interest from each source*			
DIVIDENDS FROM U.K. COMPANIES AND UNIT TRUSTS	13	Name of U.K. company/Unit Trust Self Wife	*Amount of dividend* £	*Amount of tax* credit £	
OTHER DIVIDENDS INTEREST ETC. TAXED BEFORE RECEIPT	14	Name of payer *Enter the gross amount for each holding*		Self £	Wife £
RENTS FROM FURNISHED OR UNFURNISHED LETTINGS	15	Address of property	Gross income	Expenses *(enclose statement)*	
PROFITS FROM TRADE OR BUSINESS	16	Type and address of business			
OTHER INCOME	17	Maintenance, alimony or aliment received *Gross amount before tax deducted* ▶			
	18	Income from abroad *Nature of income and country of origin*			
	19	Any other income not entered elsewhere *Nature of income*			

page 3

OUTGOINGS: Year ended 5 April 1979

	See Note	Details			Amount for year Self £	Wife £
INTEREST ON LOANS *(excluding bank overdrafts)* **FOR PURCHASE OR IMPROVEMENT OF PROPERTY**	20	**Only or main residence** Interest payable —to a building society or local authority	Name of lender	Account number	*I will be advised of amount by lender*	
	21	—to anyone else including a bank or insurance company **Let property** number of weeks let ▶ —address			*Enclose certificates*	
	22	Other property where loan incurred before 27 March 1974				
INTEREST ON OTHER LOANS *(excluding bank overdrafts)*	23	Qualifying loans	Name of lender		Self £	Wife £
	24	Any other loans incurred before 27 March 1974			*Enclose certificates*	
OTHER OUTGOINGS	25	Maintenance, alimony or aliment *(excluding voluntary allowances)*	Payable to			
	26	Payments under Deed of Covenant or Bond of Annuity			Enter GROSS amount before deduction of tax	
	27	U.K. property rents or yearly interest paid to persons abroad				
ALTERATIONS IN UNTAXED INCOME OR OUTGOINGS SINCE 5 APRIL 1978	28					

CAPITAL GAINS and Development Gains: Year ended 5 April 1979

	See Note	Details		Self	Wife
CHARGEABLE ASSETS DISPOSED OF	29	If total proceeds exceeded £5,000, tick "√" here .. .. ☐ If total net gains exceeded £1,000, tick "√" here .. .. ☐ *If you have ticked either box please state—* Date of disposal │ Description of asset(s) *The note explains the position regarding losses*		Amount of gain £	£
CHARGEABLE ASSETS ACQUIRED	30	Date acquired │ Description		Cost or acquisition value £	£

page 4

from the company who made the loan

this might be a loan for a car used in your employment

show the gross amount, and also the net amount if you deduct tax. If you don't deduct tax, say so

you should have already deducted tax before paying these

there's nowhere to put capital transfer tax on this form — unlike the form for the high earners — presumably because you're not thought to have sufficient money. But if you have made gifts above the allowances, you must declare them

ALLOWANCES: Year ending 5 April 1980

See Note	BEFORE MAKING ANY CLAIM READ THE APPROPRIATE NOTE
31	**Married man living with wife or wholly maintaining her** Wife's Christian or other forenames If you married after 5 April 1978 please state— (a) date of marriage (b) wife's former **surname**
32	**Age allowance for persons born before 6 April 1915** ☐ If you or your wife were born before 6 April 1915, tick "√" here ▶
33	**Children** *(IT IS PROPOSED THAT CHILD ALLOWANCES SHOULD BE WITHDRAWN FROM APRIL 1979 EXCEPT FOR CERTAIN CHILDREN LIVING OUTSIDE THE UNITED KINGDOM AND CERTAIN STUDENTS)* If you require the special form to claim for a child living outside the United Kingdom, please tick "√" here .. .. ▶ ☐ If after reading note 33 you wish to claim the allowance available in respect of certain students who were on a full-time course at 31 December 1976, give below the full name of the child for whom you wish to claim. If you require the special form to claim for a child who receives no grant payable out of public funds, please tick "√" in the **box**. ☐ *Full names of child (surname first)* ....
	Children for whom you claimed an allowance for 1978-79 whose earnings exceeded £500, or whose other income exceeded £115 in 1978-79 |	*YEAR ENDED 5 APRIL 1979*
Full name	Earnings £........................... *Other income* £........................... |	£........................... £...........................
34	**Additional personal allowance for children** Details of child in respect of whom your claim is made—

Full names of child (surname first)	Child's date of birth			Child 16 or over on 6 April 1979, name of university, college or school or nature of training	Does the child live with you?	Is any other person claiming the allowance for the child?
	Day	Month	Year			

If your wife is incapacitated

What is the nature of the incapacity?

Is this likely to continue throughout the year ending 5 April 1980?   *If so please tick "√" here* ▶ ☐

page 5

as it says here, child allowances are to be changed, and so this part of the form will probably change too

this is for single people with children or for husbands with incapacitated wives (not the other way round!)

here is another page of allowances, which are straightforward come to £1,535, your code number will be 153. If you are puzzled, ask any tax office or even the accounts or salaries office of your employer firm to show you the tax tables, which should clarify it for you. The employer deducts according to those tables.

There is also a letter after the figures with your name which symbolizes your marital status so that everyone knows instantly whether you are married or single. However, the Revenue is nothing if not tactful and, if you don't wish such facts to be known, you say so and the letter 'T' will be against your name (just as though it stood for Tact). It can hide a multitude of things about you which the employer will never know but which is on your dossier at the Inland Revenue and they never tell.

Never take your coding for granted, because the Revenue staff are all human beings and can make mistakes which they are always only too ready to right. Ask your local office or query it with your employer if you seem to be paying more than you think your should or did at the last job for similar salary. You may be on a temporary or emergency coding while the officials catch up with a new job or different earnings and the later, permanent code will be adjusted to take account of any overpayment. Schedule E should not frighten you, as it is one of several schedules, but it is the one under which the majority of people in Britain pay, being salary or wage earners with deductions of tax at source.

The Tax Form

The tax form is something I have referred to often enough and it will in any case be familiar to most of you. It is rather like a truth game, being a form that asks you to disclose every single penny you earn as well as any allowances or reliefs you may claim. Do not worry when it lands on your doormat, looking fat and awesome, every spring (pretty soon after April 6th). Part of the fatness is the leaflet of notes which are designed to help you fill in each

section and answer the printed questions. The language of the brochure gets simpler as years pass but may still be confusing, so, if in doubt, go straight to your local tax office or employer for advice. Never worry about genuine mistakes since you will be in good company — many, many people make mistakes on their forms and have to correct them. Most people should be able to manage these forms but, if there are extras like unearned income, company cars and such, some might need help. Just remember, and I cannot repeat it too often, to put in every bit of income, earned or unearned, and every benefit like the company car.

Wives may resent the terse message that asks them to pass the form to a husband if married. But, as I said, that will change as the Revenue workload allows, so overlook it and be patient. In the meantime, single women still have no special heading so they should fill in the column marked 'Self', just as though they were men, and leave out the section headed 'Wife' which ignores the fact that single women make tax returns. The ugly word 'spouse' creeps into more and more forms now that women are more and more often the principal 'fillers-in' of forms.

The self-assessment form

There are a number of experiments in the minds of the tax people, all aimed at simplicity. One is the 'self-assessment form'. This puts the taxpayer on his honour to return everything concerned with income and allowances or reliefs and to arrive at his own assessment of what tax he should pay: perhaps even to work out his own code number (though this might involve changing the code number system we all now know). I think this kind of reform will come slowly; it would inevitably operate side by side with the familiar coding method for a fair time yet. It would relieve the Inland Revenue of some of the burden of overwork and already works pretty well in America, for instance. There they operate a kind of self-assessment 'honour' system, but the Internal Revenue Services (their equivalent of our Inland Revenue) has terrific powers to investigate and to pounce, with strong penalties for fraud, where they suspect even the slightest anomaly or lack of integrity.

About separate tax returns
Wives may prefer to make separate returns from their husbands. In fact, husbands may prefer it too even though, as yet, her separate tax return does not relieve him of the final responsibility for paying the couple's tax dues to the Government. But at least this provision for separate tax returns removes some of the liberationists' complaints that women continue to be treated as mere chattels, classed along with children and idiots when it comes to handling their own personal finance. As long as women remember that, with equality and equal opportunity, comes equal responsibility, which they don't all remember.

There are two ways of being 'separated' for tax though married. The first is

Separate assessment
This means quite simply that each is separately assessed so that both allowances and tax are properly apportioned into shares directly in line with the income of each spouse. It makes not a bit of difference to the final total of tax paid, no matter what the combined earnings, but it does mean that the wife gets her share of the married allowance, and that her refunds are paid to her. Nor does it particularly hide the affairs of one from the other since anyone with a fair knowledge of tax levels can guess at what the other must be earning. It does not quite place responsibility squarely on her shoulders as does separate taxation, but that will inevitably come.

Either spouse can apply for separate assessment provided he or she does it before July 6th of the relevant tax year and the other must accept such a decision. In fact, separate assessment has been around a lot longer than most people seem to realize

though it has been comparatively little used until more recently, when married couples have a tendency to fight anything that looks like sinking personal individuality.

Separate taxation
This must not be confused with separate assessment because this treats each spouse as a separate individual. To get such separation, the couple must apply jointly so that the Revenue is sure both want it. It can save money for the couple on really high combined incomes. The reason is that each spouse gets the personal tax allowance and then gets each 'band' of tax rates. Thus each gets the £750 band above the tax-free allowances on which only 25 per cent is paid. Each gets the £12,000 on which no higher rate than 30 per cent is due. Now if a couple is taxed together, they get that £12,000 between them and then start paying the higher rates of tax at £12,001. Suppose each earns £12,000. All the tax would be paid, if they are separately assessed, at the standard rate (apart from the lower 25 per cent band). They would gain on the deal considerably. There was a time when it paid even more handsomely to be separately taxed so that a number of couples got legal separations, easy enough when they had two homes and could use two separate addresses for their tax returns however much they might have been united in marriage and in bed behind closed doors. The higher tax for two affluent marrieds used to be called Sin Tax (though it was actually a tax on morality) or the High Cost of Loving Nowadays, there is no disadvantage to marriage as regards earned income if you elect for separate taxation; but unearned income cannot be separated thus.

Such tactics are no longer needed under separate taxation rules but it must be said that it does not pay a couple to elect for separation until their joint income reaches just under £15,000 (if both are on P.A.Y.E.). The total varies where one or both is freelance since the deduction of costs and allowable expenses play havoc with these figures if they represent gross payments to freelancers.

There are other variations on the combined income, since the advantages of separate taxation may vary according to how much of any one income is unearned or earned. To choose, one needs to think of the characters and natures of the couple concerned. Many may prefer separate taxation despite the extra trouble of two returns, two lots of envelopes falling through the letterbox and so forth. You don't make the choice because it may or may not benefit you financially but because that's the way you like it. Incidentally, separate taxation does not necessarily mean that you keep your income secret from your spouse or vice versa. You can have a jolly good guess at each other's earnings by how much tax is being levied. In fact mutual trust means that neither wants to know nor to hide too much: it means that the couple know roughly what each can afford or what they can jointly spend without even wanting to ask too many questions. But, again, such things depend very much on the couple's nature, and some may hate secrets, even regarding them as disloyal, while others don't even think of a lack of knowledge as meaning that secrets are being kept from them.

Divorce

Now we have a very different story, not always a happy one; quite apart from the emotional miseries of marriage breaks, there are often financial complications at a time when one is feeling unable to cope with them, when depression and anxiety bring on the kind of exhaustion that makes money problems loom large even when they are small (see Chapter 4 on insurance to provide a little against such eventualities as death and divorce).

Divorced spouses are immediately deemed to be two separate people, even if they continue to live at the same address, which often happens in these days of costly and difficult housing. They are deemed to be running two separate households, even at this same address so that each gets his or her allowances as single people (plus the additional personal allowance already mentioned for whoever has the child or children).

Each becomes, therefore, a single person for tax. Now a husband may continue to make payments to his ex-wife after divorce or separation (or vice versa if she is the breadwinner). The deed of parting will state whether the sum of money is supposed to have had the tax deducted or whether the wife must pay tax on it. Although this makes a difference to the amount the ex-wife receives, it is really a detail; the husband will deduct the tax, he will then pass it on to the Inland Revenue since he will be paying tax on his income in the normal way. However, if his ex-wife has no other earnings, she is entitled to her personal allowance on her maintenance payments; there will therefore be some tax to reclaim, since in effect she has had 30 per cent of her maintenance payments deducted. In these cases, it would be better for the husband to pay the ex-wife gross (deducting the payments from his taxable income) and for her to complete her own tax return.

If the children are living with her, this makes even more sense, since she can claim the Additional Personal Allowance and this will reduce the tax she must pay on her maintenance and the maintenance of the children.

If the payments made are 'small' (i.e. under £21 per week or £91 per month) then these are always paid gross, and the recipient again declares them on her tax return. Payments for children who are under 21 fall into the 'small' category if they are under £12 per week or £52 per month.

I would emphasize that these rules apply to payments made under court orders and that legal agreements between the consenting parties might lay down their own terms as long as they are acceptable to the Inland Revenue. The point is that two people do not pay tax on the same lump sum of money, whoever earns the income; but one of them has to. Since you will almost certainly have a solicitor in such cases, this kind of agreement is automatically handled by a professional but, if in doubt and without legal advice, go to your local Inland Revenue office.

To take an example where the husband pays the wife a net figure for maintenance and pays over the tax to the Inland Revenue: let's say the monthly maintenance is £300, and he earns £10,000. The wife has no other income:

Maintenance payments per annum
= £ 3,600
Less 30% tax = £ 1,080

Net maintenance payments per
annum = £ 2,520

Husband's income per annum = £10,000
Less personal allowance = £ 1,165

Taxable income = £ 8,835

Tax payable on:
First £750 @ 25% = £ 187.50
Balance @ 30% = £4,425.50

Total tax = £2,613.00

To take an example of a 'small' payment, where the wife is paid a gross figure and the husband may deduct his payment to her from his taxable income: let's say that the monthly payments are £70 and that he earns £10,000 per annum. She is earning also £3,500 per annum:

Husband's income per annum = £10,000
Less personal allowance = £ 1,165
Less maintenance payments
per annum = £ 840

Taxable income = £ 7,995

Tax payable on:
First £750 @ 25% = £ 187.50
Balance @ 30% = £2,173.50

Total tax = £2,361.00

Wife's income per
annum = £3,500.00
Maintenance per
annum = £ 840.00

Total income = £4,340.00
Less personal allowance = £ 1,165

Taxable income = £ 3,175

Tax payable on:
First £750 @ 25% = £ 187.50
Balance @ 30% = £ 727.50

£ 915.00

Mortgage-interest reliefs go to the person who is actually paying the mortgage and, by the same token, tax reliefs on insurance premiums only to the person whose life is insured. In some cases, a spouse may take over the mortgage covered by insurance on the life of the other spouse. In such cases, the tax relief on the insurance premiums is not granted to the paying spouse. In such cases it might pay to surrender the policy and start another under his or her own name. But such cases are relatively rare and, for the most part, the marital home is sold, the proceeds divided (often equally) and each starts again somehow.

Death
A surviving husband may disclaim any tax due on her income in the year of her death since he is not bound to pay it. His late wife's estate would, however, be required to meet the bill is she leaves anything at all, along with anything else the Revenue may claim from her estate. If she leaves nothing, her dues remain unpaid.

The self-employed (Schedule D)
So far, we have dealt with only one schedule, the Schedule E that draws tax from the majority. The self-employed come under Schedule D, which also covers income from savings, investments, rentals, freelance fees,

and a lot of bits and pieces not covered by other schedules. The thing is that it deals with income received gross, or without prior deductions for tax. The recipient then pays his tax, as stated, twice a year in large lump sums, sometimes frighteningly large, for it is one of the drawbacks of getting gross income that too few people remember that the taxman has to be paid. It looks so lovely, all that money going into the bank account, but the man or woman who fails to put aside enough for the taxman is heading for trouble and many, many actresses and writers have been badly in hock for arrears of tax. One of the difficulties is that earnings can be exceptionally high over one year and that the taxman's bill comes in the next year, when they have fallen. There are provisions for spreading income over more than one year, putting some away for the lean year, which too few people recognize or use.

There is a popular misconception that the self-employed get a real bonanza, that they can charge all their normal living expenses against their earnings and get away with it. Some do well, it has to be admitted, but the vast majority get away with very little and certainly never see that alleged licence to print money. For one thing, goods and services have to be invoiced (even more essential since VAT was introduced), which means that officialdom has a double-check on earnings. For another, the firms that pay such invoices (or even non-invoiced fees) are going to claim such costs against their earnings as tax-deductible so that a record of who was paid what exists from that source. It is no good the self-employed asking for backhanders or cash payments because the payer becomes increasingly reluctant to pay in that way, since he wants to record all his payouts as legitimate expenses. As it is, the Inland Revenue is pretty good at recognizing tricks and assiduous at double- or triple-checking income returns. Once the whole business is properly computerized, they will find it even easier since one or two buttons will be all they need to see a taxpayer's entire earnings (and

history, if they want it) thrown up on a small screen. Every payment will be centralized, every illegal evasion highlighted.

Few taxpayers in this category can have failed to notice how quickly the Revenue catches up without even computer help. I have occasionally written articles under pseudonyms and have very soon afterwards got a form addressed to the pseudonym asking me if I make returns of my income and to which office because the name is a new one. I know some get away with it and they cost the country dear but government is catching up on this 'black economy', as they call it. It costs the country an estimated £9m per annum in unpaid taxes.

The dossiers are formidable and taxpayers would be amazed to know how many cuttings or historical and biographical details are filed under their names. A showbiz star who boasts of unduly high earnings could get a nasty shock when the bill comes in and could find himself having to prove how little he really did get. Mistakes are forgiven. Fraud is not and the fraudulent find themselves queried, almost hounded for ever until they show themselves to be reformed characters. Incidentally, I would like here to explode a persistent theory that contends that you are not liable to pay taxes that are still outstanding after six years, that they are what is known as 'time-expired'. It is true that the Revenue reckons six years without a demand for tax dues is long enough and that demands cannot be made after that time has expired. However, as long as a demand has once been made in — say — 1972, and the argument has gone on since, even in dilatory and desultory fashion, then the 1972 payment remains either due or arguable all the time. The case is always open, as it were. Similarly, if a sum has been agreed and new evidence comes to light showing that it was too little, the Revenue has the right to re-open the case and to demand further payments, even after six years. The only thing to which time-expiry applies is the agreed payment on which no new evidence arises. The case remains closed.

Every organization you deal with financially is bound to disclose your affairs, be it bank, building society or employer. The many pieces of your personal tax jigsaw all get put together one day, slowly or fast (faster with computers). So be honest now, not sorry later.

Allowable expenses

Let's get back to the self-employed. They can and do get allowances for some of their living costs in a sense, such costs being deducted from their gross earnings, thereby reducing the income on which tax has to be paid. They are allowed to charge some light and heat, some cleaning and even some articles of furniture if such be essential equipment for the job (like a desk for a writer or an easel for an artist). They can even charge for a cleaning lady. But they need to beware of charging any normal household expenses such as a portion of the mortgage or rates. To do so would be to run into capital gains tax liability on the profits of the house when sold. The self-employed man would not pay tax on the whole of the capital gain between the purchase price and selling price of his house. But he would be liable for a proportion. For instance, suppose he owned the house as his owner-occupied home (which is exempt from capital gains tax) for ten years. During that time he uses one of six rooms solely for business purposes and claims that proportion of his mortgage against tax. He would be liable for tax on one-sixth of the capital gain. It is not quite that simple as a sum, and this should be seen only as a rough guide because there are deductible costs against capital gains tax, such as work done to convert the workroom into a darkroom, studio or whatever. But the principle is that you pay on the working portion, as it were, for any rooms set aside solely for an office or studio or darkroom. If a living or bedroom is used only partly as workroom, then you should be all right. Normally you will have an accountant to argue this point with you

and then with the Revenue. The Revenue keeps files of the kind of costs to expect in each job or profession and will only query unreasonable claims. An accountant's job is to know what is reasonable and not to exceed it, so be honest with both.

Rent of business premises is totally deductible provided it is for solely business purposes and you are not living there, though one would overlook a divan for the occasional night when one works into the small hours or on which one sleeps during a slack hour in a busy day. One may also charge all relevant equipment such as cameras for professional photographers or photo-journalists, typewriters for writers, medical equipment for doctors, and so forth. Anything that is bought essentially for the trade or profession is chargeable and even some gifts to people who might commission work might be deductible although they need to be declared on your accounts (and the recipient might be asked about them so keep them small in case he gets a tax bill for their estimated value).

The secret is, as I have already stressed, to keep careful accounts. If in doubt, enter it anyway and let your accountant decide whether it might or might not be allowable. If making your own returns, attach a note against doubtful costs or make a note at the foot of the page, then let the Revenue allow it or delete it. As long as you are honest, that will not be held against you. A second camera, a tape recorder used in the home as well as for interviews, or anything of that kind might be borderline so do ask.

If your job takes you out to meet people, and depends on the effect created by your personal appearance, you may get hairdressing and clothes allowances — actors, journalists and such can always apply, though not all will succeed, especially where clothes are concerned. I staple all my bills, small and large, to large sheets of really cheap paper. This not only makes them easier to keep and find, and easier for my book-keeper to file, but it also gives me space to scribble along the bottom of the paper the exact purpose of the purchase or service such as 'new bookshelf in office as old one broke/was too small/etc.' Your accountant can then instantly answer any awkward questions the Revenue might put (or you can if dealing with your own tax affairs).

I cannot stress too often the desirability of having an accountant as honest as yourself, one with a good reputation at the Inland Revenue, who does not boast of all that he can avoid. These days, you also need a firm with a fair turn of speed since interest is charged on overdue tax.

Property

Rentals from property count as investment or unearned income, though there are some grey areas here. For instance, you might have a guest house or rooming house, even a bedsitter house or a house converted into small furnished flats.

Suppose you maintain the garden, clean all the 'common parts' like stairs and corridors, do much of the general maintenance, and so forth, then you might get all or part of the rent as earned income. You may have to keep a diary showing how many hours you put in and to prove that you even do some of the building work yourself. You may be entitled to be paid for your work, but the Revenue may not allow you the full rental income as earned income. Once again, sort this out in advance and get it looked at in the possible light of your selling the 'investment' house one day and making a large capital gain. You cannot have it both ways and, if you have been earning money from the house all along, you will have to pay your capital gains tax in full, not deducting the materials and labour already put into the house as deductible against an annual income. Either you keep all your bills, all your costs accumulating against the eventual capital gain. Or you claim as you go. Which you do depends much on the size of the income, the potential size of the capital gain, the time you plan to keep the house, a myriad

things. You may even be running the place as a business, as an asset of your own little property company, which will bring you into the company taxes like corporation tax. Your personal rental income is chargeable under Schedule E, whether earned or unearned. There are fewer confusions about furnished property but there are still many so take professional advice. When it comes to unfurnished property, you could come under another Schedule, namely Schedule A, of which more towards the end of this chapter. So, for that reason, let's summarize the schedules so that we can do just that, forget them unless we want to look them up:

Schedule E

Not such an illogical start, even if it is not the first letter of the alphabet, because it is the one that most people pay. It includes all earned income on PAYE, pension and social security income and/or benefits, all of which must be returned on your annual form, as I've already said.

Schedule D

Unearned income like interest, payments from annuities, rents on investment property, profits from a trade or business, etc. Freelance earnings, self-employed earnings, etc. There are several classes of Schedule D.

Schedule A

Deals with rentals from property or unfurnished buildings.

Schedule B

Concerns woodlands run as businesses, some rural or similar land that does come under farmed land, etc.

Schedule F

Mainly concerned with company dividends, and with companies.

So much for direct taxes on income. There are other direct taxes such as

1. Capital gains tax (CGT)

Oddly, few people recognize it by its popular name, in tax and financial circles that is, which is simply by the three initial letters of CGT, run together.

CGT is paid on anything that can be called a 'chargeable gain', from the rises in the prices of stocks and shares to th appreciation on a valuable painting. If you buy shares or a painting worth £5,000 and sell for £7,000, the tax is due on £2,000. Gains of up to £1,000 a year are free of tax and the proceeds from the sale of personal possessions (called 'personal chattels') are tax-free up to a maximum — at the moment the chattels must be sold for under £2,000 to escape. On gains of between £1,000 and £5,000, the tax is 15 per cent on the gain only, not on the whole of the sale price. Then comes a sliding scale of rates up to a top rate of 30 per cent payable on gains of more than £9,500 in a single year.

You declare any such gains on your annual tax form; you can carry forward losses from previous years — and even in inflationary times it is all too easy to lose money on shares, merely by buying the wrong ones. But such losses can only be used to offset against capital gains of more than £1,000 in any one year which is hardly a hardship since it is rather nice to be able to make such capital gain anyway.

CGT is really a pretty inexpensive tax compared with some and utterly painless since it is not even due until after the proceeds are all received and the expenses paid, after which tax is levied on what 'profit' is left; expenses, such as brokers' commissions, stamp duty, maintenance on buildings, and so forth, can be deducted. In fact, you get three months to pay, just to make sure you have been able to include and settle all the outgoings first.

There are certain concessions on standard capital gains tax. For instance on unit trust and investment trust gains (see Chapter 8). And there is every hope that a new type of capital gains tax might be introduced in the very near future.

The new CGT could well be based on the American pattern and called a 'tapering tax'. This would mean that investments held for a long time get a tapering relief. Thus, gains realized only a year or so after the original purchase would be subject to high tax, while those sold in the medium term would attract medium CGT. Investments held over a long term might attract little or nothing in tax. The obvious aim is to encourage people to invest rather than merely to speculate, gamble or to buy and sell. In other words, there might be some distinction, though probably not in name, between genuine investment at lower tax rates and 'merchanting' for quick gain (or so they always hope).

2. Capital transfer tax (CTT).

A very complicated tax this, of which most people are largely ignorant and hope to stay that way, yet it is something that affects nearly all of us now that property prices are going throught the roof. CTT is a tax on gifts, in life or death, whether by will and testament or merely by default of leaving no will so that the next-of-kin inherits. Many people still tend to think of it as estate duty, but it can be levied in life and not on the 'estate' at death only. If in life, then you declare any liability, again, on your tax form.

CTT is due and payable on the accumulated total of all the gifts made in life and at death though the rates charged on lifetime gifts are lower than those charged after death. Thus, if you can ever afford to live without your home or capital or part of the latter, give away what you can while you live. It is also a lot more fun to give while you can see and enjoy the pleasure you give to those you love.

The giver ('donor' in financial language) is responsible for paying CTT and not, as you might think, the recipient ('donee'). Of course, the giver and the recipient can arrange for the donee to pay the tax but such cases are rare. The donor has to declare what gifts he/she makes but I would advise anyone receiving a gift to make sure that CTT has been paid or there might be a frightening tax bill after the gift is spent. The CTT has to be paid by someone and, in time, the gift will become known. When the Inland Revenue computers come fully on stream, such knowledge will be quickly collected, stored and retrieved.

To give here the full details of CTT would be impossible — the Inland Revenue's own book on the subject runs to 146 pages including the index and it is free to anyone who asks for it from the Capital Taxes Office, if you think you can understand it. A free book is cheaper than an accountant or solicitor but, unless you can understand it, less helpful than an adviser. So, for the sake of brevity and understanding, let us look at what gifts are exempt from CTT on the basis that you should assume everything else to be liable, and go about finding out what to do about it:

1. Any and every transfer between a husband and wife, in life or after death. That includes all such assets as houses, stocks and shares, jewels, money in the bank, anything at all. Even works of art or antiques, thought by some to be subject to CTT. Not so.

2. Any transfer (gift) of up to £2,000 or a collection of several transfers amounting to under £2,000 in total in any single year. So you could give each of four children £500 without liability (but you must declare the gift for your tax dossier). You may carry forward any unused part of your £2,000 for one year only. Also, in your lifetime and at death, you may give away a total of £25,000 tax-free. All these levels are subject to change as inflation lessens the actual cash values of money and gifts in kind so keep an eye on changes. You may be able to give away more than you think.

3. Any gifts that can easily be made out of your income or capital without in any way affecting your standard of living and gifts up to a maximum of £100 a year to each individual donee. These small gifts are allowed even if you have already given away the £2,000 in that same year.

4. Wedding presents. A parent may give up to £5,000 when a child marries and grandparents or great-grandparents can give £2,500. Anybody can give anybody £1,000 as a wedding present. These amounts have been raised since the beginning of capital transfer tax to keep more in line with costs and inflation so do check on current sums before you start giving as changes can be made and you might wish to give more if you are allowed to do so. It is highly unlikely that the permitted sum would ever be lowered.

5. Donations to charity with no limit as long as they are made more than a year before death. Within a year of death or after death gifts are limited to £100,000, anything above that being subject to CTT.

6. Gifts to the nation, provided they go to art galleries, museums, universities or some such place where they are for public pleasure or good. The giver cannot simply decide what is or isn't for the public use or benefit so must put a case to the Treasury, whose objectivity has led them to refuse some such intended gifts — historic homes, for instance, because the nation just cannot afford to go on repairing and maintaining them.

7. Donations to political parties (and the definition is that a party is not a party unless it has two elected members in the House of Commons or one member elected by more than 150,000 votes). The same rules apply as for charities, which I find rather funny — is a Parliamentary party a charity in official eyes? That is, no tax up to within a year of death and tax on anything above £100,000 after that time.

8. Woodlands and agricultural land carries some exemptions and concessions, in order to keep some estates together in certain circumstances. For instance, two deaths very close together might erode an estate — if the son inherits and dies soon after the father, a double set of taxes could mean the sale of the entire farm or estate, the farm being the sole means of someone's support. If the deaths are within four years of each other, some benefits are available.

If you receive a gift from a will, you may be sure there is not tax due on it from you and that such CTT will already have been paid out of the estate; CTT is first taken before all the bequests are made, levied on the sum total of all bequests. You will be notified that this is the case unless something goes wrong, but do check if you are not told exactly what the position is.

There have been many discussions on the way that family businesses can suffer from CTT, which may force the sale of shares in such businesses and perhaps even the loss of the business to the family. Every effort is being made, even as I write, to get some reforms on to the Statute Book and to see them implemented, even by the overladen tax collectors of Britain. Indeed, it is seen almost as a priority to find some way of relieving family businesses, but they obviously must be real family businesses, not mere you read this.

I have not covered all direct taxes, but certainly those that concern most of us, since the rest have to do with companies, investment in new plant, land development and that kind of thing. So let us, just for light relief and before going on Indirect Taxation, look at some of the benefits that escape taxation.

Gratuities for extra service in the nation's armed forces attract no tax which seems more than fair. Educational grants are tax-free, and employers are even allowed to give small cash prizes to employees who win exam-style competitions and even some reward for passing exams essential to advancement in the job. Endowments from insurance policies are tax-free, as is the repayment of *capital* from an insurance annuity (see Chapter 4), but more of that under the relevant heading of annuities in that chapter. Do not get confused. Remember that income from an annuity and all pensions taken as income are taxable.

There have been a number of arguments about certain prizes, awards and such and always will be. For instance, a designer might win an award for design and the Inland Revenue just might argue that it was won on the job, as it were, and was part of the earnings of the job. Awards for journalists can run into £2,000 or so and can be tax-free. However, if somebody is taken off his normal day-to-day work to prepare — say — designs or articles solely for entry in a competition, the Revenue might argue. The whole thing pivots on whether or not the money is earned or won by someone who can make a continuing business or source of earnings out of what he does. It is not easy to argue that one can make a business of winning awards which are judged by an authoritative panel of people unknown to the competitor. But there might be borderline cases.

Certain types of income are not subject to tax except in special circumstances. For instance, the interest on National Savings certificates, bonuses on Save-as-you-Earn (SAYE) schemes, on Defence Bonds, National Development Bonds, British Savings Bonds, and post-war credits (stock issued by the Government to help finance the 1939-45 war).

Prizes on premium bonds, football pools, the gaming tables, at bingo or in lotteries are tax-free, as is any gambling win. Social security benefits are also not subject to tax but, obviously, those who get such benefits are assumed to be earning too little to exist anyway. Disability pensions and pensions for the war-wounded or victims of serious crime are also tax-free. You get housing grants from local authorities for home improvement without having to pay tax; but, if improving a house other than an owner-occupied home, you would need to deduct the grant from all the building expenses that you plan to offset against the capital gain on the property.

To repeat, compensation payments for loss of job or office are also tax-free up to a maximum capital sum which may vary and has been moved up to £10,000 over recent years. Obviously the theory is that such permitted levels of compensation would rise more or less in parallel with inflation, but it is rather simply a nice theory. In practice such increases lag behind inflation. Ten thousand pounds can be very little compensation for loss of earnings today but anything above that is taxable until the next increase. Until then the golden handshake has decidedly a leaden look.

English people living abroad do not have to pay tax in two countries, the one in which they live as well as in the U.K., because there are mutual agreements between countries that exempt income already taxed in one country from being double-taxed. But, since you will have been told all this when you left Britain for your new job or your retirement abroad, I am probably telling you nothing new. If you plan to move abroad, go and see your local Inland Revenue Office first.

Indirect taxes
Indirect taxation is a good deal simpler, and becoming a way of life. The last three governments, at least, before the Conservatives came to power in 1979, had all made noises about moving towards indirect taxation something that has been in a number of pipelines for at least twenty years that I know of and maybe for longer. When VAT moved sharply upwards to 15 per cent, almost double the previous rate, while direct income tax was reduced, we were on the way at last – again. The first tentative steps were taken when VAT was introduced in 1973.

VAT (VALUE ADDED TAX)
Value Added Tax is the most familiar and important indirect tax and it is collected for government by the Customs and Excise departments. Other indirect taxes include stamp duties payable on contracts or on sales and purchases of property, stocks and shares or such. Then come the duties on petrol, beers, wines, spirits and tobacco in any form.

We all pay VAT, most of us simply on the goods we buy. The maker and seller of such goods return the tax to relevant government offices and all these must be registered for VAT if their annual sales come above certain levels. In other words, you may be liable to register for VAT if you are in any trade, profession, business or vocation, whether you are selling goods or services.

Registration is compulsory if your business turnover is more than £10,000 a year. An author or journalist, restaurateur or hairdresser all come under the same ruling. Their services must be charged with VAT added if in excess of that £10,000 level (which has changed only once since 1973, upwards, so might be due for another change to keep more in parallel with inflation). Returns and payments are settled quarterly. It may, however, pay anyone in trade or a profession to register even if their turnover is below £10,000 and likely to be for some time to come. The reason is simple enough. VAT-registered businesses may offset the VAT they pay on the goods they buy against the VAT they collect on what they sell before remitting the change, as it were, to the Government. In effect, they can claim back the VAT they have paid. For example, a commercial photographer may sell his services for £2,000 in one quarter. Included in his services are some very costly materials, like film and chemicals, on which he has paid VAT. The materials (excluding VAT) are deductible against his income for direct tax purposes but he may also claim the VAT back on his indirect taxation.

Let's assume that his invoices total £2,000, then he will have to charge his buyers a total of £300 VAT (15 per cent on his invoices). Suppose his materials came to £400, which is very feasible, he will have paid out £60 in VAT; he may then deduct the £60 from the £300, sending on to Customs only £240. The VAT he charges comes under a heading called 'outputs' while the VAT he pays is an 'input'. He would naturally lose money by not being registered, even if his annual sales were as low as £6,000 and, since anyone may register voluntarily whatever the level of business, he certainly should do so. By the same token, he can offset other VAT payments such as those to builders decorating

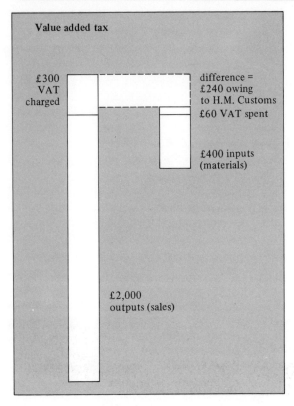

Value added tax

£300
VAT
charged

difference =
£240 owing
to H.M. Customs
£60 VAT spent

£400 inputs
(materials)

£2,000
outputs (sales)

the studio, legal contracts, petrol for his car when carrying goods or going on locations, and all that kind of thing. It could be downright foolish not to recover the VAT he's paid and he may even find one quarter's input coming to more than the output.

A writer, on the other hand, might choose not to register. His materials are relatively cheap, his VAT costs low, and he will have much smaller sums to deduct from his output. Even so, his petrol for going to interviews or research trips, his typewriter maintenance and repairs, ribbons and such all carry VAT.

If you are not registered and suddenly discover your sales rising, you may have to tell Customs and Excise about the trend, so keep a note of what the VAT levels are. If you earn more than £3,500 in the first quarter of your year, you must inform on yourself. If sales are £6,000 or more by the end of the second quarter, regardless of how low they might have been in the first quarter, you must also inform. And, should you not

reach those levels in the first two quarters, you must still tell Customs if your earnings top £8,000 by the end of the third quarter. You may not have to register because the reasons may have been freak reasons, unlikely to be repeated, but you are breaking the law if you keep quiet. These days, earnings of £10,000 (including normal business espenses) are not so high and there should be few traders or professionals unregistered, for their own sakes. But, as I will often repeat, life is to be lived according to one's own comfort and convenience within the law and the happiness of those for whom you are responsible, so feel free to decide that you will 'lose' a little money to save yourself the quarterly inconvenience of making VAT returns. It is not an arduous task but it is a chore, naturally.

There are two categories of goods and services which carry no VAT at all – exempt and zero-rated. There is an important distinction between these two classes. If you deal in 'exempt' goods, you may not claim back any of the VAT paid out for the premises on which you sell exempt goods, or any of the VAT you pay to get essential raw materials, etc. You keep records, but you neither charge nor claim VAT (which is not the same as zero-rated, and distinctly less advantageous, as few people realise).

Zero-rated goods carry a nil per cent VAT, which means that no tax at all is currently placed on these goods but they are within the VAT structure and could become subject to VAT at any time. If you deal in zero-rated goods, you may claim back the VAT you pay out as expenses. Let's look at the two lists (not fully comprehensive but long and detailed enough to give you some idea of the Government thinking and object of not overtaxing the poor, elderly, infirm or children).

Zero-rated

Children's clothes and shoes: but only up
    to certain sizes for young children
Food: excluding ice cream, soft drinks,
    alcohol, pet foods (the subject of many

a complaint), snacks like potato crisps and other oddments

Books: excluding diaries, sundry stationery items, except printed letterheads and some items supplied for businesses, professions, etc.

Heating fuel and power: excluding petrol, diesel, etc.

Transport: excluding taxis, hire cars, pleasure boats and such

Newspapers and newspaper advertisements

Building: but only the actual construction, all architects', surveyors' and similar professional fees being subject to VAT. Repairs are also VAT-able, as are sales and purchases in builders' merchants, etc.

Caravans: when they are larger than certain specified lengths and widths so that they are not strictly 'domestic' caravans but probably industrial trailers, temporary housing for workmen, etc.

Exports: subject to other tariffs or imports, maybe, but not VAT

Bank notes: not so odd as you might think since some commercial banks in England and Scotland print and issue their own notes (see Chapter 10) and could have to charge VAT on each note, which would be very curious since we should be paying more than £1 for a £1 note and could not afford that for long

Water supplies: excluding distilled water, mineral water, bottled water, etc.

Crash helmets: but not decorative or fashion helmets

Charity donations

Drugs, medicines, surgical aids, medical appliances of all kinds, but only as long as they are bought from registered chemists and pharmacists so the local herbalist should charge for his panaceas

Blind people's needs such as wireless, talking books and suchlike

Exempt

Land leasing: except for hotels, camp sites, parking, timber, mooring or sporting rights, etc.

Insurance: of any kind, on life, cars, personal belongings, pets, etc.

Postal services: except telephones, telex and telegrams

Betting, gaming, lotteries and such

Finance services: excluding brokers' commission, unit trust services, consultancy services, etc.

Health treatment by doctors: excluding health farms and such

Education: excluding secretarial colleges, correspondence courses and similar

Burial/Cremation

VAT has varied, both in the percentage rates added to goods and in the fact that we have had two-tier rates at some periods — higher percentages being payable on various luxury or semi-luxury goods and lower rates on life's daily or periodic needs. The Government can change rates to reduce or to boost consumer demand, to affect its national economic policy and that, for the most part, is how indirect taxation has been used in the past.

Leaflets from any of the VAT offices, listed under Customs and Excise in your local telephone directories, cover every conceivable aspect of this tax and all the advice is free. They get a good deal of criticism but my own experience of VATmen and women is that they are helpful, lenient and far from aggressive. But, as I have often said, one gets the contacts one deserves. Be honest, treat them right and they will never treat you wrong; or not for long, anyway, not as soon as you've genuinely asked for help and advice.

Taxes hurt, it is true, but they are fair, being levied on what one has, not on the basic income needed for breadline existence. There are anomalies, and it is far from easy to save for our declining years, with inflation gnawing at our lifetime efforts; but the country does operate a savings and pensions scheme, with supplementary benefits for those in real need, so our taxes buy us some cushioning for those later years. Our taxes help to educate our children, pay for medical treatment and for further education. Our grandparents and older ancestors undoubtedly paid much less tax but they lived in times when some were rich but many starved; when many brains got no education to speak of and no opportunity for further training and advancement; when people died of mild illnesses because they could not afford to call a doctor; when babies and children not only had a high mortality rate but were born to weakened and exhausted mothers.

We are a long, long way from Utopia and we do pay more tax than many, many countries. The scroungers, those shadowy people of the Black Economy who cost the nation £9 million a year and whose losses to the country have to be met out of the pockets of the honest people, are probably going to be reduced in number as computer checks become better and better. On the whole, our social security system works well and is worth paying taxes to maintain.

If you lived, as I did, through the 1920s and 1930s, you saw real poverty, deep human misery and degradation, frustration and sickness, death and decay of our people, our cities and our country. There is so much less of it today, so much, much less. I remember that every time I write those ghastly cheques to the Inland Revenue and thank God I earn enough to have to pay them. And I feel that much better about the hole in my bank account.

Chapter Three

Housing

Unless you are rich enough to buy your home outright, you will have to borrow most of the money you need for a house, and the chances are high that such borrowing will be linked to an insurance policy, so that this chapter and the next will often be inter-related.

The loan itself will most often come from a building society (in the form of a mortgage), but there are other sources. For example, some insurance companies do their own lending and give mortgages, like National Mutual Life (one of the first to do mortgages at all, now 150 years old, nestling in the shadow of the famous St Mary-le-Bow church, the Bow Bells church, in the City of London, indeed in the churchyard itself) or Norwich Union — well, the list of companies doing their own lending allied to endowment/ life insurance policies is very long and brokers, whether they deal in mortgages or insurances, will be able to tell you about most or many of them.

Banks also do home loans. Mostly rather short-term, by average standards, and at higher rates of interest than, say, building societies and many of the insurance companies. Then there are loans from employer-companies, especially banks and insurance companies, who usually charge staff exceptionally low rates of interest and who occasionally have special schemes involving either gentler repayments of the final charge on the property (without profit to themselves) or something similar. I do not propose to deal with such loans since every member of the relevant companies will be told all about them when they are employed and they are not available to the vast majority of us.

There are also housing associations, where loans can be made by a national body to groups of people wanting to buy or convert property and I shall deal with those in more detail later in this chapter. And there are private loans, often made through solicitors or accountants with clients looking for this kind of investment. Private loans are rare and becoming rarer since the return on invested capital is so often better with commercial concerns.

Usually the building society will be the one to help us. Britain is way ahead of any other country where this kind of lending is concerned, and banks more often finance European home-buying so that our own building societies are finding Europe a natural ground for extending their businesses, exporting the experience of many years to where it is being welcomed by buyers who like the gentler repayment terms.

History of building societies

More than 8 of the 10 million homes in Britain have been bought through building societies. Thanks to the societies, more than half of all British householders own their homes (the others being in local authority housing, and a few in rented homes). In any year, well over 750,000 people will seek a building society loan and roughly half of them will be first-time buyers. It adds up to enormous sums of money.

For instance, building societies are probably owed something approaching £30,000 million. Divide that down among 5 million people with their loans still outstanding and it looks less frightening, but it is a lot of money out on a good deal of trust.

We take the system very much for granted and it was not really until Clive Thornton, dynamic and far-sighted head of Abbey National, pointed it out to me that I realized how much like a kind of reverse of Robin Hood the societies are. They borrow from us all, more often from lower income groups and low taxpayers than from the rich, by taking our money on deposit and paying us interest on it (much as a bank might, but without the bank services). In theory, they take from would-be home-buyers to lend to home-buyers; Clive Thornton's point was that the money does not always go back to the people who saved it and who probably need it most — hence some of his revolutionary ideas (by building society standards), of which more later in this chapter.

The industry was born about 200 years ago. In 1775 a man called Richard Ketley wrote of a society he had set up in 1775 and the idea caught on in other areas. The early societies were no more than groups of people all wanting homes that none could afford. There might be 20 of them, each with a little money and the wish to save more. They pooled their funds and bought small parcels of land. Then they would start building homes, one by one as they could afford it, and the homes would be allocated to the members. Often, they simply drew lots to decide who would get the next house. The lucky owners had, by agreement, to go on subscribing to the homes still to be built for other members and, when everyone had achieved their homes, the society was wound up; they were more often than not called 'terminating societies', a phrase you hardly hear today in Britain though similar 'communes' exist in Europe and other parts of the world.

At that time, since the small societies paid interest on the subscriptions they received, people who did not want or need to buy homes began putting their money into them, where they thought it would be safe. The

safety was born of trust in people who longed for their dreams of homes to come true and who were prepared to work and to save to that end. Thus the investors felt they would not be let down as they might be investing with rather less worthy citizens.

Building societies won legal recognition in 1812, when Napoleon was being routed in Russia, but before our own victory at Waterloo. By 1836, an Act of Parliament had gone through, whose object was to regulate the affairs of the societies for the protection of all subscribers and citizens. And, by 1845, the first 'permanent society' was established as a continuing company to receive deposits and make loans.

The drawing of lots was still the principal method for allotting homes, which drew too many gamblers to the societies, hoping to win homes that they could let out for income or re-sell at profit. Not all societies were as careful as they might have been about keeping out the rogues, so more laws were passed in 1874 and again in 1894 to lay down rules of management. The final Act in 1894 banned balloting and drawing of lots, so that few new societies were formed and those that already existed began putting their affairs into very much better order.

The industry's growth was slow until after the First World War. For one thing, tied houses were still very prevalent and many, many employer companies, factories, coal-mining businesses and others as well as farmers and engineers had cottages for their employees. For another, there was plenty of property to rent and rents were not high, even compared to earnings in the pre-war era. There were also many huge houses after the Victorian fashion so that families often lived together even after marriage. And there were a great many young people in service in towns and cities, living below stairs in the large houses.

After 1919, the Government brought in a number of rent restrictions which made it uneconomic for owners of houses to let their property if they were to pay for dilapidations, and a good many homes came on the market for sale. Smaller and cheaper homes were in great demand, and modern roads were being built which made it possible for people to move further out of the crowded city centres and former factory or commercial areas. Houses were generally being built alongside the roads because of the ease of transport, and 'ribbon develop-ment', as it became known, was the major development.

Builders wanted to sell their houses and were quick to see the advantages of being linked to building societies. Houses were anything from £200 to £800 in most 'dormitory' areas and in the growing suburbs of the major cities: sums which few people could hope to save out of their weekly wages of from £2 to £12 a week, even when income tax was low and there was no PAYE. Close links between commercial builders and the societies put savers at risk; bribery had become fairly prevalent because home-buyers were prepared to find that little bit extra to give builders just to get a home. Rents were soaring − even a single room was anything from 15s to £1 per week and homes to rent were scarce at £1.10s a week, which was a pretty high rent.

In 1939, the rules were again tightened considerably and building societies started the Second World War with a lot of regulation around their necks amid a population of men at war and women at work, with little prospect of prosperity. Whole sectors of the country, where bombing attacks were feared, were virtually emptied of all but those whose whole lives had been there or whose work took them there. One lot had homes, the other did not want to buy. But wars end and, since 1945, the building societies have been the centre of some spectacular growth. For one thing, the Government recognized the need to encourage owner-occupation as well as savings, and was helpful about tax concessions to encourage the use of building societies. At the same time, to help Britain back to prosperity, new building and new homes were vital, so the two movements

grew together. Branch offices of nationally strong societies sprang up beside the smaller offices of local societies and, in time, mergers and takeovers became so rife that, nowadays, we have mostly the really large conglomerate groups of societies under one parental umbrella.

Savings in building societies are described in Chapter 8, but a lot of people fail to realize that the source of their home loans is the collective fund of small savings by far-from-wealthy people. You do not have to save with a building society to get a home loan from it, but it does help; and I would not be either surprised or disapproving to see more and more societies beginning to refuse loans to non-savers.

It was all too easy for societies to lend to just anybody as long as they had funds. However demand for loans has exceeded the supply for some time and, because building societies have had no need at all to 'sell' their loans, they have fashioned the simplest possible lending systems, fully protected by life insurance of some kind. And this, according to Clive Thornton, could mean that they are not living up to their social consciences. He has taken the initiative to move out of traditional loan areas, to try and give back to the savers the money they saved.

His idea of getting together with local authorities to restore poor, old-fashioned near-derelict areas of towns and cities has been a winner. It takes management time and trouble but it does not take risks with the savers' money − that being some-thing the building societies are legally bound to avoid. It takes advantage of local authority grants, of local authority land and purchasing ability. Town halls love the idea and look forward to run-down areas getting new life, which means more rates and more wealth for the city. Thornton sees it all as a man inspired so that many a city council has offered land free for the projects. Abbey National is also working on direct building as well as restoration, trying to bring back modern homes for rent as well as for sale. Thornton's team started by looking at six really grotty areas and getting local managers involved. The team is now involved in areas all over the country, and Britain will be all the better for it, since other building societies will follow suit.

Building societies are not like normal commercial companies. They work under special, strict laws and are essentially non-profit-making, though the staff are naturally paid proper salaries to work for them. On the whole, they manage to hold the costs down, having some 4,000 or so branch offices for 300 societies around Britain as compared with more than 10,000 branch offices of the Big Four clearing banks, for example. There are just over 300 societies and the number grows smaller every year as small ones get merged into large units.

Building societies must by law be financially independent and they are restricted about indulging in other businesses which might make them money. They may take deposits of money from the public, on which they pay interest and get some tax concessions for their depositors to boot. The money they thus collect from deposits is loaned out as mortgages. You often read about a queue for mortgages, money for homes running short, a mortgage famine and so on. The problem is that, unless people save or invest with the societies, there is a shortage of money to lend to home-buyers and, when inflation hits hard, people save less.

The law governs how much (or little) a building society may lend. It may never lend a sum that is greater than the value of the property concerned for the obvious reason that the over-optimistic borrower might find himself in deep debt if he ever defaulted on his payments — the society would have to ask him to pay the balance between the sale price of the property and the borrowed sum. Building societies do, therefore, make a practice of lending only against a certain percentage of the property's market value — anything from 60 per cent

to 90 per cent according to the type of property and the valuation, though they obviously sometimes lend far smaller percentages. The valuation, though done by an independent valuer, is commissioned by the building society and the borrower cannot refute it. He can and often does (sometimes successfully) argue that he needs more than the percentage offered to him.

As a rule, the mortgage a building society will give you will be about 2½ times your annual salary, but there are other limits. For instance, no society will lend more than £25,000 and will often baulk at anything over £15,000. Never forget that a building society chooses you, not the other way around. The law and building society tradition both try to ensure that mortgages are as much as possible readily available to middle- or low-income borrowers. It doesn't always work out that way, but that is the object. Therefore the law and the societies also act in such as way as to protect the borrower from over-committing himself.

They cannot advance more than 10 per cent of their available funds in special loans, such as to corporation organizations (companies, commercial concerns of various types mainly), though they are allowed to make big advances to housing associations (which are described later in this chapter). The history of inflation is such that house-buying has been the best protector of one's money on a consistent basis ever since the end of the last world war; houses rapidly become more valuable than the sums borrowed on them.

The Building Societies' Association monitors the annual percentage increase on the selling price of all houses bought through building societies which, as we've seen, represents the vast majority. Opposite, you see this gives you a 264.5 per cent compound interest over the last ten years, provided you stayed in the same house — removal expenses would reduce your total gain if you had moved. Compound means, of course, that the percentage growth each year is on the already 'swollen' sum of the previous year.

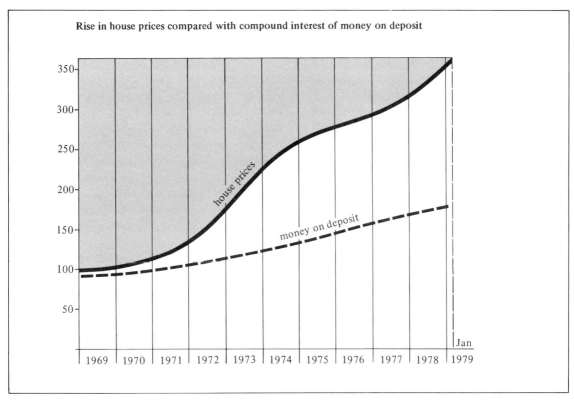

Rise in house prices compared with compound interest of money on deposit

house prices

money on deposit

350
300
250
200
150
100
50

1969 1970 1971 1972 1973 1974 1975 1976 1977 1978 1979

Jan

It is a satisfying piece of arithmetic because it will make the interest you pay on your loan look small. You would be unlikely to have made as much money by depositing it at the bank or in some other investment. To do so would have meant picking the winner among investments, never easy even for the experts. And all the time you win, you are enjoying warmth, comfort, shelter, happiness. The best buy in every way is your home.

Buying a house

First, before we borrow to buy our home, we have to find it and, even more difficult, to find one that we can afford. Most people have a good idea of what they want and where they want it, but not everyone remembers all the extras that arise to ruin the family budget when house-buying begins. Apart from the actual mortgage and insurance-cover repayments, there are going to be all sorts of expenses, some one-off lump-sum payments due during the processes of buying – to surveyors, legal firms and suchlike; and others which will continue, such as heating and lighting, rates and maybe even higher fares to work.

You can find out very roughly what mortgage loan you might get on your income or joint incomes and what it will cost you at your age (the age makes a difference both to the term over which you can borrow and to the insurance premiums). As I said before, you are usually allowed to borrow a sum 2½ times your annual salary or slightly more if both of a couple are earning. This gives you a price range when it comes to visiting the estate agents or studying the property advertisements. The advertised price will very likely be higher than the price you pay after a little bargaining, unless you hit one of those periodic booms when sellers manage to offload their homes in days rather than weeks; or unless you fall in love with the most desirable property at the most desirable price in which case others will recognize the value of the place too. You might then be 'gazumped', meaning that someone will make a higher offer than you even if yours has been verbally accepted. You can always gazump back if you can afford it and think it worth while. Otherwise, just make an offer below the asking price. How much below must depend on market conditions, how keen you are not to risk losing the place and so forth. It should be enough to show the estate agent and the seller that you are serious. The margin could be anything between £500 and £5,000 but is normally nearer 10 per cent reduction, depending entirely on the market state.

Before offering, try taking a builder round to give you some idea of the cost of repairs and/or renovations and conversions. Not all builders will do this for you but you may have a friendly local man with whom you have previously dealt. His opinion in no way constitutes a survey, just an estimate of cost.

Ask your solicitor (you will need one) or the estate agent to give you a rough outline of legal costs, stamp duty and so forth. Stamp duty is payable on properties costing more than £15,000 and is levied on a sliding scale – it is a tax that goes to the Government.

Stamp duty (1st quarter 1980)		
More than	but not more than	payable
£15,000	£20,000	½%
£20,000	£25,000	1%
£25,000	£30,000	1½%
£30,000	without limit	2%

You get a Certificate of Valuation to prove what you paid for the house. If, in the case of leasehold property, there is a rent exceeding a certain sum, you may not be able to use the official Certificate of Value so that all stamp duty would be at the top rate of 2 per cent. Ask your solicitor, of course.

Furniture

You may have some or none. If some, do make sure of your additional needs and add that into your mental arithmetic about initial costs of moving. If none, your outlay will be greater. Obviously, you will manage with very little at first, just the bare essentials, but how they can add up these days. Cooker, refrigerator and bed can be very costly and, just in case you think of them as being easy to buy on credit, remember the credit repayments could be more difficult once you have mortgage or bigger mortgage repayments to find. Curtains – you will need some privacy – can be devilishly expensive and it is just not sensible to buy make-do things to start with. The theory that you can always replace with better ones later leads into even more cost and a good deal of wasted money as well. Check every single thing carefully. You just might need a bigger mortgage than you thought (if you can get it).

If you are in love, move heaven and earth to buy the place anyway, even if it means bare floorboards and sleeping bags at first, with a calor gas stove that you rescued from a camping holiday.

Where?

Don't be blindly snobbish or stupid about the area in which you house-hunt. You can buy excellent value in less-than-nice areas, most of which are being constantly and rapidly improved by thousands of home-buyers who, just like yourself, are having to buy what they can afford wherever it might be. Thus the area will become as nice as many already-smart ones and the value of your home will grow enough to enable you to move to your dream area if you still want to. Obviously some areas build up more slowly than others so use your judge-ment. See what the potential is. Is it close to a railway line or a proposed building development? Are there shops, buses and other transport? Are there schools – they aren't building many and nothing keeps an area depressed, short of young energetic people who improve their homes and neighbourhood, like a dearth of nearby schooling? Are you near some friends and/or relatives who might babysit. Try to get a glimpse of some of the people who will be near neighbours. Ring a bell or two and ask some questions. Most people love to tell you about the place and few will shut the door on you unless they are hectically busy. A home is too important to sacrifice to such traditions as snobbery but you will be spending so much time there that you must not risk unhappiness, isolation or the kind of ugliness that might eat into your very soul.

If you live in a council flat or house, you may be offered the chance to buy it (probably, since you are a sitting tenant, at a reasonable price); this can be a good buy, but do consider the price and state of the property. Get a surveyor round, and, if he has major criticisms of the place, argue with the council about the price.

You might feel like joining the satisfied if small army of people who found their homes through the Department of the Environment list of property for sale or rent. This list, sent free four times a year, carries rough details of anything from an old school, a disused railway station (but probably with a still-used railway past it) a Gothic chapel to a haunted house with thatched roof and even some derelict town cottages of the Industrial Revolution era. It is sent free by the Historic Buildings Bureau, 35 Saville Row, London W1X 2BT. One word of warning: there are probably special regulations about what you can and can't do to nearly all the buildings on this list — you would not be allowed to remove particular characteristics, like turrets, for instance.

Ask the Council

When you finally decide to buy, you will hire a solicitor, with whom I shall deal shortly. He will ask many questions that seal the decision to go ahead or start house-hunting all over again. But you can, before committing yourself to the expense of hiring

him right away, make a few enquiries at the local authority office or Town Hall. They can tell you whether a main road or nearby motorway is proposed, whether plans have been passed and suchlike. They can fill you in about schools, churches and amenities like sports centres or markets, new shopping centres and local transport. You might find a new airport is due to come close to you or a bus centre is destined for the end of your road.

None of these apparent drawbacks need matter. That depends entirely on your nature, on how they would affect you emotionally and mentally. But they could make a difference to the re-sale value, upwards or downwards according to whether they might improve or spoil the locality. In the end, someone will buy your house if you did, but it could be difficult to find buyers in a problem area. If you plan a long stay, this may be less important than if your lives and circumstances might entail a move before too long (such as working for a firm with many branches or factories, a firm that might 'post' you).

In any case, your selling price will undoubtedly be higher than your buying price because inflation ensures that. As the cost of labour, bricks, cement and land soars, new houses become more and more costly and old 'secondhand' homes move up in parallel. Yours is bound to improve; if you modernize it that helps. The profit will usually pay for your labour and the materials. As I already said, such profit is not taxable on your owner-occupied home, of which you are allowed only one per couple (and their children until the latter grow up).

Service charges on flats

You may be looking at a flat rather than a house. Look carefully at the running costs. There will almost certainly be a service charge, which probably rises in line with such increases as the cost of fuel, labour and building materials. It may even rise annually, or be subject to two-, three- or four-year reviews. You might find a flat in a building where the management is by a tenants' association which pays for essentials as they arise, not automatically. Each tenant has a vote.

There will, apart from the service charge which should make you pause and study it, also be a ground rent if you are buying a leashold flat. In such cases you should also take note that towards the end of the term, the lease decreases in value. More and more, this is small and there are even some freehold flats as well as some with peppercorn rents, meaning tiny nominal rents just to meet the demands of a lease or trust governing the whole building. The law about selling parts of large properties, such as flats, has become clearer year by year and it is now a lot easier to buy and sell them and to get mortgages on them. I have seen flats where the ground rent is 'one red rose on midsummer's day' and another where, suitably since it was in London's Mayfair, they asked for an orchid. In both cases, the buildings were managed by the firm who owned the freehold of the land on which the block of flats stood and the service charges were far from low though they included the provision of such services as sauna, swimming pool, gymnasium and all. Fine, if you want those things but not if you do not since you will be paying for them anyway. If service charges and ground rent are high, the actual purchase price may well be lower than for a home. That is, a four-roomed flat may well cost less than a four-roomed house.

I am not saying that the service charge is necessarily expensive, but it usually is. Do not get the idea that your freehold house carries no service charge. Everything you spend on redecorating the outside, keeping it safe from intruders, maintaining the roof against leaks and so forth is actually a service charge. With blocks of flats or apartment houses, there are all sorts of proper laws about fireproofing, extra doors, cleaning and other activities for the protection of

the inmates' safety and health. In your own freehold home, you might accept scruffiness and danger. That would be cheaper. Unless the place burns down and the insurance company decides the fire might have been your fault so that either it pays out less than you hoped or the place costs more to put right than they pay.

Think about the heating bills and whether or not the house already has adequate and relatively inexpensive heating systems. Look at the rates payable, the water rates, the fares to work and school, everything. Frightened? You probably will be. Still in love with the house? Then forget fear and forge ahead. Loves does conquer most things in the end, even love for more or less inanimate things like houses.

Solicitors

You are now probably going to need a solicitor. Maybe you have one, maybe you will ask your building society, if you already have one, since they do recommend reasonable ones. Or write to the Law Society, Chancery Lane, London WC2, for the address of a few near you so that you can interview them and see who you like, get an idea of the charges and generally choose somebody (the local Citizens Advice Bureau can also help you find one).

A solicitor is expensive. But I would never hesitate to say you ought to have one. Nothing is as expensive as making a bad mistake, all too easy when you don't know what you are doing. There are firms who do cheap conveyancing, claiming that it is such a simple matter that it can be cheap and that solicitors are overcharging. The report on the solicitorial profession (the legal one, I mean) last year criticized conveyancing charges by law firms and they may have dropped a little now. So do shop around for your legal adviser and ask bluntly in advance what it will cost you, then compare the prices.

My own view is that a solicitor is necessary for so many things that you need him. There

Land Registry Fees Price of Property	First Registration (Payable where the property is being registered for the first time)	Dealings (Payable where the property is already registered and is being transferred from one owner to another)
£10,000	£17.00	£25.00
£12,000	£20.00	£30.00
£14,000	£23.00	£35.00
£16,000	£26,00	£40.00
£18,000	£29.00	£45.00
£20,000	£32.00	£50.00
£25,000	£39.50	£62.00
£30,000	£47.00	£74.00

Where, to finance the purchase of the property, a mortgage has been raised, it is registered free of charge, whether on first registration or on a transfer of land which is already registered. The only condition attached to the free registration of the mortgage is that it must accompany the conveyance (or transfer) when the latter is sent for registration.

may be very rare exceptions such as if you are buying a new house with nice, tidy title deeds. But such cases are rare, and I keep recalling the terrible story of the people who bought a house on a new estate in Essex and gradually found the field on which the homes were built subsiding so badly that they were all in danger; they had no redress, either with their insurance companies or with the builders. A builder's guarantee, after all, usually covers only the actual structure and not compensation if the land settles (as long as his foundations were not faulty).

There are all sorts of other things that need legal advice. Such as whether to own the property yourself, let your spouse own it or settle for joint ownership; who should be the 'mortgagee' (meaning the borrower of the mortgage) – or you can be joint mortgagees. It may be well to halve the 'equity' of the house (its asset value) and for each to have equal shares or to have shares in some other proportions – friends, 'good' friends, homosexual lovers and relatives may be applying for a home in which to live together. Buyers are not only single people and married or engaged couples. It used to be

very difficult to buy unless you were the latter; building societies thought that single people could flit off easily and that other relationships didn't have the stability of heterosexual marriage. The taboos are dying and, with them, building society resistance to people in curious or unusual circumstances. Gradually, but positively, building societies are becoming less discriminating.

Your own solicitor's fees will be from about £200 to £500. The charges may be based on a number of factors including the time involved, the complications of the 'search' (which means finding out everything there is to know about the house, its history and area), deeds, registration and other things. For instance, it could take longer to 'conveyance' a country cottage of which the deeds and boundaries are obscure and subject to argument than a large new house which is properly registered and legally 'identifiable' without complexities of law. Houses built since 1925 should be registered under the Land Registry Act of that year, but many, many others are registered now that so many have already been sold, bought and legally conveyed. The solicitor may also charge for

Purchase price or valuation	Mortgage advance (say 80%)	Building Society's solicitor's fees (where the purchase and mortgage are contemporaneous)		Building Society valuation fee (as recommended by the Building Societies Association)
		Registered land	Unregistered land	
£6,000	£4,800	£21.50	£28.00	£14.05
£8,000	£6,400	£23.18	£36.00	£18.36
£10,000	£8,000			£22.68
£12,000	£9,600			£27.00
£14,000	£11,200			£31.32
£16,000	£12,800			£34.56
£18,000	£14,400			£36.72
£20,000	£16,000			£38.88
		On advances of over £7,000 the charge is fixed by arrangement		For property over £40,000 the fee is fixed by negotiation

special skills and knowledge. And the value of the property may be taken into account in the legal fees – this is the issue on which so many people argue fiercely, so do try your own arguments. On top of everything, we get the dreaded VAT at the end of his bill. Normally, the solicitor pays stamp duty and other official costs so that they appear on your final account. In some cases, he might ask for an advance payment, depending on you, your background and the circumstances in which you hire him. Mostly, he merely receives the money from you with his charges added. The vendor's solicitor receives your money and deducts his charges before sending the balance to the client, the vendor.

The legal procedure is that you agree a price and a sale and purchase 'subject to contract and survey' – more about surveyors very shortly. This means that you can change your mind up to the time that you exchange contracts. The solicitors will arrange for their respective clients to sign identical contracts and then, when everything is satisfactory to both sides, contracts will be simultaneously exchanged by the acting lawyers or their representatives. Until contracts are exchanged, any initial deposit you made is returnable. Once the contract stage is past, your deposits are forfeit if you change your mind and you will be liable for the legal costs so far incurred, including those of the vendor, though there are sad cases where vendors find such costs hard to get out of the offending mind-changer.

Your solicitor may help you find a building society, if you haven't already got one, or an insurance company to lend money. He may also recommend a surveyor (though estate agents can sometimes do both or either and they often have a good knowledge of the neighbourhood which can help to find the right professional advisers).

At the stage that you hire your solicitor, you will begin to sign various papers as events move towards the completion of the sale and purchase. Never, never sign anything before getting a solicitor. When the estate agent lets you know the vendor (the seller) has agreed to your offer (after some negotiations, as a rule) you may be asked for a deposit to prove your honest intentions. In theory this is 10 per cent but in practice very few people ever pay that much, and the agent might agree to as little as £100. Anyway, be sure to suggest that and try to insist upon it. It does not go into his pocket, since he gets his commission from the vendor but he may act as 'stakeholder', meaning he holds the stake until things progress. Your solicitor will deal with the vendor's solicitor and with the building society (or other lending source) and you pay some of the legal fees of the lending company.

This table shows what you might have to find for the building society and you can see it is small. These charges must be paid in cash, they cannot be added to the mortgage.

You will notice that legal fees are less where the land is registered. Do not worry overmuch if it is not because the registration costs are not very high, though there is some legal labour involved over and above the basic registration fee.

After you have paid the deposit and agreed the price, but before exchange of contracts, the solicitor will find out all the hidden snags. He will also make sure that all outstanding debts on the property — rates, ground rent, service charges, instalment or hire-purchase payments on home extensions and improvements or central heating systems, water rates and everything of that kind — be paid up to date. There will be some more to pay on some of these things between signature of contract and completion (which is when the actual money is paid, and usually takes place about a month after contracts are exchanged); he may agree with the vendor's solicitors to a final settling at the time of completion, but he must make sure what you are buying, something amateur conveyancers are very bad at doing thoroughly. The money does not change hands until completion, as I have said, so these things are discovered before it is too late. He will also carry out a 'search' which reveals any and every development planned for the area over the next 50 years as far as it is known.

Surveyors

Whether you have your own surveyor or not is very much your own decision. The building society surveyor will value the house before they OK your mortgage but he will be deciding how large a mortgage he would recommend, looking for faults or damage that you may have to put right after moving in. He will specify essential repairs or changes such as replacement of broken basins or WCs, roof tiles that let in the rain and anything else that threatens the actual structure of the house. These give you a clue to the probable faults of the house and, if you are actually there when the surveyor goes round, you might guess something from his face and attitude. But he will make his own date directly with the householder if the place is occupied, without telling you when that is, and you may never meet him. If the place is empty and the estate agent is admitting him, you could be lucky and coincide. But you are not his client (even though you have to pay the building society a fee for his services), and he is not bound to tell you anything at all. Nor is the building society, though they do try to be helpful if there is any bad news about your potential home, especially if they are going to turn you down.

Your own surveyor will cost anything from about £85 to £150 depending on the value of the house, perhaps more if there are any complications, travelling to isolated places, etc. Make sure your surveyor has the letters A.R.I.C.S. or F.R.I.C.S. after his name, meaning that he belongs to a reputable association of surveyors, and try to use a local man, not only because it costs less but also because he knows the idiosyncrasies of local property values.

If the house is old, I think you should hire your own surveyor. Don't despair if he turns in a bad report of dry rot and wet rot there, or even worse. He will also tell you how to put it right and you can get your estimates from local workmen of the kind he recommends. Your solicitor will then seek a corresponding reduction in the price, since all this will be happening before

Immediate Cash Requirements

Value of House	Personal Stake or Deposit	Amount of Mortgage	Legal costs of Conveyance (with VAT at 15%)	Fees Building Society Valuation fee (with VAT at 15%)	Building Society's Solicitor's fees (with VAT at 15%)	Total Fees	Total cash Required
£	£	£	£	£	£	£	£
4,000	400	3,600	69.00	10.35	25.30	104.65	504.65
6,000	600	5,700	86.25	14.92	37.38	138.55	738.55
8,000	800	7,200	103.50	19.55	43.55	166.60	966.60
10,000	1,000	9,000	120.75	24.15	47.43	192.33	1,192.33
12,000	1,200	10,800	132.25	28.75	50.74	211.74	1,411.74
14,000	1,400	12,600	143.75	33.35	53.93	231.03	1,631.03
16,000	1,600	14,400	155.25	36.80	55.91	247.96	1,847.96
18,000	1,800	16,200	166.64	39.10	58.50	264.24	2,064.24
20,000	2,000	18,000	178.25	41.40	61.09	280.74	2,280.74
22,000	2,200	19,800	189.75	43.70	63.68	297.13	2,497.13
24,000	2,400	21,600	201.25	46.00	66.26	313.51	2,713.51

Notes:
1. The figures have been calculated on the assumption that the purchaser can provide a 'deposit' of 10 per cent.
2. The figures for legal costs are very approximate and apply only to unregistered land. They do not include search fees, stamp duty wher applicable, or other small disbursements.
3. No allowance has been made for the cost of an independent survey or removal expenses, nor for the indemnity premium on a higher-than-normal loan.
4. Where the amount of the mortgage exceeds £7,000 the Building Society Solicitor's fees is 'by arrangement' and the figures shown are estimates, based on the former statutory scale.
5. Where the advance exceeds £24,000 the borrower should consult a building society about the immediate cash requirements.

exchange of contracts; the original price was agreed, if you remember, subject to survey; before you (maybe even the vendor) knew of such horrors.

Some of the costs

A booklet written by the Secretary-General of the Building Societies Association includes the table below as a guide to some of the basics that you will have to fork out for that dream home.
Remember that the table includes the very basic essentials and please do not overlook the fact that stamp duty, search fees, and some other costs are not included. Nor, of course, are moving costs and they can be hefty. Do always get at least two estimates and three are better because you will find quite a wide variation between one firm and another. You can sometimes reduce the bill by doing a great deal of your own packing — say, china and kitchen things — but you will then be entirely responsible for breakages and some firms may not even agree to such an arrangement.
Other omissions from above include the insurance premiums for the building, which are compulsory and will be demanded early on by the lending society. They will probably

give you a list of insurance companies from which you may choose one; if you have a favourite with which you are already insured, or work for a bank or insurance company, you will be able to ask to use your own company, and such permission is unlikely to be refused in normal circumstances.

Finding the loan

I have already mentioned some people who could be helpful in finding a building society, such as friendly estate agent, insurance broker or other financial adviser. The matter may however already be settled by the fact that you are a depositor, a saver with a building society, which will make them sympathetic. In fact, I believe the time will come when many societies will refuse loans except to their depositors and they undoubtedly deserve the priority their applications now get.

I need hardly say that a mortgage is like a hire-purchase agreement on a washing machine except that it is on a house or flat. You borrow a large sum for an agreed term (usually 20 or 25 years); in return you pay interest on the sum and repay the capital at the same time, which means that, as you repay more of the capital, you pay less interest because the interest is on the

reducing sum; alternatively you may not repay the capital, but may take out an insurance policy that guarantees to pay out the sum you owe the building society at the end of the 20/25 years. In this case you pay premiums to the insurance company and interest only to the building society. Either way, you pay out a good deal more than the sum borrowed. The table shows what you pay a building society if you are repaying capital as well as paying interest.

Interest rates are liable to vary according to the minimum lending rate – though they do sometimes come down, they are more likely to go up.

For a list of Britain's building societies, write to the Building Societies Association, 34 Park Street, London W1Y 4AL. Ask, too, for their leaflet *Hints for Home Buyers*.

Nearly all home loans are covered by some kind of insurance policy, if only on the life of the borrower or by term insurance, meaning that the insurance lasts only for an agreed term such as the period of the mortgage (see Chapter 4). There are fewer uncovered loans though they do exist.

The amount that a loan costs you looks a bit terrifying but tax relief makes the final sum a shade less daunting. You can claim tax relief on interest payments: if you pay

Monthly repayments on repayment mortgage for a term of 20 years					
			Rate of interest		
Amount advanced	12%	13%	14%	15%	16%
1,000	11.16	11.87	12.59	13.32	14.06
2,000	22.32	23.74	25.18	26.64	28.12
3,000	33.48	35.61	37.77	39.96	42.18
4,000	44.64	47.48	50.36	53.28	56.24
5,000	55.80	59.35	62.96	66.60	70.30
6,000	66.96	71.22	75.54	79.92	84.36
7,000	78.12	83.09	88.13	93.24	98.42
8,000	89.28	94.96	100.72	106.56	112.48
10,000	111.60	118.70	125.90	133.20	140.60
11,000	122.76	130.57	138.49	146.52	154.66
12,000	133.92	142.44	151.08	159.84	168.72
13,000	145.08	154.31	163.67	173.16	182.78

tax at standard rate of 30 per cent, every £100 of interest is actually costing you only £70 because you have not had to pay £30 tax on the £100 worth of earnings. If your interest is £250 a month, and you pay standard rate tax, you will 'save' more than £75 monthly. If you pay at higher rates of tax, you save even more; but, now that the high rates come into effect on much higher levels of income, there may be legislation to allow tax relief only at standard rates.

This tax relief is one of the Government's more useful generosities even though tax relief is allowed only up to a limit of £25,000 on one house only (no loans on second homes are eligible for tax relief). Married people living together count as one for this purpose so, even with separate taxation, you cannot have a home each for either relief on mortgage interest or for escape of capital gains tax.

It may surprise you to learn that the average mortgage is only about £10,000. Sadly, that does not mean people want to borrow only £10,000, but that it is all they are actually able to borrow. Obviously, some loans are double that and some are smaller. But it is rather a pathetic average considering how much houses now cost. The £25,000 ceiling might rise with inflation but hopefully not yet, as such a move might just make houses more expensive. Not that the buyers would abound because, however high the ceiling, loans for mortgages are just not available in sufficient quantities for people to borrow. Nor can their incomes (the £25,000 mortgage means you must earn £10,000 p.a.) justify the high loans. There are ways of topping up the mortgage loan which, as I said, we'll study later in this chapter. They are of little help to most low-income earners but they do exist. Any building society will base his consideration of an application on the following main factors:

(1) The age of the applicant (not the sex, as discrimination is illegal and women should be able to get mortgages without argument).

(2) The occupation and income; here women might find themselves being very slightly victimized on the basis that their incomes might fall or vanish if they have babies, so that this might be considered too. Fair enough, really, as the new mother might lose her home and she ought to consider this point. It is not legal to penalize a woman because she is young enough to have babies, but there are more ways of killing a cat than wringing its neck; the refusal just might be due to such an eventuality even if nobody is prepared to admit it.

(3) The sum needed, the period for which it is borrowed, and insurance cover.

(4) The applicant's references and credit-worthiness. Some societies are still rather careless about checking references but most have been caught out by good references being supplied by worthless referees and are pretty demanding. Anyway, computers and such have made our credit-worthiness an open book, so they have other ways of checking up on us.

(5) The property in question: whether it is a flat or house, leasehold or freehold, good value or overpriced, and that sort of thing. They can be difficult about the unconventional, the societies, because such properties are hard to sell. But fewer buildings are now unconventional and the market for homes is such that either old-fashioned or modern monstrosities are saleable. But churches, old schools, or old railway stations and such might prove difficult for them to accept and they may ask for promises and plans of conversion and renovation.

(6) The condition of the property, naturally. If it needs much repair and restoration, the estimated cost may be added to the sum borrowed (because it is legally part of the value of the house) and therefore paid off over the same period as the mortgage, as part of the mortgage.

The society's object is to discourage any borrower from taking on more than he can afford. Very roughly, and it does vary from one case to another, your monthly outgoings to the society should be no more than a full week's earnings; or, putting it another way, the total loan should not be more than 2½ to 3 times your total annual income.

Whether the borrower wants his loan over 20, 25 or 30 years is partly up to him and depends much on his age. The longer term means comparatively small reductions in the monthly payments and does add a good deal of interest to the total bill. A long-term debt reduces so slowly that it could mean awfully little profit for a borrower who sells within a short time of buying the house, and my own advice is to make 25 years the maximum term. Obviously, older people (or people in poor health) might have to borrow for shorter periods like 10 or 15 years.

On leasehold property, societies will normally advance limited sums. These vary, but a popular calculation is that they will lend for a term equal to one-third only of the leasehold, so that it might well be difficult to borrow on leases of under 60 years; the final decision naturally depends much on how much is being borrowed and what percentage of the total price it may be. Other societies will consider short leases, even of 20 years.

Married couples can get slightly larger advances if the wife is working and earning though, once again, her potentiality towards motherhood is taken into account, officially or otherwise.

Any would-be borrower will be asked for – say – 5 per cent minimum deposit though this will be based on the building society's valuation which, as I have already remarked, may be lower than the asking price. There are however special arrangements which can be made for 100 per cent loans, involving guarantee schemes, but only for properties costing less than £14,000 – and they are hard to find these days.

The building society has the right to vary the rate of interest at any time after giving proper notice of the change. All mortgages can be paid off before their time, but three months' notice is usually required, which is easier than one might think since the normal processes of selling and buying a house take as long as three months. There might be a small charge, and there will be legal fees, but there is usually no charge unless the repayment is very early in the original mortgage term and most companies waive their rights to it anyway.

A mortgage at the moment is usually settled on one property and started again on another. In fact, the building society, if you are using the same one and it has agreed to the same loan on the new property, will merely repay itself and then lend again, as it were, so that you do not go through the actions of closing down and starting again and the mortgage is actually, if not technically, transferred without much trouble to either you or the society. Obviously, there is quite simply a new contract for the new property and the building society has not asked you for money to lend out again. However, they have the right to take your settlement and then lend again. The timing can make the difference.

As a rule, you may not sublet or let part of a mortgaged property, but permission would be granted to do something of this kind if it helped you make payments that would otherwise be difficult to manage. Societies are reasonable as long as you ask, tell and do both honestly. You might get an overseas job, but want to keep the house to come back to – they would agree in such a case.

Never fall into arrears without warning the society first and asking for help. You may get a temporary moratorium, a period of rest from repayments if you are in genuine trouble and have been a good payer in the past. When things get better, you re-start the payments and the missed period is tacked on to the other end of the mortgage term. As I said, societies are understanding and human.

However human and understanding, a society will dispossess a persistent defaulter of his home; it is only fair, since the loan can then be extended to a possibly homeless family. A dispossessed property must by law be sold for the best possible price by all normal methods so the idea that the building society gets a quick sale at a discount is totally false, if rather prevalent. Having sold, the society pockets its debt and any out-of-pocket expenses, then passes the profit to the former mortgagee (borrower).

There are several kinds of mortgage. In some cases, you pay off the capital as well as making interest payments. In such cases, you are paying large slices of the total interest that would be due over the agreed term of years of the loan and rather less capital. Actuaries, men with highly skilled mathematical precision, work out the combined total of interest over the years and the capital repayment, converting it into equal monthly terms. But, since the element of interest is so high at first, you may find you owe more capital than you think if you sell within the first few years. In other cases, you might merely be paying interest to the building society, your loan being secured by a life insurance company, as it were, which has an endowment policy that matures when the time is up. In such a case you might be making monthly payments to two different firms, a building society and an insurance conpany, the first being interest only and the second being premiums to gain the eventual endowment. But let's look at some of the different kinds of mortgage:

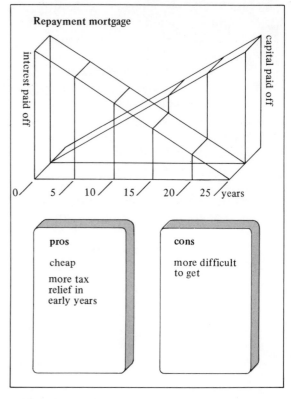

1. Option Mortgages

These are very much for the low-income earner who is also a low taxpayer and therefore unable to take advantage of the full benefit of tax reliefs. When he gets his mortgage, he relinquishes all rights to tax reliefs, even if in future his income grows to attract standard rate or higher income tax. In return, he gets an annual subsidy from the Government, which is a small percentage of his annual debt if he is repaying both capital and interest; or a slightly smaller percentage if his loan is covered by an endowment

policy. In hardship cases, where you might have started with an ordinary mortgage but find it too much of a burden, you might get a 'late option'. Sometimes incomes fall unexpectedly, and this right to change is a great help. In reverse, you can apply for a change to an ordinary mortgage after four years of option mortgage, but in most cases the decision is taken at borrowing time and stays that way.

To qualify, the borrower must be the occupant of the home and it must be his only or main residence though dependent relatives are naturally allowed also to live there. The mortgage may not be more than £25,000, which it is very unlikely to be in such cases anyway. Joint borrowers can elect for option mortgages. The capital debt of the mortgage is reduced fairly quickly even in the early years of the loan because the subsidy is paid by the Government to the building society. Though the option subsidy is not fixed but can be varied from time to time according to the interest payable on

Normal Rate of Interest under Repayment Contract	Lower Rate for Option Mortgages	
	Repayment Mortgages	Endowment Mortgages
Exceeding 7.0% but not exceeding 7.6%	2.5% less	2.25% less
Exceeding 7.6% but not exceeding 8.2%	2.7% less	2.45% less
Exceeding 8.2% but not exceeding 8.8%	2.9% less	2.65% less
Exceeding 8.8% but not exceeding 9.4%	3.1% less	2.85% less
Exceeding 9.4% but not exceeding 10.0%	3.3% less	3.05% less
Exceeding 10.0% but not exceeding 10.6%	3.5% less	3.25% less
Exceeding 10.6% but not exceeding 11.2%	3.7% less	3.45% less
Exceeding 11.2% but not exceeding 11.8%	3.9% less	3.65% less
Exceeding 11.8% but not exceeding 12.4%	4.1% less	3.85% less
Exceeding 12.4% but not exceeding 13.0%	4.3% less	4.05% less

the mortgage, the following sliding scale, supplied by the Building Societies Association, gives a guide to the difference in interest rates made by having an option mortgage (the 'normal' rates of interest given also take account of tax relief).

The Building Societies Association (see p. 63), which has explanatory booklets on most types of mortgage, supplies a very sensible one on option mortgages which is free.

2. Repayment mortgages

These are the most popular. Here the mortgage is repaid in monthly instalments. The instalments are actuarily worked out to include both the repayment of the borrowed capital and the interest chargeable. In the early years, the interest element is high so that little capital is actually being paid off. Later, the reverse begins to be true. Obviously, since tax relief applies to interest paid, the tax relief is greater in the early years too. Some covering insurance is wise and necessary.

3. Endowment mortgages

Here the mortgage is directly linked to an endowment-life insurance policy. The endowment is for the sum of the loan, though you

might take out a with-profits policy which will give you some extra money at the end of the agreed borrowing term. Naturally, the term of the mortgage and the maturity of the endowment coincide; the length may be anything from ten to thirty years according to the age of the person involved,

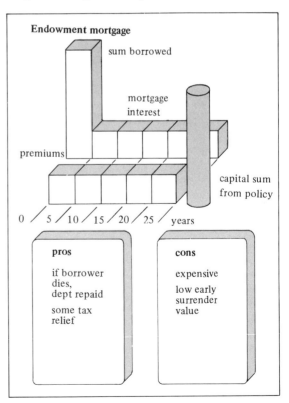

their available income for premiums and that kind of thing. If the borrower dies before the maturing date, the loan is automatically paid off and the surviving spouse, friend or whoever inherits the house might also get any profits already accrued on a with-profits policy.

The borrower pays the interest on the loan and the premiums on the policy, but is not repaying capital. Thus, if the house is sold after — say — 10 years of a 20-year policy, the borrower officially has only the capital value of the surrendered policy at that time if he does surrender. In fact, he would be crazy to do so as the surrender value falls short of the total of the premiums he has paid until right at the end of the endowment term. What he should do is to pay the building society out of the proceeds of the house, go on with his premiums and policy, then either collect the money at the maturing date or, if he is buying another home (which is more than likely) use the policy to cover another mortgage loan. There is tax relief at half basic tax rate on insurance premiums linked to mortgages (which at the moment means relief on 50 per cent); a considerable advantage over the lower tax reliefs (currently 17½ per cent) on other life-endowment policies. another Government help to house-owners. A with-profits policy will cost higher premiums and might be refused on overweight or unhealthy people, but it is usually very good value. This kind of mortgage is costlier than the others but always much easier to get; and insurance companies, who will give mortgages, insist on endowment schemes. If you haven't saved with a society, you may have to borrow from an insurance company which will mean you must use this system.

4. Interest-only mortgages
Here the borrower pays only the interest charges, which means payments are comfortable and low, but the capital remains a debt until the end of the agreed term. When property prices rise as they have, this is no

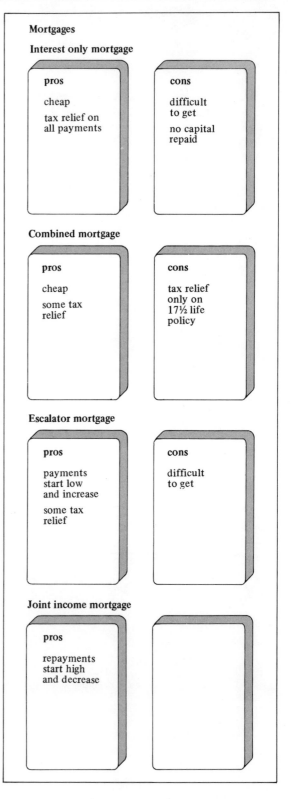

Mortgages

Interest only mortgage

pros	cons
cheap	difficult to get
tax relief on all payments	no capital repaid

Combined mortgage

pros	cons
cheap	tax relief only on 17½ life policy
some tax relief	

Escalator mortgage

pros	cons
payments start low and increase	difficult to get
some tax relief	

Joint income mortgage

pros	
repayments start high and decrease	

Mortgages	Option	Repayment	Endowment	Endowment With Profits	Interest Only	Combined	Escalator	Joint Income
Good For Low Earners	▓							
Good For Low Earners with Expectations							▓	
Good For High Earning Couples who expect Children								▓
Good For High Tax-payers					▓			
No Capital Repaid					▓			
Mortgage Paid Off At Death of Policy holder			▓	▓		▓		
Lump Sum Bonus Tax-free				▓				
Easy To Get			▓	▓				
Cheap	▓	▓				▓		

problem but it means nothing has been repaid when you come to sell, which might be difficult when you buy the next property at highly-inflated prices. It is an expensive way of borrowing despite low monthly payments because the interest charges will be high. But they do qualify for tax relief, which means that this could be a good idea for high taxpayers. Not always easy to get one, however.

5. Combined mortgages
These combine insurance and loans, the loan being guaranteed by insurance but the insurance premiums do not carry the extra tax relief, but only the 17½ per cent. Cheaper than endowment mortgages for most, just the same.

6. Escalator mortgages
Payments start low but increase as time goes by. Fine if you are positive of higher income (such as from trusts, land, etc). But the lender needs proof and you need to be absolutely certain. Interest charges are lower and repayment might be faster but obviously not many qualify for this kind of mortgage.

7. Joint income mortgages
Rather the reverse of the above. A couple take a joint mortgage based on both incomes and agree to repay high sums in the early years, such sums reducing as they have children, grow older and retire or something of that kind. The formulae vary slightly but this is useful for a couple of high-income earners who want their overheads radically reduced before the family comes along.

Local authorities
There are other ways of borrowing besides the building societies. Local authorities will have their own loan schemes for properties within their areas and residents can apply for these. The rates may be the same or higher

and their conditions will be the same as for societies but they will probably advance 100 per cent of the price (valuation may be close to the asking price unless the vendor is especially greedy). Not all councils have such schemes but, because they lend as a social duty and consider the loan to be a part of their policy for housing their residents, they are likely to be less conservative and limiting about the kind of property on which they lend.

Trustee Savings Banks
With private enterprise banks moving further into the home loans business, it is not surprising that the Trustee Savings Bank, Government-backed, has also been there since late 1979, when it earmarked 3 per cent of its £5,500 million deposits to advance to customers on home mortgages. The maximum advance is £30,000 (a generous advance and likely to be given to relatively few applicants) with repayments over either 25 years or up to the age of 65, whichever is the shorter period.

Interest on the loans was set at 1 per cent above the current building societies' rate. The object was not to move the T.S.B. rate in parallel with MLR but to move the rate only when sizeable changes in MLR occurred.

Housing associations
Then there are housing associations. In these cases, the buyer buys a share in the whole of the 'equity' of a housing association and that entitles him to one unit (or two or three according to the size of his flat or house if the sizes of the dwellings vary). When you leave, you do not sell your dwelling, but you leave it to the next one in the Housing Association's queue. However, the prices of the shares or units rise as the value of property rises, so you get more for your shares. Cheaper way of buying, but not as profitable in the long term. Your local council will tell you of local associations

which, thanks to government subsidy, can still do relatively cheap homes.

Several people may get together to form their own housing group, to buy a huge old mansion for conversion into separate flats or something of that kind. They may do most of the work themselves and hire builders only for some of the essentials – drainage or electricity (though there might be builders among the group which would help). With so many to share the conversion work, there is less work for each person and the home may not be as far away as if one person is having to do everything himself. They save money because they are buying their homes 'at cost', without the profit that developers would take for converting similar properties to sell on the open market.

The snag is that the home never really belongs to the 'owner' but to the association. There is security of tenure, naturally.

There can also be other schemes put together – always use a solicitor – which enable everyone to build their own house or converted flat and finally to own them, rather like the old terminating societies which led to the building societies. If you want to know more about either housing associations or co-ownership, get the details from: The National Federation of Housing Associations, 30/32 Southampton Street, London WC2; or from The Housing Corporation (for co-ownership), Maple House, 149 Tottenham Court Road, London W1.

Single people

It is fair to say that single people sometimes find it difficult to get a mortgage. That should not be so, under law, but building societies get a much more comfortable feeling about married couples (or just living-together couples) and families. The single man or woman is considered to be rather footloose and fancy-free, possibly inclined to take tempting jobs in tempting places and to flee the nest, leaving it sublet without permission or allowing it to get rather dilapidated. The mistrust of single people is passing, but

slowly. Do not be discouraged, because quite a few enlightened building societies now recognize that houses are bought every bit as much for their investment value as for homes. Besides, rental property is so scarce and expensive that house-buying appeals to the young singles more than once it did. Such changes in society, combined with the acceptance of homosexuals who live alone or with other homosexuals, have made building societies far more likely to lend to the unwed, whether they be young or old. A steady job helps, of course. There is also less racial discrimination than once there was, when societies dealt in properties in limited areas only, near the office or branch office, and were at great pains to make it difficult for coloureds to move in and spoil prices in that area. Societies are now becoming real, caring concerns once more.

If you have a difficult property on which to borrow, no savings with a building society, or other problems, you may be tearing your hair out trying to get a loan. First, write to the Building Societies Association (see p. 63) and ask for their directory of members. Then call on some (you may not have heard of them before seeing the directory, but can then find their addresses in the phone books) and plead. Some just may have funds to spare at that particular time. Never, never borrow from any but a member of the association or through a reputable solicitor, your local council or a housing association recommended by your local council.

Mortgage brokers

If all these simple routes fail, do not forget the mortgage brokers, but again make absolutely sure that the broker is a member of the Corporation of Mortgage Brokers (full title 'Corporation of Mortgage, Finance and Life Assurance Brokers'). Their address is 24 Broad Street, Wokingham, Berkshire RG11 1AB. Mortgage brokers charge, but the charges are small and not payable unless you get your mortgage.

Members of the C.M.B. have to conform

to standards which protect borrowers. The broker's job is not only to know where the money comes from but also when it is available. He must, as a member of C.M.B., pay any money you give him into separate clients' bank or building society accounts and not into his own account. He has a special indemnity insurance to protect you and he subscribes to the C.M.B. compensation fund in order to see that no client loses money. He is bound to produce a certificate of solvency from a proper accountant when he joins the C.M.B. and periodically as he renews his membership. He sticks to a proper scale of fees, has a licence within the laws of the Consumer Credit Act of 1974 and also observes all the C.M.B. Codes of Conduct.

The C.M.B. showed me a fascinating document, a report on 'Rogue Brokers', showing how the unwary can be gulled by such people. Sadly, it is just these sharks who get the publicity while the men who conduct their business honestly and fairly get little; because the bad behaviour rubs off on to them, they are less able to help the people who need them because those very people stay away, frightened of the consequences. Professor Gordon Borrie, director-general of the Office of Fair Trading, is bitter about how the rogues can promise the earth, exact exorbitant charges and then admit they cannot get a 100 per cent mortgage or else get one which commits the poor family to payments way beyond their means.

These rogues advertise and, despite laws governing advertisements, their claims sound reasonable, as though they were involved with respectable building societies because they use the same words and phrases. They claim to get 100 per cent mortgages without difficulty, then extract an advance from the luckless applicant and that advance is not returnable. Most of the sad letters from people who have been badly conned – and they include couples who lose all their savings and are forced to put their children into care while they both work to recoup – make the point that they knew very little about buying houses and applying for mortgages at the time, a fact that seemed painfully obvious to the con-men who took advantage of it. For that reason, though much of what is in this chapter may seem obvious to some who read it, I have taken care to give as much information and as many warnings as possible. Home-buying is the biggest decision most people ever make and the mistakes can be a handicap for life.

If at any time you do part with money that you cannot reclaim, try the Small Claims Court (see the local telephone directory for local addresses or ask the local Citizens Advice Bureau). Few people seem to know about these courts which exist in some boroughs and where, for a small sum, you can take your own case to recover sums due to you, either via unpaid bills or taken by rogues who promise to return the money if they don't procure the mortgage (or any other service) but still fail to return the allegedly returnable advance. You may not need a solicitor for the Small Claims Court – you probably will not except in complicated cases – and you can always ask legal advice of the Citizen's Advice Bureau which will be able to tell you whether the case is simple enough for you to handle alone. Local Consumer Advice Centres can also help.

The brochures of the rogues are terribly convincing, yet they protect only the rogue and not the customer. The Consumer Credit Act of 1974 rightly laid down strict rules for those dealing in financial services but, alas, did little to change or clarify the law concerning those who do not conform. The C.M.B. and others are lobbying all they can to get some sense into this murky area, but meanwhile all they can do is to hope that the public deals only with reputable members of reputable organizations who do conform to the spirit and the letter of the Act. Just because a broker is licensed does not mean he is reputable, alas, though we are moving towards that Utopia gradually. So always check on your broker with the C.M.B. or BIBA (British Insurance Brokers, described in Chapter 4). The Office of Fair Trading still issues licences to those who do not conform to C.M.B. or BIBA standards so ignore that message at the top of the literature produced by the rogues, who usually send a convincing and vocal salesman with their literature to get a cheque and signature.

It bears repeating – never sign anything without knowing exactly what you are doing or consulting a solicitor, the Citizen's Advice Bureau or someone who does know. A solicitor is much cheaper than making an error like handing over a deposit that is never returned. You will have to pay a C.M.B. broker, but the payments are for work actually done and are spread in easy payments. Sometimes estate agents can give helpful advice about co-operative building societies and private lenders, as can bank managers and lawyers or accountants. Do, however, acquire a little knowledge about such matters before asking questions because buying and furnishir a home will probably take more than all your savings anyway and every wasted or lost pound can be something like disaster. Private mortgages, for instance, should never be accepted without proper legal advice – your own solicitor's, not the lender's. Sometimes, you may be offered a solicitor who can act mutually for you and the lender or the vendor; and, just sometimes, that might be all right, but rarely so; the legal man must have a prior loyalty to one client in the event of disagreement, so that mutual professional services can only work in the simplest of cases.

Home improvement grants/loans

Never forget that you might be able to get grants for modernizing or improving your property. There are statutory grants, the kind that must be given to make the place sanitary if it has no bathroom, loo nor water supply. Then there are discretionary grants for other improvements, payable on quite a few older properties. The grants are not loans but gifts from the local council and they are based on the cost of work as approved by the local authority and not on the builder's estimate or costs to you – there may be quite a wide difference. While no local authority can commit itself to promising a grant until the applicant has put in formal application, most of them are helpful with informal advice before you start. They can at least say that such-and-such improvement would positively not attract a grant. No grant is ever payable before the local authority gives written approval, so beware about starting work prematurely.

Any local council or office or Citizen's Advice Bureau can give you the free booklet on *Money to Modernise Your Home* which covers this aspect of financial aid. There is often a long delay in actually getting the grant and therefore some discomfort, so you may prefer to tackle the building society, who might advance the money and add it on to the mortgage, as already mentioned; but you might also try the local council for an improvement loan. From time to time, the National Home Improvement Council has published exceedingly helpful booklets at low costs so do try them at 26 Store Street, London WC1. Finally, never forget your own bank and the finance houses (see Chapter 1).

Loans for extensions

If you plan home extensions, you are not likely to get a grant, though you might get a building society loan. But you are also moving into an area as populated by brigands as some of the broking areas, so once again it pays to be quite sure about your choice of builder or home extension contractor. So many of those whose advertisements appear regularly in newspapers and magazines are small organizations employing local casual labour which calls to do the job and then disappears from the face of the earth, leaving the householder with problems of damp, falling ceilings, useless loft conversions or garden rooms. Check your proposed conversion contractor with the National Home

Enlargement Bureau (and please don't confuse it with some other organizations using rather similar names). This bureau is owned by reputable architects and builders as well as other firms interested in protecting a good reputation for the kind of work that is so often done badly. The N.H.E.B. keeps its own list of rogues while building up the directory of goodies. Alas, the baddies still get customers — if a legal case in the area gets them deserved bad publicity, they simply stop advertising there for a while and return to the scene of the original crime later on when memories — all too short — have faded as far as their misdemeanours are concerned. The N.H.E.B. is at 594 Kingston Road, London SW20, and they are receptive to telephone calls as well as letters. Cut out the advertisements that catch your eye and send them along. For legal reasons, the N.H.E.B. may not be able to tell you why they advise against this form or that, but trust them. They know a lot from their formidable dossiers of complaints from customers who have been badly let down.

Topping up the loan

The upsurge in house prices over the last couple of years has made buying a second home easy for those who already own their homes because of the profit that can be realized on the first home. However, it has made it impossible for many first-time buyers even when they get a mortgage. The limit on the mortgage — usually £20,000 but often £15,000 — puts even small homes in London and the Home Counties, where it is becoming extremely difficult to find even small studio flats at under £25,000, out of reach. Building societies, once reluctant to lend on single-room flats, are now having to do so to help first-time buyers; since these are the cheapest type of property about, this creates an extra demand for such flats. The availability of mortgages on them inflates demand even more and raises the prices out of proportion with larger

properties. Many people cannot get such high mortgages because their incomes limit the amount they can borrow. Thus the banks and others have moved into the 'top-up' home loans business. These are, effectively, cleaned-up versions of what used to be called 'second mortgages' — a phrase that turned ugly when the high interest rates on such loans put many home-buyers into more or less permanent and crippling debt. Legislation and fears of spoiling the market turfed out profiteering schemes to a large extent, and the respectability of the top-up market has now become established with the entry of the clearing banks and insurance companies into the field.

Obviously, the first and most important advantage of any loan that you are offered is just the fact that you can get it, that the home of your dreams becomes reality. But, if you can get more than one offer, if you have time to do a little shopping-around for home loan top-ups, start with your own bank. If you find other bank schemes looking more attractive or even more available, have no compunction about moving your bank account to that bank. Banks have their own subsidiary insurance companies (such as Beehive with Lloyds, Forward Trust with Barclays, and so forth) which usually do the actual lending and handle the covering insurance policy — this you will need in all cases, unlike straight mortgages, some of which (though fewer all the time) are available without full cover.

Each bank will offer slight variations on the theme, and each borrower may get different offers, depending on how much the bank already knows about him and his means, and his prospects. I do not propose to go into each scheme in detail but to give broad guidelines of how they operate.

How much top-up?

Normally, the bank will lend up to 100 per cent of the existing loan from a building society, not more (depending on your circumstances, of course). That does not mean you automatically get 100 per cent, only that you may if you are lucky. There is likely to be a second restriction, which protects you, the borrower, as much as the lender: that the two loans together should not exceed 85 per cent of the purchase price of the property. Note that I said 'purchase price', not the valuation of the surveyor from the lender(s). That is a real advance on old-time lending and, indeed, I must give great credit to building societies for their thinking on this kind of thing, for their understanding of market prices and their use of local surveyors who know local markets. Inflation in house prices has contributed to much more modern thinking about home valuations but, in top-up cases, the yardstick is more often than not the purchase price.

Now the home looks a little more like reality. Say you can borrow £15,000 from a building society (on joint earnings or single earnings of about £6,000 to £7,000 per year). You might also borrow £15,000 from the bank. That leaves quite a bit to find on top of the loans if you want to live in or near London, unless you are prepared to go to one of the less popular areas and wait for it to improve (there are so many of these now that the wait might not be long). Outside London, the position is much easier. Being able to borrow the extra £15,000 may make a crucial difference – provided you can pay it back.

What does it cost?
The interest on a top-up is likely to be anything between 2 and 3 per cent above the current building society rate. Some borrowers may have to pay more, of course depending on their credit rating and such. It is high, but it is available.

You might find an insurance company cheaper, so try a few directly (it often pays just to search your local yellow pages for local offices and call on them with your problem). The Norwich Union and many other companies have been offering top-ups on the basis of a life-endowment policy to cover the loan (working the same way as

endowment mortgages, see p. 67). Obviously, the young will find these top-ups cheaper than the elderly – in fact, many loans are cheaper for the young – for two principal reasons. One is that the premiums on any covering insurance policy are lower than for older people. Another is that the loan repayment can be spread over a longer period like 30 years instead of 15 or 20. Of course, the second longer-term scheme does not actually make the loan interest cheaper, but it does lower the monthly repayments so that the effect is the same as far as the borrower is concerned. Having to pay less per month is what we all want.

Be warned on one point. Insurance companies may offer lower-premium endowment policies than do the banks and their insurance subsidiaries but they do sometimes charge higher interest rates on the capital. The moral is, as always, to shop around and compare prices. Go directly to the insurance company offices or to insurance brokers who are members of **BIBA** (British Insurance Brokers Association). Get everyone to spell out exactly what you have to repay and to itemize them so that you can see what you pay in interest and what in premiums. Get them to show alongside such items what the tax relief is in your case. And then decide.

If only one scheme is available, then you will naturally have to accept it. But it is always nice to feel that you chose the cheaper or better of more than one if at all possible.

First-time buyers should really hunt for the kind of property that is in low demand, such as anything from tumbledown old agricultural cottages to industrial-revolution styles of building in poor areas of large cities. Building societies are becoming more co-operative about this kind of thing, while local authorities are waking up fast to the need to improve sub-standard, old housing. They are becoming far more alert to the need to preserve local communities without chasing away the kind of inhabitants who are the mainstay of the place – such as the elderly retired in Worthing or Blackpool, the young in Gateshead or Oldham, the young to middle-aged marrieds in Eastleigh or Guildford.

Always go — and I do mean *always* — to the local council when house-hunting, but remember that some are much less alive and co-operative than others. Ask them where to look for lower-price property. Ask them about grants, repayable or otherwise. Ask them about loans to bridge the gap between the builder's final account and the grant and about temporary housing during the repairs or modernization. Judging an awards scheme run last year by the National Home Improvement Council and seeing some of the work done by councils in conjunction with the Department of the Environment, I found that much was being done by a few councils, and more and more are thinking about intelligent help for home-buyers.

One council was offering free front walls of brick, which made many a householder order side walls to match (offered at a discount). Another was offering cleaned-up brickwork, repointing and protective coating, which encouraged house painting and improvements. These were extra and imaginative things, aside from the usual sanitary and other improvements connected with grants. Most of the councils I saw had made many, many efforts to take their gospels of rescuing old property and helping new buyers or old residents to improve right into the heart of their areas. But please go to your council, whether you live there or merely hope to do so. Their advice, even their loans, could be invaluable.

If this chapter has frightened some readers, it has done a good job and a bad one. Nobody should ever commit themselves to more than they can afford and the dream of a home is enticing enough to lead many into temptation. On the other hand, nobody will ever offer a better investment than the home — even two homes if you can afford it — and do not mind the extra work and overheads involved. Many a couple nowadays have two homes simply because each had started home-buying before their union. And my own advice would be not to rush into merging the homes unless they must. I still think couples should behave like individuals, keeping their own assets as far as possible as self-protection in the event of separation and homes are the greatest assets they can probably ever own.

The golden rules are think, think and think again. See and trust only the most reliable and longest-established professionals you can find and get their advice, then listen to it and heed it — they don't want you to default any more than you do. Mistrust those who are too profligate with the loans any time. Search before you buy, and then serach again to make sure you aren't going to make a mistake you cannot live with. Never let the dream of a home become a nightmare.

Chapter Four

Insurance

The day we are born is the day on which we become immediately vulnerable to sickness, injury, disablement and, finally, death. On that day we start a difficult journey which inevitably brings much sorrow, much anxiety, much heartbreak, as well as our fair share of happiness. Fortunately, bad fortune rarely comes all at once but builds up slowly so that we are more or less ready to face it. Most disasters mean loss of money in some way, whether through ill-health and a drop in earnings or through loss of treasured possessions. Insurance can never protect us from misery or loss, but it can at least cushion the blows. Almost anything is a little easier to bear if your basic financial platform is strong and insurance can at least insure that for all of us. It is not cheap but it is good value.

How it began

Historically, insurance was started to protect commerce from the elements, the storms and seas that wrecked so many commercial ventures when ships were the mainstay of trade. A slow ship could cost many a trader dear, while a sunken ship wiped out merchants and companies altogether until, one day, a group of Italians got together to work out something very similar to the kind of insurance protection we all know today.

That was 600 years ago, and the Italian idea spread rapidly to other countries visited by the trading ships. In the late fifteenth century, when sea routes to India were being discovered and rapidly building up trade, a whole new land was shortly to be discovered, to come into our ken and to make sea routes even more lucrative as ships plied their way to the newly developing America. Elizabethan gallants from Britain, fired by the thought that still more land might be awaiting human discovery, explored and traded further and further afield, insured against storms and even piracy. The sea bandits became as active as merchants and sailors, ending the life of as many ships as were attacked by the elements. Britain's era of wealth could easily have turned to one of disaster had she not followed the fashion for insurance.

Insurance as a British operation began under Sir Thomas Gresham, merchant and economic adviser to Queen Elizabeth I. The first insurances were carried out, with Royal blessing and the close interest of the Queen herself, in the Royal Exchange, London, near where the Bank of England was much later to be built. The men who offered insurance were called 'underwriters', because they wrote their own names under their promises of compensation for adverse happenings. They collected the premiums personally, invested the money profitably and were normally able to pay out on any claims without destroying their own profits.

They continued to deal almost entirely with marine and shipping insurance until the Great Fire of London in 1666, thought to have begun in or near a baker's shop close to London Bridge. The dry, high wind fanned the flames through hundreds of timbered homes all the way to the great cathedral of St Paul's. For the first time since they had heard of insurance at all, the men who offered it realized the threat to homes and people on dry land and the first-recorded fire insurance company was set up in 1680, many little firms having done inland and domestic business on a small scale up to that time. Insurers used to meet in the coffee house of Edward Lloyd, near the Royal Exchange, and that coffee house was the forerunner of Lloyds of London.

There were no fire engines except those owned by insurance conpanies and these went to put out fires on insured property only. Such property, once the first premium was paid, had a Fire Mark on a metal plaque fixed to its walls (very, very few still survive). Buildings without Fire Marks were allowed to burn to the ground while looters turned up to make things worse. The firemen on those private-enterprise company machines were as much guardians of the contents of a home as firefighters, carefully screened and picked as honest men who wore liveries and badges to identify them from the pillaging thieves. By 1833, the many small engines and brigades were amalgamated and a larger, well equipped brigade was formed, owned by a consortium of the insurance companies. Eventually, the London County Council took over the brigade and the firefighting responsibilities, making the service available to everyone, insured or not. London, and the famous Lloyds of London which has outgrown the original coffee shop, by the eighteenth century had become the world's insurance centre.

Lloyds underwriters, then and now, were and are proud of their flexibility, their broad-mindedness and ability to cover any eventuality foreseen or unpredictable. The premiums we pay for the benefits we might have to claim are worked out by special accountants called 'actuaries', men who are really sophisticated bookmakers, adjusting the odds to realities of life. Life insurance probably started in the early days of marine insurance, when a ship's owner took out insurance for his captain, just in case he was kidnapped and held to ransom, a favourite

sport even centuries ago. In the old days, the employer paid the premium for his man's life insurance, but also took all the benefit, giving nothing to the grieving widow. The system naturally left a lot to be desired and, in those days when life was considerably cheaper than money, ship's captains worked hard to protect themselves as well as to run to time with their cargoes, just in case the employer might be tempted to get compensation for commercial losses by sacrificing his skippers' lives.

Inevitably, men began to insure themselves so that they paid the premiums and their families got the benefits. At first, they would do this on a single journey basis, taking out new insurance for each voyage, but the idea of full insurance for the whole of a seafaring life soon grew out of that idea and, at last, the kind of life insurance we know today. During the eighteenth century mathematicians were hired to work out how much each man should pay according to his age and state of health, to be the forerunners of latter-day actuaries. Interestingly, one of the first people to make a serious study of this particular science was Edmund Halley, Astronomer Royal, after whom the famous Halley's comet was named because it was discovered under his aegis. Most of the credit goes, however, to one James Dodson, a maths teacher at Christ's Hospital, the Bluecoat School. It was he who hit on the idea, after many complicated mathematical calculations based on the law of averages and the history of human mortality, that we should be able to pay the same sum each year and still not risk bankrupting insurance companies. He laid the basis for all insurance schemes of today and there is a plaque on the site of the old parsonage in Nicholas Lane, London, to commemorate 'where scientific life assurance began in 1762'.

Nobody likes buying insurance. For one thing the idea of anything ever going wrong is something we cannot easily face. Cars are meant to go, accidents never happen to us, and our health and happiness always look safe. Life insurance is the most unpopular of all insurances because the insurer is buying a benefit for someone else to enjoy. So there is mental resistance to buying insurance, just as there is to making a will.

For this reason, it is compulsory to buy some kinds of insurance, such as National Insurance which eventually becomes the old age pension (sorry, senior citizens' pension), and which also covers sickness and disablement. It is also illegal to drive a car uninsured. Animal insurance may well become compulsory as owners are already liable for the damage done by their pets and working animals. Some large awards have been made to the victims of accidents caused by dogs, whether it be a car accident or the chasing of a prize bull over a cliff edge. Some dog owners have been impoverished for life and insurance is pretty cheap to buy, so every one should have it.

Life insurance

Life insurance is the single most important form of insurance and, apart from our regular National Insurance, it is not compulsory. There are various kinds, covering anything from simply benefit on death to benefit for accidents, injury or illness and benefit after an agreed period. There are quite a number of variations on the theme of life insurance.

Term assurance

Which can sometimes be called 'temporary 'assurance'. You pay your regular premiums and the insurance company agrees to pay a stated benefit if you die within a certain term, also previously agreed and set out in the policy. The idea is to get temporary protection for a certain period such as the term of a mortgage or when the family is young and would be hard-hit by the death of the breadwinner, the widow being unable to go to work.

Term assurance is the cheapest form of life insurance because so few policies actually result in claims. The insurance company therefore has plenty of funds available for

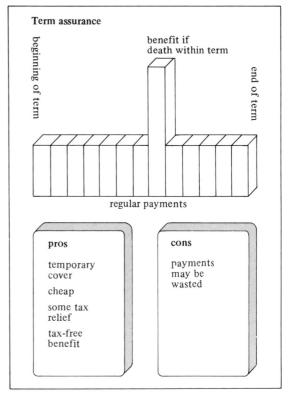

payouts when they do happen. For most, this is a better idea than

Whole life

The whole-life policy is still relatively cheap, though costlier than term insurance. It does no more than insure benefit for the survivor at the time of the insured's death. It gives no endowment (lump sum) in life if the insured lives almost for ever, and he has to go on making the payments all his life, which could be difficult after retirement.

It has the additional drawback that the insured may actually resent making the payments, because he is the one who will get absolutely no benefit therefrom and money is supposed to make you happy, not sore or jealous. There is, from some companies, a 'limited payment policy' which means that the payments could stop at retirement or when the wife (the potential widow or survivor) dies. The final benefit, if death comes first, would be smaller (or the premiums higher) than on some whole-life policies. I dislike whole-life policies

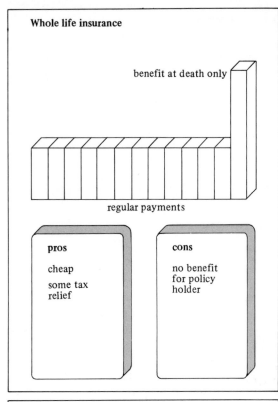

Whole life insurance

benefit at death only

regular payments

pros	cons
cheap	no benefit for policy holder
some tax relief	

because every one, except perhaps the limited payments type, must result in a payout and the insurance company therefore cannot build up nice big reserve funds of the kind which allows them to give greater benefit for less premium.

Another way of doing whole life is to buy a 'decreasing whole life with profits' policy. The premiums are based on the assumption that the benefit, the sum insured, loses value over time, because money loses value due to inflation. In this case it does not because the profits (provided the insurance company's investments are good and profitable) more than make up the decrease. Thus the insured eventually stops paying premiums and the 'swollen' policy stays 'frozen' in the insurance company until his death, when benefit is still paid out, the insurance company having, as it were, had the use of the man's money between his final payment and up to the time of death.

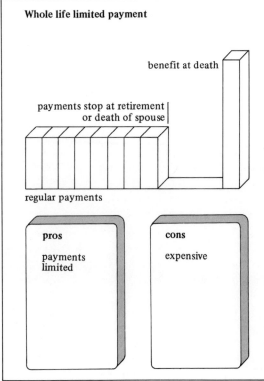

Whole life limited payment

benefit at death

payments stop at retirement or death of spouse

regular payments

pros	cons
payments limited	expensive

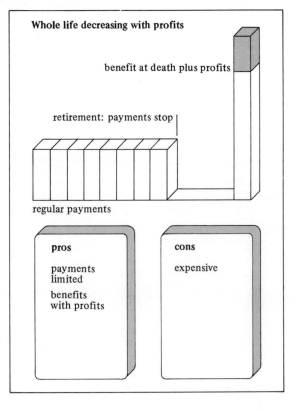

Whole life decreasing with profits

benefit at death plus profits

retirement: payments stop

regular payments

pros	cons
payments limited	expensive
benefits with profits	

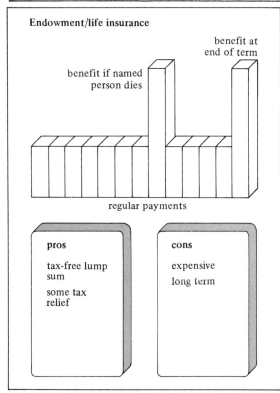

Endowment/life insurance

benefit at end of term

benefit if named person dies

regular payments

pros

tax-free lump sum

some tax relief

cons

expensive

long term

Endowment/life policies

For a healthy young couple, a whole-life policy is not a good idea. For one thing, who insures whom? Her earning power today may be higher than his, her expectation of life less now that women are able to take dangerous jobs. Once babies arrive, there might be some point since her earning power must be assumed to be impaired, at least for some time. But even then it is much, much better to consider other types of life insurance.

The most popular policies are, rightly, endowment policies of some kind. They never look very cheap when you add up the total cost of premiums over the agreed number of years but at least the insurer gets back a lump sum at the end of the period, his money or more if he bought with-profits schemes. And this lump sum is free of tax. All he has to do is to survive for the agreed term of the insurance policy. If he dies before that date, the named dependants get full benefit. It is important to note that I said 'named'. In fact, the beneficiary, or heir to the policy, may well have been named at the time it was taken out. In the case of married persons, the automatic heir is the surviving spouse. But it is just as well to leave a letter with the bank, insurance company, solicitor or whoever to make sure the right person gets the money. The best way of all is to include all insurance policies in one's will.

Endowment policies can be used to cover all kinds of eventuality from school fees to a cruise round the world on retirement. One can take out several policies, maturing at different times. You get partial tax relief (see Chapter 3) on the premiums for endowment-life policies but only up to a permitted upper limit — a percentage of your total income which the Government varies from time to time. If, as mentioned in the previous chapter, your mortgage is to be repaid by an endowment scheme, then the tax relief is greater (see p. 68).

Obviously, you can take out as much insurance as you like, but you cannot claim tax relief beyond a certain level of premium. Up to 1979, when the system began to change, one merely entered the premiums on one's return of income together with all the relevant details of number, insurance company, etc., and part of all those premiums automatically qualified for tax relief, which showed up in the code numbers of PAYE taxpayers or were deducted for the self-employed schedules. The new system, simpler all round, allows one to pay premiums of up to £1,500 to the insurance company less the sum one would get in tax relief. The insurance company then gets its money (to make up the difference) from the Inland Revenue, claiming in bulk for all its 'customers'.

The thing to remember about insurance is that any benefit is going to look jolly small by the time it comes to be paid — inflation takes care of that. So do insure for as much extra as you can comfortably afford. And do consider a policy which makes some provision for accident as well as death prior to maturation of the policy – some do but many don't and it may pay to take out extra policies, outlined later.

With-profits policy

The premiums will be more for a policy that eventually gives you £5,000 plus profits than a straight £5,000. That is obvious enough, but the profits element can look like really good value if you are with a firm that has a good profit record and, since the good ones proudly publish their figures, it is well worth studying them and even asking for them when you go shopping for policies.

The method is that part of the premium goes towards profitable investment schemes. Then, when the time comes for benefit, the share of profits from these investment schemes is added to the original sum assured (assurance is really a technical word for insurance so don't be worried by the apparently indiscriminate use of these two words). The rest of your premium goes towards the final sum payable at maturity. Therefore you will have to remember, when they show you the final sum for which you are insuring, that your whole premium is not reflected therein. It is worth thinking of this when you add up your premiums and realize that you don't seem to be getting much out of the deal. The profits should more than make it a bargain and you will get, each year, a statement of what the profit for the year is and what difference it makes to your benefit.

Do not overstrain yourself. Remember that you just might have to surrender your policy if you cannot keep up the payments, and that proves expensive since there is obviously a kind of penalty for doing so. The insurance company has been promised so much a year for so many years and naturally gears its investment policy to that promise. If you surrender early, it cannot make all the money it promised you (and itself), so you do risk losing on the deal, very much so in the early stages and much less later on.

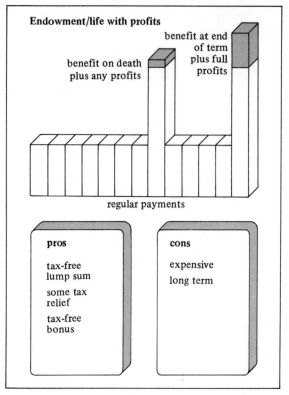

Endowment/life with profits

benefit on death plus any profits

benefit at end of term plus full profits

regular payments

pros

tax-free lump sum

some tax relief

tax-free bonus

cons

expensive

long term

Convertible

If your income looks like changing as you grow older – usually for the better, but who can be sure – you might look around for a flexible or convertible policy which means that you can trade your original policy in for a more valuable one later on.

Divorce

Married partners might work on the idea that getting married qualifies one for divorce and divorce statistics, alas, do make it quite clear that nobody should base their financial planning on the happy-ever-after dream. More and more companies are now looking at schemes by which the insurance can be separated when the couple separates. Clearly, this is a sensible type of policy for a man (or a woman) to take out if the spouse is not earning. My own advice would be that each and every earning person, married or not, should take out his or her own independent policy. As I said, money cannot itself make for happiness or lessen the misery of loss or parting, but it is a devil of a lot easier to be miserable with a little financial security than without it. Even if it is a small policy, with low premiums and small benefit, it is nice to have something all one's own, something that cannot be the subject of legal hassle.

Annuities

An annuity is an assured and guaranteed annual income paid by an insurance company in return for single lump sum 'loaned' by you to the company (though there are annuities that can be purchased out of income, as it were, by annual premiums). An annuity can be for a limited and agreed term or for life. The latter is a kind of gamble on the expectation of life, with you betting you will live to a ripe old age and the insurance company betting on an average expectation. They will pay to death, and I know several old ladies who glow with pleasure at counting up by how much they have defeated the insurance company by getting more than they gave. Die before your capital is repaid and you 'lose', as though you gave. Never, never leave yourself in a position of worrying about money.

Women are always deemed by insurance companies to have a longer expectation of life than men as long as they are fit so they tend to get smaller annuities for the same sum. There are various ways of buying annuities.

Capital sum annuities

First those you buy with a capital sum. The company then repays you the capital sum in annual instalments plus a modicum of interest on the basis, as I have said, that you will get an income until death even if all the capital has been repaid before that time comes.

That it all very fine if you have no heirs and wish to leave no inheritance. Then you can put all your capital into getting yourself a nice income and you can normally buy quite a bit of comfort for your money if

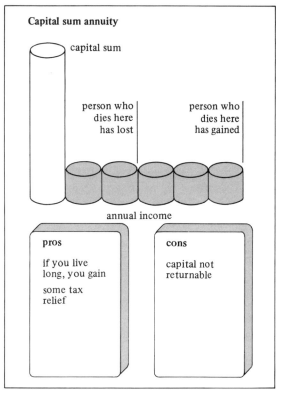

Capital sum annuity

capital sum

person who dies here has lost

person who dies here has gained

annual income

pros	cons
if you live long, you gain	capital not returnable
some tax relief	

you wait until you are pretty elderly; and, since few people want to buy until some time after they lose the ability to earn income, the annuity is very much an older person's favourite.

If you have heirs, you may want to leave something and not risk the insurance company getting it all if you die young. You can take out

Guaranteed or capital-protected annuities

This means that any unspent portion of your capital payment is paid out to your heirs at death. There are some deductions for legal fees, etc., but not too many. Your annuity, your annual income, will be smaller than for an unprotected annuity but you don't lose. If you have no large capital sum and would like to buy yourself an annuity out of income while you are earning you can look around for a deferred annuity.

Deferred annuities

This is the kind of annuity that should be bought by the self-employed (as well as by

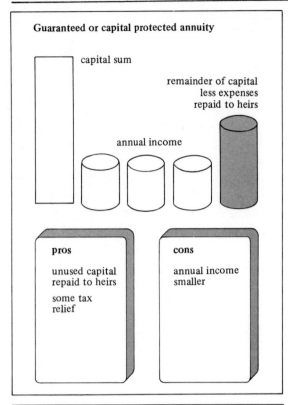

Guaranteed or capital protected annuity

capital sum

remainder of capital
less expenses
repaid to heirs

annual income

pros	cons
unused capital repaid to heirs	annual income smaller
some tax relief	

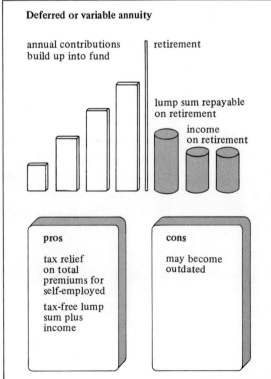

Deferred or variable annuity

annual contributions
build up into fund

retirement

lump sum repayable
on retirement

income
on retirement

pros	cons
tax relief on total premiums for self-employed	may become outdated
tax-free lump sum plus income	

others). For the self-employed, the premiums, paid annual, are totally tax-deductible, unlike the premiums on ordinary insurance policies which attract only partial tax relief. You start buying some time before the payments are due to begin, thus lending an annual sum to the insurance company. Your instalments add up to a fund which begins to pay you an income at a certain, prearranged age (though even this can be varied if you wish, the income naturally being smaller if you start receiving at — say — 60 instead of 65). Since annual premiums may have to vary according to what the self-employed person earns, they are mostly called 'variable annuity funds'. Some of the fund may be taken in cash when the time comes (tax-free), which could be invested to provide a slightly bigger income than it might if left in the fund — the reason being that it is being loaned at a later age.

There are, however, deferred annuities for everyone, not just the self-employed. It simply means spending now to receive much later, when the money you 'spent' has grown by reason of being invested and winning interest so that it grows before the insurance company has to start paying. My own view is that, while there are cases where such an annuity may be a good idea, I would want to explore other forms of investment (the self-employed policies being in a different category from the lump sum variety).

The reason is simple. Annuities depend quite a bit on interest rates as well as age of the person. Also, insurance companies become more and more sophisticated in their investment and benefit policies and there may be a better policy for you to buy than when you first started your agreement. And, not least, taxes vary from one year to another as do tax benefits and reliefs — for example, age allowance for the elderly is a comparatively new benefit. Thus it may well be a good idea to take a lump sum, reducing the annual income originally agreed, and buy another annuity. Cash payments are also a major factor in

Minimum annunities

These guarantee a fixed income for so many years — probably five — and the option to take the rest in cash at the end of that term. Useful if circumstances change or just to buy another annuity. Married couples might like

Joint survivor annuities

These allow for continuing annuity to the surviving spouse. The survivor's income is obviously a good deal smaller than the joint annuity (probably by about one third or so) but these are pretty good value.

Reversionary annuities

These are for non-marrieds who want to leave something to a surviving friend, lover, mistress, partner in business, companion or some such associate. The snag is that, if the lover, mistress or whoever dies first, the annuity dies too. While these may be a good idea in some small businesses, I think they are not often a good idea and should never be bought without sound advice.

Tax on annuities

When you start getting your annuity, you will seem to be paying much less tax on your income than you might expect. The reason is that the proportion of it representing repayment of your own invested capital is naturally tax-free; you will probably get an income double what you might have expected from investing the capital in many of the more ordinary ways, such as for interest at the bank or buying shares. However, do remember that all your capital is gone for ever, even with a capital-protected scheme which benefits only your heir. It may be more reassuring to live on a smaller income derived from the good yields often to be had from Government stocks and to preserve the capital for as long as possible) even making some capital gain). Never buy an annuity for a lump sum until you are over 60 and mostly not before 65, as the value grows as you grow older, when

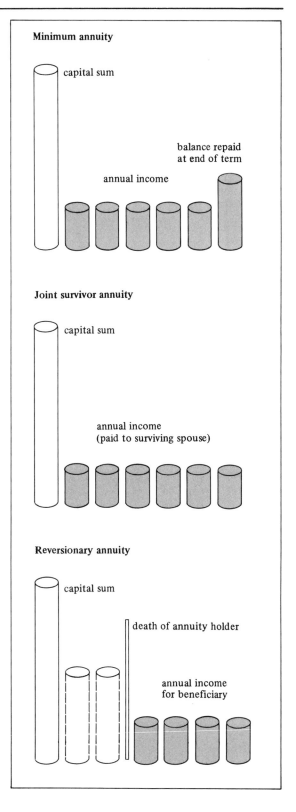

the insurance company's risk of having to pay out a large sum over many years grows less. Self-employed annuities are different, owing to the premiums being tax-deductible.

Choosing a policy

Those are our principal insurances apart from household and car policies, but there is, under each heading, a terrific variety, which can be wildly confusing especially as the variations seem so small as to be almost unnecessary. If you are sure of your ability to read, digest and understand small print and statistical tables, then buy your own policy, after a lot of shopping around for brochures and talking to visiting salesmen, directly from the insurance company. Normally, you will see an advertisement that catches your eye and, when you reply to it, a salesman will automatically call. Don't be persuaded by him. See several of them. Sign nothing. Listen, read and then, if in any doubt consult a professional friend or relative. If none, then take your particular problem to an insurance broker. BUT, and it should be the biggest BUT, do not go to any old broker you might find listed in the phone book or see advertised in your local newspaper. Make quite sure that the broker is a member of 'BIBA', which is not the name of a fashion and cosmetics designer for our present purposes.

BIBA stands for The British Insurance Brokers' Association. It was formed in January 1977, and it incorporates all the four original broking associations that insisted on certain standards for their members. The reason for consulting a BIBA man, woman or firm is the need of members to perform ethically, honestly, fairly, objectively to a high standard. Always remember that a broker is not himself (or herself) accepting a risk when he takes your money. A broker is putting your money through (you hope) to an insurance company that does take the risk but protects you in so doing. An unscrupulous broker could just pocket your money and do nothing for you — would you ever really know until the disaster struck? BIBA

tries to keep us all informed on insurance broking matters and there are 23 regional committees of the central association. When I tell you that there are about 4,000 member brokers or broking firms, you will see how difficult it is to choose one and yet how easy. So never use a non-BIBA salesman. See the initials on the letterhead — every member will boast about membership. BIBA is at Fountain House, 130 Fenchurch Street, London EC3M 5DJ and they would naturally confirm whether or not your intended broker was a member.

Door-to-door salesmen may be agents for one company or for more than one, but there is a strong lobby for outlawing this kind of selling, especially where your money is concerned. If they work for several companies, well, so do brokers in a way, but independently. If only for one, then what benefit do you find when the best way to buy insurance is to compare one policy with another? Banks, law firms, accountants and solicitors may also be agents for insurance companies. Mostly they will not press anything on you but will supply leaflets and brochures of the companies with which they deal and then will actually handle the business for you. In no case should you pay for the services of an agent or broker because their payment comes from the commission paid to them by the insurance companies.

When you want insurance, tell your broker all about yourself and be honest, honest with yourself before being honest with him. Sit down with a pad and write out all your needs, aims, responsibilities and dreams. Look at your income, the income you expect to be earning and then look at your nature. Are you lazy? Might you want to retire early? Are you a gambler and might you want to take a small risk for a big gain (insurance is not for gamblers since it plays safe, but there are more exciting variations in some policies)? All this is important, so that your broker or adviser can find exactly the right tailormade policy for you. Having bought a policy, look at it from time to time (not every year, but every two or three) and think about whether you are still doing the right thing in the possible framework of a changed life and circumstances.

There can be no set plan for any person but the Life Offices Association and the Association of Scottish Life Offices give examples that might be quite useful as a starting basis. Their booklets, explanations of how insurance works and what kinds you can get, are free from either organization: Aldermary House, Queen Street, London EC4N 1TP or 23 St Andrew Square, Edinburgh EC4R 1AD. Take out policies only with companies that are members of either association because, apart from conforming to special standards, they pay decent and fair commissions to brokers, who can then balance the vices and virtues of policies without being financially favourable towards one or the other, since the commission from all or any deal is the same.

It is a good idea to plan some kind of programme, to match each stage of life with the most suitable policy for that stage. One might start with a term policy, especially as the building society may well insist upon one for the term of the mortgage. Then one might buy an endowment policy, linked to some kind of investment and yielding some profits. Finally, one might cash in the endowment for an annuity. There can be no hard and fast rules, no set advice. The only thing that can be said is that nobody should ever commit himself to more than he can comfortably afford. Something like *half* of all insurance policies are surrendered, with some loss for the insured, within ten years of being started. The fact is significant, so do step carefully. I do think everyone should have insurance, and there are few better ways of saving money, of converting income into some capital sum (apart from a mortgage) because there are some tax concessions on the premiums. But try to avoid planning too far ahead — long term might be ten years in your case.

Medical insurance

Such policies are offered by BUPA (British United Provident Association), or P.P.P. (Private Patients Plan) and one or two others. These two are far and away the biggest with, respectively, 78 per cent and 19 per cent of the total market, and I certainly favour size when it comes to insurance, especially of this kind. More than 2.4 million people in Britain have some kind of medical insurance, paid for by their companies. But — and it is an important but— you can pay medical insurance and still find yourself with a hefty bill that is not 100 per cent covered by your agreement. It is an expensive luxury, and one that attracts no tax relief at all, so think about it very, very carefully. National Health has its drawbacks, and you may decide the expense of private medical insurance well worth while. But it costs plenty.

Your employer company may have a sickness fund, which would make medical insurance unnecessary. And, if loss of income through illness is a dire threat to the family, you might look at some schemes which give you cash while you are in hospital for a private or semi-private room, for your family's fares to visit you, for spending money, for anything. You could, for about £30 a year, get £5 a day while in hospital. It looks good, but would you be in hospital more than six days every single year? Think about that — it might be better to start your own private fund. If you do plan medical insurance, start young because it works out more cheaply. BUPA is at Provident House, Essex Street, London WC2R 3AX (and branch offices). P.P.P. is at Eynsham House, Tunbridge Wells, Kent TN1 2PL.

Accidents or disablement

Insuring against accidents at work or at home is cheap enough — though premiums would cost more if you are in dangerous work, or in jobs where you probably need accident insurance most. A steeplejack clearly pays more than a grounded construction worker, and he pays more than an office worker. Such policies cover real disablement and not normal sickness. The benefits are usually lump sums for the loss of a limb or partial sight or a small income over a longish period – say up to a couple of years. Employer companies sometimes have their own schemes to benefit themselves, their staff or both. Some endowment schemes have injury provisions.

Women

Men are pretty used to insuring themselves, but women are terribly careless about it and most of them really resent spending money on premiums. Single women are becoming better about it, regarding their future security as their own responsibility and recognizing that personal freedom, comfort and convenience do depend largely on what they buy themselves in those departments. Married women, whether they earn or not, hardly ever insure themselves. This is lunacy, on both selfish and unselfish grounds. Selfishly, there is always the problem of divorce or his death. However he is insured, she may get no benefit therefrom on divorce and little at death. If she earns, then it is easy for her to buy insurance. If not, she must just grab what she can from the housekeeping or ask for more. The asking should not be a pleading, begging session but a practical one, showing that insuring her is really to the family good, an unselfish action that might prove very welcome if she is ill or injured.

She could run the Mini into a tree or break a leg picking the apples, fall down stairs while painting the ceiling or merely running across the road for a pound of sausages. Suddenly the breadwinner has to run the home, look after the children, and cope with everything at once – grandparents may not always be unemployed, close at hand or even young enough to help out. His job could suffer since his company is unlikely to give him indefinite leave while she is in hospital or immobile in the upstairs bed-

room. He could lose promotion, perhaps even his job and go out of his mind with fear and worry.

If she is a working wife, they might be pretty strapped for cash while she is ill or injured. Either way, she ought to be insured too, for everyone's sake, even if it means his insurance being just that little bit smaller so that they can meet the premiums. Try a flexible sort of policy – one that begins to pay out only two or three or more weeks after the accident because most people can struggle for a few weeks and the whole thing is much cheaper that way, involving lower premiums. Or the injury might attract a cash sum.

Savings by insurance

The endowment plan, which we have already discussed, is in itself a savings plan, but there are others from insurance companies. Before even thinking about them, ask yourself four questions and write the answers down honestly.
1. When do I want some savings to mature (retirement, middle age, when the children leave school, get married, etc.)?
2. How much do I think I shall want? (It will always be more than you think, so make it larger than you think now. But don't overstrain yourself. Buy only what you can afford.)
3. Is my eventual lump sum going to be more than I put into it in premiums? (Add the premiums up and compare it with the guaranteed benefit.)
4. Is my money at risk in any way?
5. What tax do I pay on the eventual lump sum?
6. Is my money shut away for ever or can I get at it if I suddenly need it before I expect to?
7. And, finally, how much will I get?
From the answers you can decide whether you want a short-, medium- or long-term plan.

You will be able to buy the savings by instalments (annual or monthly premiums being put to some variation of an endowment policy) or with one large, lump-sum, capital payment called a single-premium. As a rule, every benefit at every age and stage is tabulated for you to see clearly so that you can compare one scheme with another. They will have strange names at times, like bonds, or granny bonds, or some such thing. They are all forms of insurance.

Self-employment

As I have already said, rather briefly, the self-employed are allowed by law to pay premiums that are *totally* tax-deductible on special policies to secure themselves annuities in old age, or a lump sum plus annuity. This is different from premiums on ordinary insurance which have partial tax relief on premiums. If self-employed, it really is essential to do this to whatever extent you can afford – the Government limits the amount you pay in any case to a certain sum or percentage of your free-lance or self-employed income. The permitted sum changes periodically to keep more or less abreast with inflation, so check that when you start on such a scheme. The amount of premium can be varied from one year to the next which makes these schemes different from the more ordinary insurances where you pay a level premium every year. This is essential because the self-employed, which covers actors, writers, lawyers, accountants and a host of others, earn different sums every year. The pension schemes are usually called variable annuity funds and such schemes are regularly and frequently advertised, the brochures and tables are carefully laid out and it is not very difficult to buy a good one although brokers might advise you on these. They look more complicated than they are.

These schemes do not carry endowments (apart from the smallish cash sum you take optionally at final benefit time) and there is no provision for injury or accident. There is nothing for your heirs (though you might use the lump sum when you get it) and no death benefit if you die before taking it out – which you can do ahead of the agreed date subject to a reduced annuity of course. Again, as with all insurance there can be variations. But, to qualify for tax deductibility, you must be buying an income scheme, often called a 'variable annuity scheme' – not because the annuity varies, but the annual premium can be varied according to fluctuating earnings.

House and home

Since I have covered home insurance under the appropriate chapter, it is pointless to say much here other than that it needs carefully planning every bit as much as other insurance policies.

Children

Parents and grandparents can take out policies for children and there are some tax advantages. It makes a nice gift for them and elderly grandparents can even insure their lives so that premiums will go on after death if that occurs before the policy is fully paid up. Capital transfer tax clobbers money gifts in life beyond a permitted level, and it may be difficult in any case to give lump sums away, so it might be nice to take out some sort of child scheme. Such policies are actually another form of endowment policy and handled by the same companies.

Employees

Not being here concerned with companies so much as people, it is enough to suggest here that you ought to have some cover for the cleaning lady, the gardener, the help that comes to do that sort of job – if any these days. Builders and such will have their own insurance and you will not be liable. But the cleaning lady who breaks a leg on your loose stair carpet? She might claim loss of earnings (less the State sickness benefit if she subscribes properly) for some weeks. Most householder comprehensive policies will be able to include a clause covering simple accidents of this kind in your home.

State insurance

You have no option but to pay National Insurance because it buys your old age pension. But it also pays you sickness benefit. Obviously, the sum varies from year to year in that never-ending but not-always-successful struggle to stay in parallel with inflation. No sickness benefit is payable for three days or less absenteeism from work and most humane firms will cover you at least for that time. Some firms keep staff on full pay for longer, but even most of those will deduct the State sickness benefit from the weekly salary, which is only fair. If the sickness benefit is too small for the family needs and there is real hardship, there is provision for an earnings-related supplement for 26 weeks, though it is not paid for the first 12 days.

Earnings-related benefit

It is not paid to the self-employed at all, though the self-employed can claim the *basic* sickness benefit upon receipt of a doctor's certificate and, virtually, too much

proof that he or she is really and truly ill (the mistrust of the unemployed victimizes the honest army of them because of the sins of relatively few itinerant construction workers who have always moved on to the next site before the Inland Revenue or anyone else catches up with them). On the whole, State sickness benefit is kind enough for the few times that most of us need help and, except for the self-employed, there should be no need to take out any additional sickness insurance at all.

Cars, holidays, animals and the rest — the first two are normally offered when you book the holiday or buy the car. If not, ask the vendor or the selling company and they will give you the information. Animals — go to Canine and Livestock Insurance Association, Calia House, 610 Chiswick High Road, London W 4.

If asked to define insurance, I would say that for many people it is what helps to make their dreams come true. The outlook for our declining years would be very drab without it and, though many do live on their old age pensions, most people in this country nowadays do supplement that basic income with something from the insurance companies. It is usually the best present you can give yourself.

Savings and Pensions

Savings

It cannot be helped, you are bound to find here a good deal of repetition from previous chapters, especially because so many savings schemes are linked to insurance, unit trusts and building societies. Much the same applies to pensions and pension schemes, but here we go anyway.

Naturally we should start with the Government's saving schemes; bear in mind that new ones come on offer from time to time, just as changes take place in those that already exist.

National savings

The National Savings Bank (see Chapter 1 on banks), which used to be the Post Office bank and which pays interest at low rates (the first £70 is tax-free) on ordinary (or current) acounts with slightly higher rates on investment (or deposit accounts withdrawn only with prior notice). The return on your money is low but children over seven can use these accounts and there are so many branches all over the country – wherever there is a Post Office. However, there are so many much better ways of getting capital growth and, apart from the convenience of perhaps being more local than the bank or working longer hours, there seem to be mainly disadvantages.

Savings certificates

All the interest on these is tax-free. Great – but these are long-term investments so the money is inaccessible unless you want to lose some benefit. When you see what looks

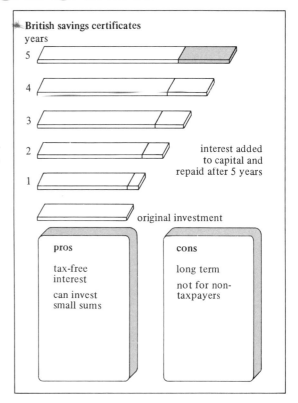

British savings certificates

years

5
4
3
2
1

interest added to capital and repaid after 5 years

original investment

pros	cons
tax-free interest	long term
can invest small sums	not for non-taxpayers

like a low rate of interest (about half MLR), remember that it is all free of tax, which makes it good, particularly for the higher-income earner. New issues appear at irregular intervals, each one tending to be better than its predecessor, but it is possible to switch your holdings from the old into the new. You can invest from as little as £5 up to a maximum that is currently £2,000. The money is withdrawable at eight days' notice but only at a sacrifice of some of the interest. The latter is not paid out, as with dividends or most interest schemes, but is announced so that you know what it is, then added to your holding. Say you bought £100 of the 17th issue. In four years it was worth £134 and still growing. You don't pay any tax on the £34 – or whatever the gain is.

Buy them at Post Offices, banks, Trustee Savings Banks, etc. Guard your card or keep it in your bank. Be ready to hold them for five years.

Not to be bought by those with little or no tax to pay, since the point of these is that they are tax-free.

Retirement savings certificates

These are index linked, i.e. the value is based on the rising cost of living. Limited to people eligible for the old age pension (currently 60 for women and 65 for men but that is likely to be equalized, probably merely by raising women's seniority to 65 also). These so-called 'granny bonds' (men – don't let this put you off) are excellent value. They can be bought in small units from £10 each from Post Offices, T.S.B.s and such. They

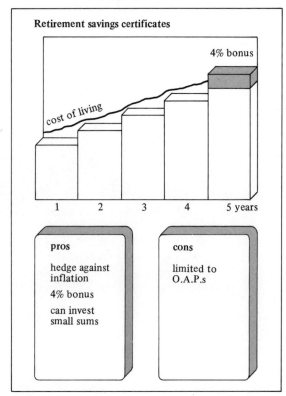

hedge against inflation and also provided a 4 per cent bonus at the end of five years (tax-free at that). Say you bought ten units at £10 each in July 1975. After each year, the percentage increase in the cost of living was added, so that by the end of five years they could be worth double the original investment and the money is free of tax including CGT. Fine as long as inflation and the rise in the cost of living is going up more steeply than interest rates. I suppose the cost of living could fall, but what a long time since it did! It is based on samples of all that we have to spend on housing, food, clothing, even household goods and watch repairs, for instance. Premature selling means less gain.

If prices stopped rising, these would not be a good investment. You decide.

Save as you earn

You make equal and regular monthly payments to build up capital over five years. The payments are anything between £4 and £20 and you must be over sixteen. If you miss a payment, the end of the term is simply postponed, but you may not miss more than six payments. If you do, you get your money back but you will get a low rate of interest on what you have already paid in (and you naturally get your capital back).

You may not withdraw cash sums, though you may cancel the whole contract and take it all out, on the basis of reduced interest.

Your total contribution is revalued in line with rises in the Retail Prices Index (R.P.I.) and the rises are added to your five-year total as a tax-free bonus. Very good investment for people who are earning and cannot get the retirement index-linked benefits. Get the forms from your Post Office and send them off to the Durham address. Pay by monthly banker's order to save trouble all round. Then watch the R.P.I. Say it stands at 180 when you start and you are putting in £20 a month. At the end of five years, the index may be 220 (my figures are arbitrary, so don't use them except as examples). At the end of give years you get

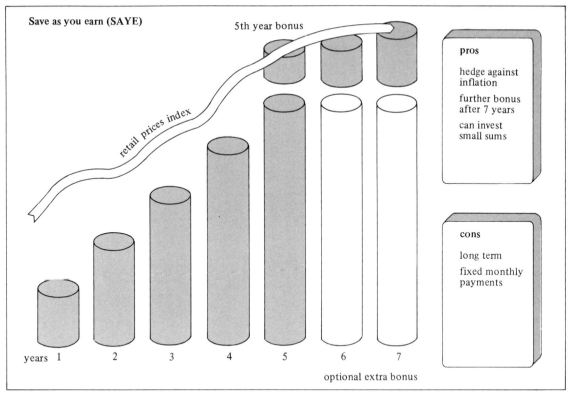

$$£20 \times \frac{220}{180} = £24.40$$

Thus your bonus or profit is £4.40 per unit of £20, or £264 for 60 units (over five years). You can take your profit or you can leave your money intact in the scheme to get a further bonus, after two more years. Then your investment is valued again and raised in line with the R.P.I. You also at that time get a bonus of twice your monthly payment, in this case £40. Early withdrawal does, as I said, mean loss of benefits. An excellent scheme for high taxpayers, and do ask your employer as he may be running a group scheme. Don't get into it unless you are sure you can afford the promised monthly sum and do try to maintain the investment for the full seven years (recalling that payments stop after five of them).

Trustee Savings Banks
Pretty well covered in Chapter 1. I need say

little more here. They are becoming more like the clearing banks we all know, the Big Four. Their savings, investment and other accounts offer few advantages that you can't get anywhere else, in many cases at much better rates with more growth.

Premium bonds
The football pools of the Government, the gambler's investment. You get no interest on your money but the chance of a nice fat win of tax-free cash. You do not lose your original stake — and the bookies and the gaming casinos never go that far — but your money is worth less as time goes by because inflation erodes it.

The numbered units are raffled every month in 'Ernie', the Electronic Random Number Indicator Equipment that 'draws' the lucky numbers. Top prizes are now £100,000, with runners up of £50,000 and £25,000 — only one of these each week, so don't get too hopeful. The balance of some £6 million of prize money handed out every month is split up into 70,000 prizes, of which the smallest is £50. You can buy bonds in £5 units up to a maximum of £3,000.

You can hold the bonds for three months before they become eligible for the raffle, but the odds are very much against your winning – they are something over 11,000 to 1, which means you do have to be very lucky. If, with amazing luck, you win more than one prize in a month (there being two draws), you may receive only one of them and that is automatically the higher one. Numbers are listed in most newspapers and unclaimed winning numbers are also often listed. They are published quarterly in the *London Gazette* and the Post Office can let you see copies. Of course you are informed of your win by post, but so many people fail to notify the Premium Bonds department of changes of address that many prizes do lie unclaimed, and there is no way of notifying the owners if mail is not being forwarded. Although one may buy premium bonds for children, actual purchases may only be made by those over 16 and parents or guardians only may buy for children (because some people disapprove of gambling it is thought right to give the choice only to parents or guardians).

Not exactly a good investment, but you could be lucky. The self-employed might like to consider using them. As I earn (being self-employed) I set aside the money that will be due in tax and I buy premium bonds. Thus my bonds are often being cashed and I am buying new ones, but at least the money might win me a small fortune before I have to draw it out to pay my tax demands. There is so little lost interest on the money during the short waiting period that I might as well gamble for the big win since I can draw the money fast anyway.

Banks

You can open a deposit account and attract interest at anything from 2 to 4 per cent below Minimum Lending Rate. The rate varies, and it is adjusted upwards or downwards as M.L.R. changes. The interest is 'paid' daily by being added to your deposit but it is naturally taxable at your own tax rate so may not be quite such a healthy yield as it looks – 12 per cent before tax is only 8 per cent net if you pay standard rate tax. Most banks have schemes to pay higher interest on money on long-term deposit; for instance, should you say you will give three months' notice before withdrawing. Useful if you are thinking about what to do with your money or for sums you might shortly need to draw out, but there are better schemes for long-term savers if you are able to lock the money away. Also useful for people who pay no tax and therefore get the full interest rate. Better than building societies (see Chapter 8).

Money market

A market for short-term loans, the principal business being carried on by brokers specializing in bills (not the invoice kind but bills that mean money, rather like cheques might but with all sorts of dates and other complications), by discount and issuing houses, commercial banks and such. They deal in bills of exchange, Treasury bills (such as short-term bearer securities that mature in 91 days) and such. If you have over £10,000 to invest for a short time, your bank can help you put it on the money market. And I have no intention of explaining any more fully since, if you are dealing in the money market, you will know a lot more about it than I do. If you know less than I, you have no business at all being there. Danger for the uninitiated.

Finance houses

Invest in these through your bank so as to be sure you have a good one – they borrow short and lend long like the building societies (which means they are vulnerable if everyone demands their money at once) so you must have a sound one. Your bank will put your deposits into one and you will get better interest for leaving it in for longer periods, such as on 'three-month' call (see above).

Thoroughly recommended for those who pay no tax as the higher rates of interest can be very attractive.

Insurance

This too has been covered in Chapter 4, and I feel that it is really not worth repeating. Suffice it to say that many an insurance scheme is a savings scheme, because you buy a capital sum out of income, as it were. You pay premiums to the extent that you can afford — monthly or half-yearly or annually. The insurance company invests all those premiums and, at an agreed time, you get a lump sum. You should buy with-profits schemes, of course. Most insurance company schemes are advantageous because of the tax reliefs on the premiums on life and endowment types.

Bonds

A bond is a lump of equity, of stock, of insurance, of investment capital, or it is any large investment bought for a large sum. You can buy bonds in countries, in property, in almost anything. Mostly such bonds, apart from those offered by governments, are offered by insurance companies. You pay — say — £1,000 or £5,000, in return for which you own part of the property or investment portfolio of the company, which might be Hambro Life Assurance, Abbey Life, Scottish Widows or any other familiar insurance company. Other types of bonds exist, of course, and they are mainly managed by insurance companies too. They are well advertised, usually with rather lurid headlines, and their managers seem to use every conceivable tax-avoidance scheme possible. You will see them called 'Guaranteed', or with much the same names as for unit trusts. They are safe and they may be really worthwhile investments, but

you should consult a good insurance broker or professional adviser of some kind — as long as you remember that their advice could be biased since they could get a better commission from one insurance company than another and be more likely to promote one scheme than another.

However, their reputations are to some degree at stake; also there are so many different types of bond for so many different circumstances that they will almost certainly choose one that best suits your particular requirements.

I suppose the easiest way to describe these bonds is to say that they are like single-premium insurance policies. You pay a large lump sum down (if you have it) for some future reward in terms of either a lump sum (payable to you in the future) or some mixture of income and capital in the future. The fact that you lend a huge lump sum instead of paying premiums in driblets is such a great advantage to the insurance company and its investment policy that it is prepared to pay well to get your money this way. Thus the return, be it in growth or interest, is likely to be better than for small-premium schemes. But bonds are not easy to understand and there are so many of them that you will probably need professional advice before embarking on them.

Pensions

Though savings are often for retirement or old age, and though many a savings scheme is partially a pension-buying scheme, there are different and special provisions for pensions, which are geared to the fact that you will not be withdrawing any of your premiums, contributions or whatever until you are old, unlike savings, which you might draw suddenly for crises. The company (or Government) that is providing a pension, whether for the employed or self-employed (done via insurance companies), knows that it will go on receiving a weekly, monthly or other regular contribution to its funds and, because of such predictability and consistency, it can afford to be more generous than most of the participants in savings schemes.

The sooner you start providing for old age the better. The younger you are when you begin, the cheaper will be your premiums or other payments and the more growth you will see because there is more time for growth.

First, for all of us, there is always:

The State pension

How it started

State pensions were first introduced in 1908 for people over 70, but not for everyone. To receive a pension you had to suffer a means test and, believe me, you had to be poor, almost on the breadline, to get any money. It was hardly a State pension, more a charitable handout, and those who got the money were usually made to feel thoroughly ashamed, not only by friends and neighbours, but by the officials who distributed this alleged largesse. Poverty was for so long considered shameful that it is quite incredible how long it took for this or any nation to give its people a real chance to lift themselves up by just a little more than their own boot-straps. Education for the children of the poor was aimed at the idea that the offspring would always be as poor as the parents, that improvement of one's lot was not a right but an occasional stroke of luck or crookery. For the poor to struggle for wealth was thought to be outrageously bad behaviour, ungrateful to the rich who dispensed periodic charity, and really not done.

By and large, the wealthy not only took over much responsibility for helping the poor but actually seemed to take enjoyment out of what they saw as plain duty, so that there seemed little need to change the system in the days before the Middle Ages. The fact that the helped were so often and in so many ways almost the

slaves of the rich and that they sold their freedom and individuality for the right to have food and shelter deterred few. The rich and the poor knew their duty or their places and stuck to the traditions.

Where individuals failed, the Church took over, using its own powers of fear of after-life or of persuasion, according to its own particular gospel, to collect money from the rich and hand it over to the poor.

Henry VIII, that extravagant and profligate monarch who spent money faster than he beheaded or divorced wives, put a stop to that by dissolving the monasteries whose earnings largely supported the Church (he also 'stole' from the coinage of the realm, see page 172). His daughter, that alleged Virgin Queen whose reputed love affairs helped Hollywood to riches, had a conscience about the terrible birthright she inherited from her dissolute father and about the fact that a sickly brother and bitter sister who had reigned before her did nothing to right his wrongs. Noting that the Church was back in power with a small degree of wealth, she decided they should again help the poor and, if they could not or would not, the State would order them to do so. She brought in the Poor Law, which made the religious parishes responsible for their local poor.

That was the first time the State ever took a hand in helping its own poor people. The hand was weak, it is true, since the law was rather vague, difficult to implement and took little account of whether the parish could actually afford the help or not. There were changes and amendments, but the State still dragged its heels badly over the lot of ageing poor until the beginning of the twentieth century. And the State really did very little at all until 1948, not much more than thirty years ago. Yes, our present system, based on what was in 1948 called National Assistance, is a post-war phenomenon.

The Industrial Revolution of the early nineteenth century did more for the poor than any dutiful obligations or charities, whose work had naturally been patchy, and served only a lucky few, could ever have done. The beginnings of the Trade Unions, the Friendly Societies and the Co-operative Movement were based on the unity of the poor to coerce the wealthy, especially the wealthy employers, to give employees more money by right, to bring earnings up to decent human levels. The dole came into being – and it was doled out with the old-fashioned mixture of reluctance and benevolence though the unions tried to cloak it with the respectability of the description 'unemployment pay'. Compensation for injury, some rudimentary types of sickness benefit and even forms of insurance came into being – the premiums on insurance being collected door-to-door in coppers for the most part.

The State moved into action at the beginning of this century. Perhaps 'action' is a bad word because the State's early participation was slow indeed. As I said, there was a means-tested pension from 1908, but thousands of people never dared take it because of the stigma attached to such handouts. It was 1926, the year of the General Strike, that gave birth to the idea that shame must be killed and that the handouts should be rights rather than privileges. Contributory pensions began, and they were to be payable earlier, at the age of 65. A National Insurance scheme to cover compensation for ill-health and unavoidable unemployment had been started back in 1912 but it began to be developed further during the 'twenties. Obviously, since so few people contributed, there were small funds to meet the real needs of people so that, in the mid-'thirties, extra funds were allocated by Government to Unemployment Assistance and Supplementary Pensions, reforms that were even further developed between 1935 and 1942. The extra money was still based on the hated means-test method.

The war changed attitudes and Sir William Beveridge (later Lord Beveridge) was made chairman of a committee to investigate latter-day poor laws and to make better recommendations. The Beveridge Report, usually referred to as the 'Beveridge Plan', came out during one of the worst periods of the war and was universally hailed as the most marvellous piece of social reform ever heard of in this or any other country (and it has since become an international pattern for social security).

Though the war was going badly, there was a feeling that our heroes needed to come back to a much better world, to say nothing of how brave, how competent and how tough women in factories were turning out to be so that they, with their trade unions, were demanding much, much more in the way of financial rights. The Beveridge Plan caught the nation's mood and the whole thing looked like a pattern for living. His report was a masterpiece, not only of practical commonsense but also of human understanding. It spoke of peace and the planning for peace. It emphasized that democracies that could prove themselves strong and steadfast in war should not be found weak in peace. It pleaded for courage to face realities and it affirmed that freedom from want cannot be forced upon a democracy nor given by a democracy but is won by a democracy, earned by the people. It ended by hoping that the plan for social security would not find the British people wanting, that we would all play our parts in achieving both social security and the justice upon which security depends.

The main principles are commonplace enough now but I wonder how few people now realize that it took centuries and the outspoken courage of a handful of men to 'sell' the idea of social security. And it might interest you to see what the proposals and benefits were then, when Beveridge became a national hero in an age packed with war heroes. For the following extracts, I must credit the Department of Health and Social Security, who give us this fascinating record of the beginnings.

It was 1948 before the Beveridge Plan could be fully implemented. The main principles, very briefly, were that:

- All citizens should be covered.
- A flat rate of benefit should be paid for all contingencies — retirement, widowhood, unemployment, sickness.
- The scheme should be financed by contributions from insured people, employers and the State. Contributions, like benefits, should be at a flat rate.
- The needs of families should be catered for by paying family allowances for all children after the first in each family — the cost to be met out of taxation.
- The new Insurance scheme would, in the long run, greatly reduce the need for National Assistance, which would continue only as a safety net to provide means-tested benefit for the minority who could not satisfy insurance conditions for benefit, or who had special needs.
- Administration of this new scheme was to be unified under a new Ministry of National Insurance.

These proposals formed the basis of the Family Allowances, Industrial Injuries and National Assistance Legislation which came into full operation on 5 July 1948. The new National Health Service came into being on the same day.

In 1948 the rate of National Insurance pensions and other benefits was £1.30 for a single person and £2.10 for a married couple. National Assistance rates were slightly lower — £1.20 for a single person and £2.00 for a married couple — but rent could be paid in addition and exceptional needs could also be met. These seem small amounts today, but for pensioners, for instance, they meant an impressive increase in the previous rates of 50p, for a single person, or £1.00 for a married couple. And in 1948 the average industrial wage was only £6.90 a week.

How rich everybody felt. There was such euphoria that everyone thought we were all secure for life, that there would be no need for a change for years ahead. When Beveridge himself warned that contribution and benefit rates would need to be reviewed every five years, there was much criticism and scepticism. Surely money values could not change as fast as Beveridge warned they might. Surely his pessimism was totally without foundation. As it turned out, the post-war generation soon got its first taste of inflation; as early as 1951, only three years after the impressive acclaim of the brave new scheme, benefits had to be raised. After that, regular increases came about every other year. And, since 1971, it has become an annual process. Interestingly, if rather incredibly, State pensions have risen faster than average earnings. Not above average earnings but, if you trace the lines of the two increases as you might on graph paper, the pensions line would be steeper than the earnings line. Not, I should add hastily, because earnings have risen so slowly but because pensions started at such a derisory level.

Retirement pensions now take a larger portion of the expenditure on National Insurance than ever before (above 70 per cent). As people live longer and as more people come into the scheme, that is perfectly natural. What is rather more surprising is the high number of people taking unemployment benefit. In all, the number of poor people has not risen or fallen since 1948, not because we have as many on the breadline but because the standards have risen and people's financial means are expected to be higher.

In 1966, the State decided it was time people stopped being ashamed of taking State money which, by this time, was as much their own as the State's since more and more of the nation's workers were contributing. The name 'National Assistance' was dropped and the term 'Supplementary Benefits' was introduced; expenditure on such services is now over £2 billion, £2,000 million. Clearly, as present pensions schemes mature, because of the improved level of benefit, the money needed for supplementary benefits must fall.

By 1968 the Ministries of Health and of Social Security were merged into the D.H.S.S. with children's social services (formerly under the Home Office) and a number of other social services brought in, so that the D.H.S.S. now faces an annual social security bill of more than £21 billion (£21,000 million) a year.

What you pay

As you know, we now all pay into the national schemes compulsorily from the time we start employment or stop studying. If you cannot get a job right away, the card that holds your stamps has to be taken to the nearest employment exchange and, as long as you are not working (provided you have signed on for work), they will stamp the appropriate spaces without charging for the stamps.

The same process takes place when a working man or woman is out of work. Otherwise, a stamp has to be fixed each week, the employee paying part and the employer the balance except in the case of self-employed (who must pay for the whole of their stamps, sold at Post Offices) and voluntarily non-employed. You will have either a contracted-in or a contracted-out State pension. The latter is for those whose employer companies have their own 'occupational pensions schemes' which will automatically boost the State retirement pension.

And here, as a percentage of your earnings, is what it costs you and your employee at the moment, this 'insurance premium' for your State pension:

These rates were introduced in April 1979 and they are subject to regular revision. If you are a contracted-out payer, contact D.H.S.S. for latest tables and rates at: The Contracted-Out Employments Group, D.H.S.S., Newcastle-upon-Tyne, NE98 1YX, giving the employer's contracted-out number. Others need not go further than the nearest social security office.

If you have more than one job.

If you have two jobs, you normally have to pay National Insurance contributions for each one in which you earn more than £19.50 per week. But, if your total earnings are more than £135 weekly, you would end by paying more in contributions than you either should or are allowed to by law. Any surplus is automatically refunded to you after the end of the tax year on April 5th but there is usually an inordinate delay about such refunds (especially if your own tax return is late). So do something about it. Get Form CF 28F from your local social security office or write to: The Refunds Group, D.H.S.S., Newcastle-upon-Tyne NE98 1YX, giving evidence of your payments, such as Form P60 or any other certificates that your employers will supply. These will show the categories in which you pay as well as the actual payments.

You can even prevent overpayment taking place by deferring payment in one of the jobs. Get leaflet NP28 from your local Post Office and follow the procedure clearly explained in it.

Self-employed

The self-employed must pay Class 1 and Class 2 contributions, perhaps even Class 4 as well if their earnings qualify them in that income band. However, it is possible to defer both Class 2 and Class 4 contributions until after the end of the tax year and thus avoid the need for refunds on overpayment. I do mine in about three slices by sending or taking a cheque to my local security office and having the card cancelled, also asking for a receipt to send to my voracious and demanding but salvationist book-keeper. Get leaflet NP18 from your local social security branch to clarify it all for you.

The general leaflet giving rates of contribution for all is N1208.

How many contributions?

Theoretically, you pay from the age of 18 or when you start work, whichever comes first.

	Employees	Employers
Class 1 contributions		
Standard not-contracted-out rate	6.5%	13.5%*
Standard contracted-out rate	6.5%	13.5%*
(1) on first £19.50 a week (or monthly or other equivalent)		
PLUS	**PLUS**	**PLUS**
(2) on earnings between £19.50 and £135 a week (or monthly or other equivalent)	4%	4%
Reduced-rate for married women and widows with certificates of election or reduced liability	2%	13.5%* not-contracted-out rate or 13.5%+ 9%* contracted-out rate
Men over 65 and women over 60	NIL	13.5%*
Children under 16	NIL	NIL
People earning less than £19.50 a week (or monthly or other equivalent)	NIL	NIL

*3.5% NI surcharge is included

	Employees	Employers
Lower earnings limit – no contribution payable for people earning less	£19.50 a week	(£84.50 a month/ £1,014 a year)
Upper earnings limit	£135 a week	(£585 a month/ £7,020 a year)

Class 2 contributions for the self-employed (see leaflet NI41)

Flat-rate for men under 65 and women under 60 (contributions are not payable for people over these ages)	£2.10 a week
Share fishermen's special rate (see leaflet NI47)	£3.30 a week
Small earnings exception from liability (apply if you expect to earn less than this from self-employment in the 1979/80 tax year - see leaflet NI27A (Feb. 1979 edition)	£1,050 a year (from 6 April 1979 to 5 April 1980)

*Class 3 voluntary contributions to help qualify for basic retirement pension and a limited range of other benefits (see leaflet NI42)

Flat-rate for men and women	£2 a week

Class 4 contributions for the self-employed (see leaflet NP18)

Rate payable on	5%
Profits or gains between	£2,250 and £7,000 a year

*For non-employed making voluntary payments

What you get

Main contributions and non-contributory benefit rates	Weekly Rate £
Standard rate of retirement*, invalidity, and widow's pensions, and widowed mother's allowance.	
Single people (including working wives paying full contribution)	23.30
Wife or other adult dependant	14.00
Earnings limit for retirement	52.00
Standard rate of unemployment and sickness benefits.	
Single person	18.50
Wife or other adult dependent	11.45
Widow's allowance (first 26 week of widowhood).	32.60
Maternity allowance	18.50
Invalidity allowance payable with invalidity pension, when incapacity began before are:	
Higher Rate	4.90
Middle Rate	3.10
Lower Rate	1.55
Attendance allowance:	
Higher Rate	18.60
Lower Rate	12.40
Retirement pension for persons over pensionable age on 5 July 1948 and for persons over 80*	
Higher Rate	14.00
Lower Rate	8.40
Non-contributory invalidity pension, invalid care allowance	14.00
Increase of non-contributory invalidity pension and invalid care allowance for a wife or other adult depenent	8.40
Mobility allowance	12.00
Guardian's allowance, child's special allowance, increases for children of widows, invalidity, non-contributory invalidity and retirement pensioners, and invalid care allowance beneficiaries	7.10
Increases for children of all other beneficiaries	1.70
New Child Benefit Rates for One-Parent Families	
First child	6.50
Each other child	4.00

*An age addition of 25p is payable to retirement pensioners who are aged 80 and over.

Main increased industrial injuries benefit rates

	Weekly Rate £
Injury benefit*†	21.25
Disablement benefit (100 per cent assessment)*	38.00
Unemployability supplement**	23.30
Special hardship allowance (maximum)	15.20
Constant attendance allowance (normal maximum), exceptionally severe disablement allowance	15.20

Industrial death benefit:	
Widow's pension during first 26 weeks of widowhood	32.60
Widow's pension now payable at £20.05 rate	23.85
Widow's pension now payable at £5.85 rate	6.99

*The rates for beneficiaries not over the age of 18 will also be increased.

†Increases for adult dependants and children will be the same as those payable with unemployment and sickness benefits.

**Invalidity allowances and increases for adult dependants and children will be the same as those payable with invalidity pensions.

Main increased supplementary benefit rates

	Ordinary Weekly Rate £	Long-term Weekly Rate £
Ordinary scale:		
Husband and wife	29.70	37.65
Person living alone	18.30	23.70
Any other person aged:		
18 and over	14.65	18.95
16-17 years	11.25	
13-15 years	9.35	
11-12 years	7.70	
5-10 years	6.25	
Under 5 years	5.20	
Blind scale:		
Husband and wife:		
If one of them is blind	30.95	38.90
If both of them are blind	31.75	39.70
Any other blind person aged:		
18 and over	19.55	24.95
16-17 years	12.15	

No specific rates for blind persons less than age 16.

	Weekly Rate £
Non-householder rent allowance	1.70
Attendance requirements	
Higher rate	18.60
Lower rate	12.40
Discretionary additions to supplementary benefit:	
Heating additions	.95
	1.90
	2.85
Dietary additions	1.05
	2.50

*Where the claimant or a dependant is aged 80 or over a further 25p is added to these long-term rates.

Main increased war pension rates
All ranks receive the same increases, officers' rates being expressed in pounds per annum.
Part I: Disablement benefits

	Weekly Rate £
Disablement pension for Private at 100 per cent rate	38.00
Unemployability allowances*	
Personal allowance	24.70
Increase for dependant wife or other dependant	14.00
Comforts allowance	
Higher rate	6.60
Lower rate	3.30
Allowance for lower standard of occupation (maximum)	15.20
Constant attendance allowance:	
Special maximum	30.40
Special intermediate	22.80
Normal maximum	15.20
Half and quarter day	7.60
Age allowance with assessments of:	
40 and 50 per cent	2.65
Over 50 and not exceeding 70 per cent	4.10
Over 70 and not exceeding 90 per cent	5.90
Over 90 per cent	8.20
Exceptionally severe disablement allowance	15.20
Severe disablement occupational allowance	7.60

	Annual Rate £
Clothing allowance	
Higher rate	51.00
Lower rate	32.00

*Invalidity allowances and increases for children will be the same as those payable with invalidity pensions
Part II: Death benefits

	Weekly Rate £
Widow's pension – private's widow; widower's pension:	
Standard rate	30.20
Childless widow under 40	6.99
Rent allowance	11.50
Age allowance for elderly widows:	
Between age 65 and 70	2.95
Over age 70	5.90
Adult orphans	23.30

In fact, as I have said, there are all sorts of exemptions like being a student, being ill, being out of work and such.

You stop paying when you are 65, if a man, and 60, if a woman; though, as I have said, there is probably going to be equalization in the near future, at either 65 or 64 years old.

If you have paid less than the statutory number of contributions, after allowing for permitted gaps, your benefits are scaled down. The point is that you should have made 90 per cent of the contributions you would have made during a full working career (19 to retirement age); you lose in proportion to the amount less than 90 per cent you have paid ('free' stamped weeks counting as contributed weeks if you are ill).

If you are still earning
If you are still earning at retirement age, you will not get the retirement pension, which is still more often referred to as the 'Old Age Pension', though the name was changed because old age pensioners hated it, yet the older people themselves seem to dislike the euphemism even more. For instance, British Rail says far more people ask for an O.A.P. card to reduced rail fares than for a Senior Citizens' card.

You will not get the O.A.P. unless you are earning less than £52 per week. If you earn more, your pension is reduced by 50p per £1 earned between £52 and £56 per week but, after that, exactly pound for pound. And you must declare what you do receive on your tax form. If your earnings are regular, you should tell your local pension office, and they will adjust your pension. If earnings fluctuate, such as with wages for jobs that may last longer one week than another, the process is pretty awful. You get a declaration of earnings from your employer and that is sent off by your local Post Office or pension office with the pension book, to be returned stamped with an adjusted amount for the

week in which earnings topped the permitted sum. Such a business. It surely must be a good idea — and it would avoid delay — to come to an agreement with your employer to take a flat rate (and it might be better to try to keep under the £52) and to keep a record of hours worked each week, to make an adjustment at the end of every quarter, every six months or year. To take an example: if you earn £65 in one week and £30 the week after you lose £11 of pension in the rich week whatever happens (£2 for the £4 between £52 and £56 plus £1 for each pound above £56).

Clearly, if your earnings are big after retirement age, you will merely not draw the pension at all because, once you start, that's it. It goes on, with relevant deductions for your earnings. However, if you freeze it (i.e. promise not to draw) until five years later (currently 65 for women and 70 for men) you will eventually get a higher pension. But you must make the decision before you reach retirement age. The increase in pension is one-eighth per week for each week that you work on without drawing the pension, which is an additional 6½ per cent per annum. When you reach the five-year limit, take the pension anyway, even if you are still earning.

Taxation
The pension is paid without deduction of tax but, if you are earning or getting another pension, it will affect your tax. Your annual tax return must include all income, even the O.A.P., and you are taxed accordingly (but with age allowance, of course). Some think the O.A.P. is not taxable, but it is income and therefore it is. Of course, if you have no other income, the pension is less than your age allowance and therefore you don't pay tax.

If you get another pension from an employer company (or, rather, former employer company) you may find it getting unduly high deductions of tax before you receive it. That is because your O.A.P. is being taken into account in your coding against your company pension and the whole of the tax liability is then deducted at source. I have already written about the 'granny bonds', those special retirement national savings certificates linked to the retail price index. These, which you can buy in units of £10 each up to a maximum of £700 each or per married couple, have been marvellous during the high rise in prices. In fact, had you bought your full entitlement of £500 when they were launched in July 1975, you would probably just about have doubled your money with no CGT by June 1980 (the end of the five years for which they should be held) including the terminal 4 per cent bonus for staying the course of five years. I know they were written about in savings but, since they can be such a good tax-free boost to retirement pensions, they are worth repeating here.

How to get the pension
About three months before retirement, you should get a form from your local social security office. If it fails to arrive, ask for it. You then decide if you want to draw or freeze the pension as I have already outlined. A married man whose partner has made no contributions receives the married couple's pension and, if he is wise, he pays it over to her after deducting the tax she ought to pay on it if they make joint tax returns. He will never get it back after handing it over gross. It is not difficult to work out your tax, and she should help by paying or get less housekeeping allowance to compensate. Each couple must work out their own best ways. Often, he keeps the lot and gives her the agreed allowance. Just remember that all income is still taxable subject to allowances.

A married women who has paid her own contributions must apply separately for a retirement pension form and make her own arrangements.

Company pensions
You may well have a company pension scheme to which you make regular monthly contributions subject to an upper limit which is based on a percentage of your earnings, the limit being set by law if it is to qualify for the tax relief (both you and your employer get tax relief on the pension payments; also you pay less National Insurance, because you pay at 'contracted out' rates). You can always 'buy' more pension or insurance-type income for later life by paying more but you will not get tax relief on the premiums above the legal level.

Your company will toe the legal line but make it clear to you what you put into the pension fund as well as the sum they contribute.

All pension schemes in companies are financed by a pension fund. Now that fund is totally independent of your employer's actual business, of the turnover and profits, and he cannot just draw on it to meet bad years of recession. It is managed by trustees and is inviolate, locked in a trust for distribution to employees with the trustees responsible for managing it and monitoring its investments. The trustees may be appointed from staff and management, from outsiders, from a mixture of both or even by a professional trustee company attached to a bank or some reliable organization. Each pension fund is operated under a trust deed, and every potential pensioner has a legal right to see it, if he can understand it when he does. Mostly, the employer hands out a simple booklet or leaflet summarizing the principal points. Most schemes include the following:-
- Pension due as income at retirement age
- Lump-sum life insurance paid to dependants if you die before retiring
- Widow's or widower's pension (the latter is rare in older schemes)
- And, occasionally, sickness or disability compensation.

Obviously the benefits vary, and most pensions are handled by insurance companies which leads to even more variation although, as a rule, the employer company gives a detailed brief of what it can afford and what it hopes to achieve. The actuaries advise employer companies how much can be bought in pension rights at what cost, so that the company's contribution can be worked out to the nearest pound.

I rather like the simile used by the Company Pensions Information Centre about how the funds work. They suggest you think of a pension fund as a bath with three taps flowing into it. The taps are your contributions, your employer's contributions and the income of capital appreciation from the investment of the pension fund. The bath naturally has a plug to pull out and a drain down which flows the pensions being paid out to the retired. Thus the actuaries must assess exactly how much has to flow in from the taps to keep the bath water level.

Your contributions, then, go into the pension fund, which is invested for growth with safety. Pensions funds favour gilts, Government's fixed-interest stocks, where

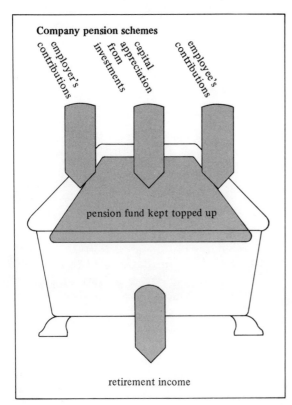

Company pension schemes

employer's contributions

capital appreciation from investments

employee's contributions

pension fund kept topped up

retirement income

they know the rate of return. They also like a substantial element of property investment which has been more than worth while in most years bar two or three between 1974 and 1976. And they also buy stocks and shares that should all swell pension funds nicely.

If you leave your job
Your employer's booklet will tell you the conditions, but you will probably have three main choices:
(1) You can get a refund of your own contributions to the scheme with some deduction for tax that now has to be paid because you got tax relief on your pension contributions. You sacrifice all rights to the employer's contributions.
(2) You might be able to freeze your pension until retirement age when the pension that becomes due will almost certainly be based on both your and your employer's contributions (though some schemes don't seem quite this generous).
(3) You may be able to transfer your pension to your next job and next employer.

I cannot tell you what to do because you can only decide according to your circumstances and the current law, but it is not usually a good idea to take your own contributions unless you need a lump sum rather desperately. Your age and length of service will also affect the decision. If young, you may take the money and start again. If near retirement age, you should probably freeze. And transfers, for the most part, are for the wide band of ages between, say, 35 and 55. Ask your employer. Some have schemes that enable you to take out special insurance policies with your pension money.

How much?
That is something I cannot answer, since it varies from one scheme or company to another. Most good schemes aim to give two-thirds of salary at the time of retirement but that involves long service and so forth.

Is the pension fixed?
Some of the older schemes are, but many

newer ones have some kind of uplift, usually every other year, to help combat inflation; quite a few socially-minded companies have, during the last few years, pumped extra money into their funds and sent out bonuses to ex-employees whose retirement pensions were low.

Taking a lump sum

You can take some of your pension as a tax-free lump sum when you retire. You will hear this referred to as 'commuting some of your pension'. The percentage of your pension entitlement that can be given in this way is restricted by law and it depends on length of service. There are rather complicated formulae but you will be told when the time comes.

Taking or commuting the lump sum means sacrificing part of your pension income. But it is normally possible to get yourself a bigger top-up income with the lump sum than you would have got if you had left it in the pension to receive as income. If interest rates have risen a lot since your pension scheme began, if you are old enough to have a short expectation of life from the insurance company's point of view, then you might buy an annuity that will exceed the sacrificed income, especially as you will pay tax only on the interest element of the annuity and not on the insurance company's repayment of the capital that you 'loaned' them when you gave them the lump sum for the annuity (see p. 85). There is a possible snag. The employer's scheme may give regular pension income increases and you also lose those.

Increases after retirement

More and more pensions do build in these post-retirement increases which are given all kinds of names like 'expansion', 'escalation' or 'dynamism' pensions — perhaps more often they are referred to as 'dynamized pensions'. More and more pensions are dynamized, though some of the rates might be rather old-fashioned.

Newer schemes could provide increases of anything from 3 to 5 per cent a year, while pensions in the public sector, such as the Civil Service, have a gearing that raises them in line with increases in the cost of living. Other companies merely inject bonus amounts into their pensions funds when they can and, even if increases seem generous and might stay reasonably in line with the cost of living, this cannot be guaranteed in private enterprise. Fixed pensions, an old evil, are dying.

Thus it could be difficult to decide about that lump sum commutation I mentioned. If you have been in the same pension scheme for 20 years or more (which might mean you have been with more than one employer but transferred the pension when you moved), you may take 1½ times your retirement salary in a lump sum, which is probably well worth doing. What you give up in pension income is on average about £1 for every £9 of cash you take for a 65-year-old man or £11 for a 60-year-old woman. As I said, the arithmetic is for the experts — those with under 20 years' service are subject to a fairly complicated formula and to agreement on each individual case with the Inland Revenue, so do talk to a good insurance broker or to your pension fund manager, personnel officer or whoever is your employer's expert (he may refer you to the insurance company handling your pension). They can work out the comparative figures for you.

Widows' (or widowers') pensions

Most pension schemes provide a pension that becomes automatically payable to the widow on the husband's death and rather more now do exactly the same for widowers, as the number of women in full time, long-term employment grows. The best schemes do not demand that the employee sacrifice any of his own pension in order to provide for the surviving spouse. Usually the survivor's pension is half that of the joint pension (though, if the survivor be the actual pensioner

107

and not the so-called dependant the full pension obviously continues for the single survivor). The most that the Inland Revenue will permit for widow's pension is two-thirds of the joint pension.

If a married pensioner dies before retiring, the surviving spouse may still qualify for pension, which would be a percentage of the income the pensioner might have expected at retirement. If there are dependant children, then some pension might continue after the widow or widower's death until the youngest child stops being dependant (earning age or school-leaving age). Many schemes stop the pension on remarriage of the surviving spouse but these become fewer as the years go by. And some schemes will provide for the husband only if it can be shown that he was dependant on the wife while she worked.

But, as I said, these can only be generalities and your company's pension contract will spell out the conditions under which your pension fund is run.

Lump sum death benefits

These are normally paid out only on death before retirement, the survivor pensions being operable as continuing income after death. They would normally be paid only to a widow or widower surviving the pensioner, but it is as well to ask about that if your spouse is already dead because you may be able to nominate a son or daughter as heir to a lump sum. There is no Capital Transfer Tax on such lump sum benefits.

Disability or long illness

Some pension schemes provide for such eventualities, some do not. Some employers may call for early retirement, others may have insurance to pay the sick. There are many possible schemes, none of them very good and it is sad but true that it often pays the family far better if the breadwinner dies rather than sustains long illness or severe disability.

Should I join my company scheme?

Yes.

You are not automatically eligible at once. You will have to reach a certain age or to have reached the stated age band by the end of your first year of employment. You will need to have been employed for a full year. And you must be in whatever is the right category for the firm. You should — though nobody ever does — try to negotiate a good pension with a good salary, as far as you can despite the company's fixed scheme. And, as your earnings grow and retirement draws near, you might see if it is possible to fund your own pension more generously by paying your own bonuses as some of your salary into the fund. It may not be possible, but do always talk about your pension as part of your salary because that's exactly what it is.

Do not worry if you are not working for ever. You will still have some benefit of some kind and it is always a good idea to start building up pension rights as soon as you can.

Do not take it for granted that the State will look after you because, while they will not let you starve, they will not provide enough to cover the comforts that are even more desirable in old age than when you are young and fit.

If you are a woman, do not assume your husband will provide. How do you know you will still be married to him, or to any other husband, when pension times comes along? If you, a woman, are earning, take out your own scheme. It is damn difficult to swap a good income for a pension at any time but a devil of a lot harder to swap two incomes for one pension.

Quite a few small companies find pensions a major problem, despite the clever and excellent help they can get from schemes offered by companies like Hambro Life, which takes all the hassle and administration from the overworked executives of small businesses. So, when arguing your salary, you might suggest to small companies without pension schemes that they look at something like this for you and their other employees.

The self-employed

The self-employed came out as being enviable creatures in the final report of the Royal Commission on the Distribution of Wealth and Income, which showed them to be among the top earners in the country, and to be well represented among those earning really comfortable and affluent incomes.

It is important to remember that this term 'self-employed' actually may include a number of employers who run their own businesses and employ staff. It also includes highly paid lawyers, doctors and actors or actresses. But it also includes a good many building and construction workers; if they can be traced, and so many of them never can, being always on the move.

They may be able to earn well but they do not get all the benefits of social security that salaried or wages staff enjoy. Besides paying for their weekly stamp at £2.10 (more than a salaried member pays and without benefit of an added contribution from the employer company) they also pay an extra sum for National Insurance to the Inland Revenue on income between £2,000 and £5,000 a year. In one way, that extra penalty, as so many self-employed people regard it, helps to swell the State's pension funds, to make up for the fact that there is no contribution from an employer to top up the self-employed's weekly stamp so that, in effect, the self-employed would be paying less per head into the State fund without this extra sum. Thus, despite the continual and strong protests about it, it is not entirely unfair.

Or, rather, it would not be entirely unfair if the self-employed were to get as much benefit as the employed people. True, they may get sickness benefit if they can provide medical certificates to prove they were totally unable to work in any week but they have to be almost at death's door, in hospital or something of that kind even to qualify for

sickness benefit. Nor do they get the earnings-related supplementary benefit during sickness that can be claimed by someone getting salary or wages who can collect such a supplement for up to a maximum of 26 weeks of illness.

Equally, the self-employed do not qualify for the earnings-related supplement on unemployment benefit and, furthermore, the self-employed will find it so difficult to collect even the flat-rate unemployment benefit that he may give up. It is relatively easy for an actor or actress, a golf professional or builder to prove that he or she is out of work and cannot find any more. But think of artists, writers, potters, designers and a host of creative people. They can be totally out of work with no more in sight, but may have real trouble in proving it enough to get the dole. And, if they are doing work on spec, hoping that someone will buy the painting or article, they will not qualify for unemployment benefit. In fact, since signing on for jobs at the local employment centre is part of the qualification for benefit, and you should in theory be ready to take a suitable job if one arises, you will see that the self-employed are rarely in the signing-on queues.

The self-employed must, therefore, arrange their own pensions and, fortunately, the Government is fairly benevolent about letting them do just that.

Flexible pension plan

The self-employed are allowed to pay annual premiums into an approved pension scheme for themselves, subject to permitted maximum premium sums as laid down by the Inland Revenue. If you were born after 1915, the total of premiums allowed is £3,000, or 15 per cent (whichever is the lesser sum) of relevant earnings (meaning of net self-employed earnings, not wages, salary or investment income if you happen to get more than the self-employed income). This annual sum may be paid as premiums into a pension fund, usually called a variable annuity fund or a flexible pension plan and all the premiums are totally tax-deductible. Not just deductible at standard rate but taken right out of the self-employed earnings and not even taken into account when tax is calculated (though the relevant policy number and exemptions must be noted on the tax return, where such payments are also detailed). See Chapter 4 for annuities.

If you were born before 1916, you are allowed to make a larger annual contribution.

Born in	% of relevant income	Maximum allowance
1914 or 1915	18%	£3,600
1912 or 1913	21%	£4,200
1910 or 1911	24%	£4,800
1908 to 1909	27%	£5,400
1907 or earlier	30%	£6,000

Though a great many insurance companies offer pensions for the self-employed, there is not a great deal to choose between them though I would always advise getting the leaflets from a goodly number and comparing the offers. Effectively, you buy a certain number of units in the insurance companies' pension funds in this particular sector. Thus you can pay in a different sum each year, hence the flexibility, which is sensible since earnings — particularly for the self-employed — may vary from one year to the next. The self-employed cannot commit themselves to a fixed annual sum. Furthermore, if they agreed to a fixed contribution, they could not be sure to get all the premiums on a tax-deductible basis since they might, in a bad year, come to more than 15 per cent of earnings.

The units may be linked to a special fund, like a unit trust fund, a with-profits insurance or something of the kind. You may, for a small fee, be permitted to switch your units from one fund to another (within the same company — for example, M & G which has insurance and unit trust interests). Normally, you may not take the pension before you are 60 or later than 75 years old. If you decide

to retire before the agreed time of retirement when you took out the scheme, then your pension is based on the number of units so far purchased. If you postpone retirement until later, then you can and, furthermore, you can go on buying units if you are still earning. If not, you can move the units already bought into some other fund or leave them 'frozen', as it were, where they are until later but you will get some accumulation on the capital value of your units, some small growth on it.

Annuities and pension schemes for the self-employed are available from many insurance companies; their names can be obtained from BIBA, Fountain House, 130 Fenchurch Street, London EC3M 5DJ.

Can I take some cash?
You are allowed, as with company pensions, to take some of the pension fund you buy in cash, to commute it at retirement age. The amount of cash is not based on earnings, as with company pensions, but it must not exceed three times the amount still left in your fund of units; it is tax-free.

If I die before retiring?
Your estate gets a sum equal in value to the value of the units already allocated to your personal pension fund.

Surviving spouse
At the date of taking the pension, you can decide whether to take all your own entitlement or to commute some to provide a pension for the surviving spouse (or dependant).

How do I pay?
With most companies, however you like — monthly, quarterly or annually — depending on how good you are at accumulating enough to meet the less frequent payments.

Illness or sickness
There is no provision for either of these, or for disability in such a plan so the self-employed really need some kind of insurance

policy (often an endowment policy) that covers them and their family in such cases. There are strict restrictions on the kinds of benefit allowed under the self-employed schemes since there are not only tax benefits for the self-employed who buy the pensions but also for the funds that underlie the pensions. Such funds are exempt from corporation tax and capital gains tax, so there is no leeway for abuse. They are strictly for the self-employed or for employed people with no pension scheme and no pension entitlement. You may well find a sickness scheme with the company holding your self-employed policy.

Part-time self-employment

If you have a salaried job and part-time self-employment, you may enter such a scheme. Say you are a staff journalist who writes freelance articles. Then you would be allowed to buy, in addition to your company pension, an additional topping-up pension subject to the Inland Revenue maximums permitted for tax-free premiums.

If you stop self-employment

You may also stop buying a self-employed pension and you will not lose the units so far purchased. They remain your personal fund, subject to rules of early retirement, stoppage and freezing or whatever. You lose nothing and you almost certainly gain something, depending on how long you kept up your payments.

The self-employed lose in many ways but gain in others. Their jobs are often very much more satisfying and, though they usually work so much harder that they are subject to a kind of self-imposed slavery, they can often choose their own hours, their own level of earnings, their own success. It is not a primrose path. But it can be good.

Topping up

Schemes of this kind may be used by em-

ployed people who have woefully inadequate pension provisions because, for instance, they joined the company too late or something of that kind. The co-operation of the employer and the approval of the Inland Revenue are essential in getting the most tax-beneficial schemes and you do need to be careful that your retirement pensions, boosted by your own payments, are being bought out of either tax-deductible or tax-relief types of premium. Since each case involves special arithmetic, talk either to the pensions or personnel officer and the local D.H.S.S. before embarking on topping-up schemes. Insurance brokers are usually knowledgeable about them.

Tax

Your pension, when you receive it, counts as earned income and you are subject to earned income tax on it. Remember, the premiums to buy the units were free of tax, so your money is not being taxed twice. Only once, and in gentle easy stages as you receive it.

Your home can earn for you

There are schemes that allow you to convert part of the capital value of your home into income (Hambro Life, Save and Prosper). If your house is freehold and free of mortgage ('unencumbered', as they say), you re-mortgage it and use the cash to buy an annuity. The mortgage can be up to 75 per cent or 80 per cent of the home's value and you agree to maintain it in mint condition. There may be a maximum on the mortgage loan, such as £25,000. You, as the home-owner, retain ownership of the property and you pay only the interest on the mortgage, not any capital repayment, during the balance of your life. The mortgage is paid up on death (with some legal charges, etc.) or when the property is sold. If the property is not sold at death, then the heirs must find the capital sum unless the estate itself can do so, which seems unlikely or the mortgage would have never have been taken out in the first place.

Since there is tax relief on the mortgage interest, which can be offset against the income from the annuity, this is a good scheme, especially for those with higher tax levels. In that way, such schemes give most benefit to those who least need it, but they are an excellent way of boosting retirement income.

Such schemes are always more valuable if, like annuities, they are taken when you really move into old age. The 70-year-old gets a better deal than the 65-year-old and it just gets progressively better as you get older. For what you can buy with cash released by by your home, see the range of annuities possible.

Drawback

The snag is that you are lessening the capital you might wish to leave to your family. If you need the extra income, dismiss the thought of providing for them. They would much, much rather you had comfort and independence than tried to scrape along with the object of leaving them the full value of the house or the equivalent in cash. Also, do remember that you can buy capital-protected annuities, which do at least leave the unspent portion of your capital for the heirs if you die before you've used it all up through your annuity scheme.

Annuities

Should be borne in mind when discussing old age, since they also provide incomes and lump sum benefits. For details, see Chapter 4.

Old age advantages

It is terribly important to be happy and to have enough money in old age. Those are the years when you need to be able to take a taxi from time to time or hire a car because bus queues, train times and walking all make outings so miserable. Those are the times when you probably want to buy some costlier

foods because you have done with all the standing at the sink and cooker converting cheap cuts into savoury dishes. Those may be the times when you want to cut down by growing flowers and vegetables, though gardening seems to be one occupation that fit people can take well into old age.

The declining years are cold ones and you need more heat. They may be arthritic ones so that you need more help – home helps, meals on wheels and all the other advantages that are offered ought to be considered carefully because, although paid for, they are normally very good value.

Then there are cheap rail fares, air fares and – in City centres – other travelling fares. Cheap seats at the cinema, free buses in many areas, and cheaper entrance tickets to all kinds of local functions. All the many and possible advantages should be taken. The local council will almost certainly have a relevant department to tell you all about them and many even run lunch clubs and a lot of other social services. It is not fun to grow old, and it is really an incurable disease of a kind. But it need not always be total misery.

For those who grew up with the Welfare State, since the beginning of the 1950s, the declining years may be much better than for those whose social benefits never kept pace with their costs, who never saved much and were unable or unwilling to buy their homes and thus save up some cash for old age (it is often possible to sell and to move to small compact homes or homes further from major cities for less money in old age). But those who will grow old in future ought to have it better than our present senior citizens. More of them have homes. More of them have pensions over and above the State pension. The State pension and other benefits are improved and improving. Physical help for the disabled and the blind are now available, even though charged. Homes for the elderly are still, for the most part, sad and awful places, dreary with hopelessness, the atmosphere of people waiting in a forlorn row to die, terrified that their money will run out before they do.

There is still a tremendous amount to be done to make the lot of the old warm, secure and comfortable. There is also a lot to be done to make the old feel they have still some purpose in life, some reason for continuing to exist. It happens slowly. But we are a Welfare State and it is happening. Not enough. So that I must say to each and every person, it is essential to provide for your own future.

The nation's welfare system works if everyone contributes his or her fair share, without dodging taxes or National Insurance contributions. Equally, everyone should take their fair share (they pay tax if they enjoy other income). The system is worked out on that basis, that all give and all take and then, if need be, give again.

Chapter Six

The Stock Exchange

Let us assume you have reached the lucky position where you are buying your home, you are properly insured and you still have some money to spare. If it is income, then you are reasonably limited as to the number of ways in which you can invest it; there are a number, and most of them are listed in the previous chapter. Inevitably, some of them will overlap with shares, unit trusts and insurance schemes, but most financial systems and schemes are so interlinked that I have had to divide them into what seem to me to be logical compartments.

Just to be contrary, I plan to start with one of the investments I rarely advise to people who know little about them, stocks and shares (which are exactly the same thing, by the way); they are bought and sold in a well known marketplace, the Stock Exchange. You will probably not buy shares unless you have spare capital, and I do mean 'spare' – capital you can afford to lose or see decreased – because shares can go down as easily as they go up. If you have shares already, you will have noticed how often other people's shares rise and how rarely your own do. That's the usual pattern except in boom periods like the heady first two years of the 'seventies when the Stock Exchange hummed and fortunes were made, many of them to be lost in the 1974 slump.

How it started

But to the Stock Exchange. As I said, this is a market in which shares are bought and sold. It evolved, as did Lloyds of London in the insurance world, from a series of coffee houses in which share dealers met. In 1801, a one-building market was opened on the site of the present Stock Exchange in Throgmorton Street; the modern skyscraper was actually finished and opened in 1973, built rather incoveniently but very efficiently, while marketing and dealings continued unchecked – during a hectic period too, as I have said, because business was booming.

It was also in 1973 that women were first officially admitted as 'members' of the Stock Exchange, something which had hitherto been impossible. There had never been any stated rules against them, but it was obvious that they were unwanted because, even when they found respectable and respected sponsors, the Council of the Stock Exchange somehow never managed to vote them in. Their blackballing was unofficial but it was effective. The old joke was that it was impossible because there were no ladies' cloakrooms in the Stock Exchange building – where the trading area is called 'The House'. That was actually true, but members do not have to be in The House in order to trade now that there are telephones and, in any case, some other representative of their firms could trade for them.

Stock Exchange members are now men and women who deal in shares of many, many kinds, national and international, Government stocks, local authority stocks, company shares, anything of that kind which members of the public may buy and sell freely. Some companies are not 'public', their shares all being held by a family, their friends, or a consortium of private owners. Such companies' shares are not marketed freely on the Stock Exchange.

Stockbrokers and jobbers

There are two main classes of members. First, brokers called 'stockbrokers'. They act directly for people like you and me, for buying or selling clients, as well as for large, institutional clients like the pensions funds of companies, investment managers of insurance companies or unit trusts, even the Bank of England itself. For anyone, in fact, who buys stocks and shares.

Then there are the jobbers, sometimes called 'stockjobbers' but more often without the prefix of 'stock' that brokers always get. Jobbers deal for the brokers, acting as 'principals', to use a trade term. They, theoretically, hold the supply of stocks and shares. I say theoretically because they do not always keep masses of shares in stock, as though they were warehouses or retail shops. They may have the shares, it is true, or they may know where to get them on demand. They specialize in various types of securities (another word for stocks and shares), but there are always at least two jobbers dealing in any one category to make sure that competition survives and the risk of price-fixing is eliminated.

A broker goes into the market by either going personally to The House, telephoning, or sending his orders and messages through a representative of his firm, which will almost certainly have a 'box' in The House, a kind of local office, even if their offices are next door. Not all brokers are as close to the Stock Exchange as they once were – the City of London used to be called The Square Mile because everyone was within running distance of the Exchange, which meant all brokers were crowded into a square mile. Modern communications have changed that.

Suppose the broker's client has asked for Marks and Spencer 'at best', meaning the buyer is prepared to pay whatever looks like the best price to be had on that particular day. The broker does not place the order immediately; he asks the jobber for a price without giving away whether he is buying or selling. The jobber quotes two prices. The broker tries the other jobbers in Marks and Spencer and he gets back more of the curious shorthand talk like 152/8. This means that one price is 152 pence and the other is 158. The higher price is the one at which the broker will have to buy, the lower is the selling price. The difference between the two is a 'spread' or a 'turn', and the jobber's profit is within that turn, depending on the fact that he can sell the shares for more than he has to pay for them. The spread can be very small and brokers can often argue the gap to shocking narrowness, even bring halves into the prices, bargaining with the jobber until they feel they have 'the best'.

The broker then places his verbal order to buy, say, 5,000 Marks and Spencer at 156. The order is scribbled in little notebooks by both broker and jobber for a secretary or clerk to confirm later when the invoices have to be made out. The whole thing is done on trust and the motto of the Stock Exchange is: 'My Word is My Bond' as it is, unofficially, in most City institutions.

The point about membership of the S.E. which involves passing exams and being carefully vetted for suitability in many ways, is that only members or their representatives (most members being on the staff of stock-broking or jobbing firms) may actually deal. The busy trading floor in the Centre of The House is known as The Floor and the only people who may walk The Floor are members or messengers, who are known as 'blue-buttons', because they wear bright blue badges in their lapels to identify their right to be on The Floor.

Messages are conveyed more by flashing lights than by shouting as in the old days, and each broker has a number which is lighted up when his partners back in the office want a word with him. The various people who work the backroom apparatuses and pass the calls or light the lights are uniformed 'waiters'. The name has been passed down from the old days of dealing in the coffee houses.

Jobbers seem to have special instincts and foresight for the ills and booms that beset a marketplace, and they are ultra-sensitive to the laws of supply and demand. They mark their prices up and down feverishly to defend their own profits but also to defend the position of a share in which they deal. If they see unexpected demand for any shares, they will rapidly mark the price up to discourage greater demand and greater buying in case the supply of such shares cannot meet the demand. In reverse, they will mark down unpopular shares to encourage buyers. You may hear the phrase 'defensive markings', which means they are taking a stand against what they fear might happen to demand rather than what is actually happening.

The Account

The Stock Exchange divides the year up into two-week (ten working day) periods, called 'the Account' during which everyone has time to collect their shares and prepare accounts before settlement. During Bank Holidays, Christmas, etc., the Account period may last for three weeks to take in the non-trading days. Suppose you buy shares on the Monday at the beginning of an Account period. The Stockbroker who buys them for you will send you a contract note setting out the price he paid per share, the total cost, his commission, the stamp duty on shares (2 per cent, which goes to the Government), and the VAT. Stamp duty may be called on the note 'Transfer Stamp', but the phrase is rarely used verbally. Since it is applied to sums in specific bands and not exactly to the nearest £1, you may find it is not an exact 2 per cent. For more about the cost of buying shares, see the next chapter on stocks and shares.

The contract note is not the account, which you would get a fortnight later, when settlement was due. The jobber is working within the same period of the Account; since he does not have to deliver the shares for two weeks (in this case) he has time to rustle up shares he sold if he has insufficient stock. Delivery on both sides is due at the time of settlement, so everyone gets themselves straight on settlement day. The Account period is what makes possible the practice of selling shares you do not own. Suppose, for instance, you are convinced that I.C.I. shares will fall, because you think that they are going to announce poor figures, or something else will make the market anxious about them or shares in general; you will then sell shares (that you don't have) in I.C.I. at the beginning of the Account in the firm belief that before the end of it (when you must deliver) you can buy them for less than you sold them. The difference will be profit for you; since payment for both deals is due on the same day, you don't have to lay out any money before you receive some. Sadly, many are tempted to do this kind of gambling when they haven't the money to pay if the shares go up instead of down.

Bears, bulls and stags

A person who takes a pessimistic view of the stock market and believes prices will fall is called a 'bear' and you will sometimes hear the phrase 'bear covering caused prices to rise'. This means that bears are rushing in to 'cover' themselves, i.e. to buy shares they have already sold (hopefully at higher prices) earlier in the Account. Their rush to buy the shares they sold without owning them in order to deliver by settlement day creates a demand for the shares which causes the price to rise solely on the basis of demand for them. A 'covered' bear is therefore all right. An 'uncovered' bear has problems that can be solved only by money, so let's hope he had enough to try the gamble.

As you can see, this kind of dealing depends on split-second timing and I would not advise anyone to try it unless they are (a) brave, (b) foolish and (c) rich enough. A 'bear market', by the way, is a market in which shares are either falling or expected to fall; bad news from home or abroad will trigger off a bear market. Suppose there were suddenly a whole lot of industrial strikes and anti-Government demonstrations, you would get a bear market. Buyers would simply be nervous of shares and their prices would fall. It can happen in special industries such as, for example, retailing when higher VAT is imposed and expected to generate resistance in shoppers. You might then see the shares of House of Fraser (which owns Harrods, among many other stores) fall a few pence on such news and probably the shares of most stores would also fall.

A 'bull' is someone who believes that prices will rise, a supreme optimist. He may buy shares in the beginning of an Account to sell before it ends. He may not have the money to buy, but will be speculating on the ability to pay for his purchases out of the inevitable profit on his sales. If only it were that inevitable.

As you can see, bears and bulls can both get badly caught with their bank balances down. Should they be in trouble when the Account ends, they can 'put through' their deals or 'contango' them to the next Account for a fee (arranged by the stockbroker). They can do that a few times hoping to make good, but the moment of reckoning does catch up with them eventually if the gamble goes wrong.

A stag is someone who 'buys' new issue shares in order to sell them at once at a profit. I think it will be easier to describe him better when we come to define new issues, but it is relevant to say here that he can get caught too. The new issue may be a failure and he may have to sell his new shares (if he has been unlucky enough to get them) at a loss. If the share rose when they were dealt in (and he has been lucky enough to get some), his profit is sure.

The structure of the Stock Exchange

The Stock Exchange has about 4,100 members each of whom has passed the qualifying exam, and a ruling council of 46 people is elected from among them. The Government Broker, as he is called, is an *ex officio* member without a vote at council. One-third of the council retire each year for replacement by other elected members. An administrative staff of about 1,000 people handle the day-to-day work of this busy market.

The members deal daily in about 8,000 stocks and shares. The companies in which they deal are listed in the Stock Exchange printed lists and you will therefore sometimes hear of public companies as being listed or having a listing, which does not mean they are in a bad way – one young lady once told me it sounded as if they were listing over and in danger of sinking. Not so. Some overseas companies are listed, especially the larger American ones and South African mining shares. Most British firms are small by foreign standards and 370 overseas listed companies actually have a capital value that is bigger than that of 2,400 British companies combined.

During the boom in railways in the nineteenth century, a number of Stock Exchanges opened outside London to handle the extra pressure of business, especially as railways were distinctly regional – some of you may remember the Great Western Railway, the London Midland and Scottish, the Southern Railway and others, all better known as G.W.R., L.M.S. or S.R., etc. The railways were not always nationalized, they were all separate companies. There are still provincial Stock Exchanges in Manchester, Birmingham, Liverpool, York, Glasgow, Edinburgh, Dublin, Cork and even poor old war-torn Belfast. Many specialize in the shares of local companies but all can deal in anything and all come under the umbrella of the Stock Exchange.

The S.E. is not controlled in any way by Government and prides itself on having a stricter code of ethics than any national laws might impose, disciplining and fining its members, even 'banishing' them for misdemeanours. Well, its prefects can be strict, and the code usually works, but they cannot deny that a good many people still get away with murder. For instance, those who commit the cardinal crime of 'insider dealings' (using their inside knowledge of a company to deal in shares) have too often got away with mere admonition. In fact, nobody with any inside knowledge of a company that might affect its shares price may deal in the shares until such knowledge is public property. Insider dealings are prevented in every way possible but some still slip through the net. Often very hard to prove because, though all deals are recorded, it is not always possible to prove they were done on inside knowledge and an 'insider' might use some other name, a friend's for instance. Leaks are so common in the Stock Exchange and rumour spreads like wildfire so an insider never has his knowledge for long and newspapers are often on to it very fast.

About two million individuals in Britain actually own shares, and these private clients account for something more than one-third of the value of all share deals done. Incidentally, deals are very frequently referred to as 'bargains', even when they are not. You will find shares under different category headings in the financial columns of some daily newspapers and, since there is some slight variation between newspapers, get used to looking up your prices in the same one each day, so that you will always know where to glance at once. The headings are simple, like Banks, or Beer, Wines and Spirits, Building Industry, that kind of thing.

The visitors' gallery

The Stock Exchange has a visitors' gallery, which you should certainly visit if buying shares tempts you. Charming and attractive uniformed guides will show you the busy Floor, where scurrying antlike figures are dealing away, chalking figures on blackboards and shouting or gesticulating like a gang of bookmakers — which in many respects they are. The guides will explain what is happening as you watch and the gallery is open during trading hours every working weekday.

Although the old unofficial uniform of black jacket and striped trousers is hardly ever seen nowadays, the old-fashioned spirit largely remains beneath the trendier suits. Many own no shares themselves, believing that this is the way to be totally objective. Sir Harold Wilson headed a committee to investigate the City and its affairs, which, rather than being found wanting in ethics, got a good many pats on the back.

The Stock Exchange maintains a compensation fund currently worth something like £600,000 to protect share-buyers. But the S.E. would pay up if more were needed to bale out share-buyers or holders who suffered from the demise or insolvency of a member firm.

Each individual stockbroking or jobbing firm must be highly solvent, with funds (which can be invested in approved securities) worth something like £10,000 per partner. There is in any case a minimum per firm of £30,000 for brokers and £60,000 for jobbers. Not only must all entrants for membership be screened for financial soundness, but also for their moral outlook and principles, and sponsors who introduce them must be anything but casual about the people they recommend. Every member must be approved by 75 per cent of the Stock Exchange Council and, in a small village like the City, reputations are pretty well known to one and all; so it is less easy for a baddie to get in than you might suppose.

There was long thought to be much abuse of the City Code during takeovers. More often than not, the offenders were members of the companies involved in bid situations rather than the merchant bankers, stockbrokers or other City inhabitants. For the most part, offences consisted of insider dealings by those who knew that a higher bid was about to be made by Company A for Company B and so they bought shares in B to make money, while members of the public could only guess at the possibility. There are other offences but, since you and I are unlikely ever to be in a position to commit them, we need not worry too much about them.

The criminals are dealt with by the City's own body called the 'Takeover Panel', a self-governing 'police' force which was set up after some prodding and many suggestions from the Bank of England. It meets informally, but its investigations into misdeeds or even suspected misdeeds are very thorough and its permission must be sought for any actions during a takeover situation; you may often notice in reports or prospectuses, in advertisements or newspaper stories, that certain operations have been cleared by the Takeover Panel. It may not be the ultimate shareholders' protection society but it works well enough for the Government to believe that no special legislation is necessary.

Times change and the Stock Exchange may have to change with them. Competition and change may force the old commission system to be replaced by negotiated fees or rates for buying and selling or, indeed, for any other jobs. Recently there has been much criticism of stockbrokers' fees. There is much freer trading in stocks and shares in America, where the fashion is for road-sweepers and bankers alike to be able to buy shares or portions of shares more easily than is possible here. Once upon a time in Britain, shares were actually sold over shop counters by many — Boots the Chemist sold its shares along with aspirin and my grandfather often told me how he had been offered shares in Harrods for 2s 6d when he bought some bacon and tomatoes. He had no half-crowns to spare, which he much regretted when he saw them go to £8 each while he was still painting portraits for a living. But under the present system share-buyers are protected. Boots and Harrods were all right, as it turned out, though Boots had a bad patch and had to be rescued by a giant American drug company, from which it was later able to buy back its British independence. But many, many shares were worthless, foisted on to an unsuspecting buyer as they could not be today.

Yes, the Stock Exchange has its faults, but most of them are errors on the right side, even if their attitudes seem a little stuffy and old-fashioned. Well, they are a little stuffy and old-fashioned.

Chapter Seven

Stocks and Shares

The Stock Exchange, then, is like a good many other wholesalers' markets, but the merchandise in which they deal is a little more complicated. The names, for one thing. Stocks and shares – usually discussed in partnership like that – are two words for the same thing. There are very fine nuances of meaning, maybe, but they have really become obsolete except to the cognoscenti and it is not wrong to describe them as synonymous.

There are other synonyms. You will hear of 'securities' and 'equities', for instance. All these words cover the same product, which is a share in, a stake in a company or organization that hopes to make profits by using the money you lend it when you buy that share or stake. For your part, if you buy them, you hope – as well as receiving income – that the shares will increase in value. Before I embark on more detailed explanation, I would like to say that, though it sounds tempting and exciting to buy stocks and shares, I honestly recommend anyone to stay away unless they have:

(a) first-class advisors or some personal knowledge of what they are doing
(b) enough money for it not to matter if they lose some, most or almost all of it
(c) strong nerves, a sunny and philosophical nature and a doctor who readily prescribes Mogadon
(d) their own home, whether under mortgage or not
(e) adequate insurance for unpredictable

crises and old age
(f) a genuine interest in the investment market so that they can read, mark, learn and inwardly digest all that is said about it and about stocks and shares

If you qualify on all these counts, still stop and think again. Money is hard to come by – even if you win a football pool, it may never happen again. And it is all too easy to lose it on stocks and shares, many of which go down as well as up. There is, as I never get tired of saying, no investment as good as your house. And, with small sums of capital or with no capital but some disposable income, you will usually be safer with your money in an insurance scheme or a building society (depending on what your tax rate is) than in stocks and shares.

If you have the money, the inclination and the nerve, then you might make money and quite a lot of it. The next bit of advice would be to spread your investment over several different companies and indeed over several different industries so that a crash in one might at least be offset by a boom in another.

The snag there is that you will feel very bad about not having every penny in the share that goes up. I remember once being told a story by a man who had made himself a nice tidy sum during the boom years of stocks and shares in the late 'fifties and early 'sixties (then again in the early and the late 'seventies). He had picked very few losers and was delighted to have seen his initial £5,000 turn fairly rapidly into £32,000. He wrote well on stocks and shares, and was well pleased until he met a man he described as a bit of a bonehead; a man who had been retired early with a lump-sum pay-off after a long term of overseas employment. My friend described to me how the lucky man had just made £280,000 in less than two years by putting the entire £37,000 into Western Mining shares.

'So you see', said my friend, 'it can still be done. You can still make a lucky strike.'

'Well, yes,' I admitted, grudging and envious, 'but you do need to have the £37,000 to begin with.'

'True,' was the reply, 'but let's face it. If you and I had £37,000, we'd never have been such bloody fools as to put it all into Western Mining.'

I'm not sure what point he was making, or whether there was a moral to his anecdote. I do know that thousands and thousands of speculators (gamblers, really) rushed to buy mining shares of all kinds, whether they were rich in nickel, copper, gold, rutile, diamonds or even just suspected of having a few seams of either. The big rush at the end of the 'sixties and beginning of the 'seventies turned into a hopeless crawl of defeat for most of them as the mines proved less than valuable. I remember watching Poseidon shares rocket from about twenty shillings to twenty pounds and then go on and on, wishing I had bought a lot. I also remember how they crashed when hopes of finding valuable mining rights, suspected of being in the Poseidon mine, came to nothing. Those who bought a few and sold before the top was reached — impossible to judge, but many made a good guess — found themselves with lovely capital gains even after meeting the tax demand (for of course capital gains tax affects these successful gambles). Those whose greed or over-optimism made them wait for even bigger increases got caught in the overnight slump and ended up sad and, I hope, wiser; alas, gamblers rarely learn, so they probably did it again when they had

got some more money together.

The point about buying stocks and shares is that you are taking a risk because you hope to make a good profit, a better profit than you could make out of interest from a bank or building society. It is more or less true that the greater the risk, the greater the profit (or loss). The less the risk, the less the profit. It is entirely up to you to assess yourself and to see which kind of investment suits your nature best. I always tell people that the most important thing about investments is never to do anything that keeps them awake at night. It is also a favourite adage of mine that you need to be honest because, whoever else you sleep with, you've always got to sleep with yourself, which means you need to have respect and affection for yourself.

So be brave to buy stocks and shares. And be honest with yourself, your stock-broker and the Inland Revenue. Your own nature is terribly important.

What are stocks and shares?

When you buy these, you are buying a slice of a company or similar enterprise (it might be a slice of a government but that will be covered later under Government Stocks). You buy the slice of the company actually from the company although you deal through the Stock Exchange (or your bank). The company gets your money to use in its business and you get a share certificate which shows how many shares you have. The company will use your money to make more goods, build a new factory, start new products, and generally try to make money. And you will share in their profits by getting dividends, explained later. You are now a shareholder.

There will be many other shareholders, and you all now own the company between you, with a right to its profits and, if they are distributed, its assets. The assets are the 'negotiable' or 'realizable' possessions of a company and may include properties, cash, stock of raw materials, plant, machinery, patents on inventions, factories, and a good many other things including even goodwill and the company or brand names. These last three may seem intangible but, whether they actually appear on the company's balance sheet or not, they are nevertheless negotiable assets. Thus you may hear assets described in two different ways: fixed or intangible. Simple enough to understand, really, as are all money terms if you take the trouble to find out what they mean, which is usually terribly logical. It is important to recall that companies have liabilities too and that a liability — heavy borrowing, a product that fails and such — can depress the share price.

Nominal value

The shares will have a nominal value which may seem to bear no relation to the price you pay for them. It is worked out like this. Every company has an 'authorized capital', which represents the value of the total number of shares that could be issued to the public at any time. The shares that are actually issued are combined to make the 'issued capital', which may not be as much as the authorized capital because there is no compulsion for the company to sell or release all its authorized capital at once. The company will issue as many shares as it needs money.

The issued capital is divided into shares, which can be of several different kinds and which I shall explain shortly. Each share will have a nominal or 'par' value — 'par' meaning the value of the share if calculated as part of the total capital in its class of share. If a company has an authorized capital of £100,000 (all issued) and it also has 100,000 shares, then the nominal or par value of each share is £1. If it issues 50,000 shares, then each is worth £2 'at par', and so on.

The price you pay in the market may be very different from the par value — maybe £5 and £9 respectively, depending on how well the company has performed and how much demand there is for those shares.

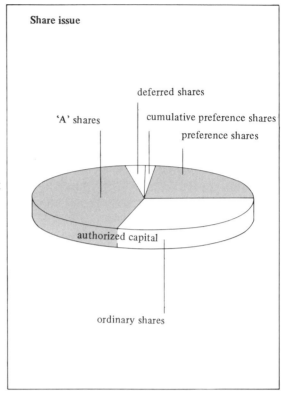

Share issue

From time to time, a company may decide that it wants to raise more money, which it does by issuing new shares (see 'rights issue' below). Market prices fluctuate a lot. When you look up share prices in the financial columns of the serious papers or periodicals and in the *Financial Times,* you may see more than one price, depending on where you are looking and on what day. When you see one price (which is what most papers give), this is the middle price of the day's average prices for buying and selling. If you remember, the buying and selling prices of shares are at opposite ends of a 'spread'. The middle price is the one quoted to keep the columns simple. The *Financial Times* has also pages that show all the prices at which deals or bargains were done. These are set out in chronological order so that they make interesting study, because you can see whether the price trend was up or down towards the end of the day. For instance, suppose you see prices marked from 128p up to 138p, with few falls in between, your share was becoming more and more popular as the day went on.

Share prices may fall behind the rise of inflation, keep more or less in parallel or rise faster – property prices tend to run more or less in parallel. So, when you are looking at a share that has performed well and wondering whether to sell it, remember to assess what has happened to the value of money during the time you owned the share as well as taking buying and selling expenses into account. For instance, £1,000 of shares bought two years ago may now be worth £1,500, which means a cash profit of £500 (not counting expenses and CGT). But a cash profit is not necessarily a real profit after adjusting for inflation. That doesn't mean you shouldn't sell. You should sell when you need the money, when you become nervous, if you are fed up with the slowing of the share price or its failure to rise, or for any other reason that you like. It's your money. They always say you should be prepared to leave a little for the other man, meaning take your own profit and leave the rest of the rise in the share price to the next buyer. If you try to reach the top, you may topple.

Never refer to the extra that you failed to make (i.e. the rise of the share after you sold) as a 'loss', as most people do. You will not have made a loss, but you will merely have made less or failed to make. If your money had been lying idle without collecting either some interest or capital gain, you would have been guilty of not 'putting your money to work', as they say.

Apart from the laws of supply and demand economic pressures and Government action can boost or slump share prices. For example, if the Government lowers VAT on some things, the industries making such things and the shops selling them look all set for profit, so their shares rise. If VAT is doubled, retail shares and shares of consumer product manufacturers tend to fall. The fall is only a few pence, mostly, but the shares are less popular for a while. Sometimes, the few pence fall may be little more than a jobber's

defensive marking to encourage buyers for those shares.

Ordinary shares (or equity shares)
I said there were different kinds of shares, and these are the shares that most of us, the 2 million individuals in Britain owning shares, buy and have. There are theoretically two kinds of ordinary shares – voting and non-voting, the latter usually being called 'A' shares. 'A' shares are most unpopular because they deprive shareholders, who take the company's risks, of the chance to have a vote in the company's affairs. Most 'A' shares have now been enfranchized, given a vote, and there are few companies left with this particular class of share. Such shares are usually cheaper but anything that is cheaper to buy also realizes less on selling. If you were lucky enough to stumble on some 'A' shares that became enfranchised soon after you bought you would make a quick profit because the price would rise to meet the level of the voting shares.

Deferred ordinary (or deferred)
Very rare, usually with some limitation such as the right to the dividend or distribution of assets being subject to deferral until other classes of shareholders have been paid. You will probably never come across them and don't look for them unless you know an inside story of the company.

The vote
Your ordinary shares entitle you to vote at either annual general meetings or extra-ordinary general meetings; to attend such meetings and, from time to time, to vote by post on special forms that will be sent to you. You may think, if you own a few thousand shares of a company with hundreds of thousands of shares, that your vote is worthless, but you would be wrong. Everyone who has a vote should use it; big decisions have been made by shareholders rallying to use the combined strength of their votes.

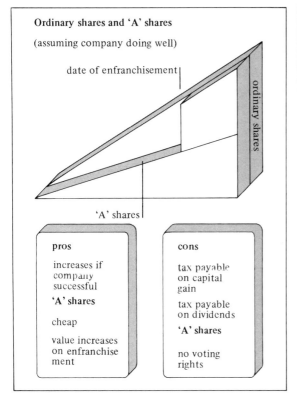

Ordinary shares and 'A' shares
(assuming company doing well)

date of enfranchisement

ordinary shares

'A' shares

pros	cons
increases if company successful	tax payable on capital gain
'A' shares	tax payable on dividends
cheap	**'A' shares**
value increases on enfranchisement	no voting rights

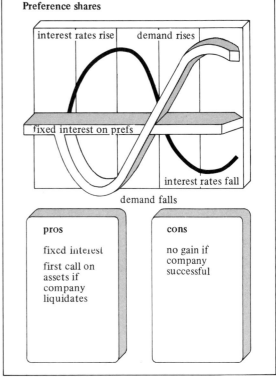

Preference shares

interest rates rise   demand rises

fixed interest on prefs

interest rates fall

demand falls

pros	cons
fixed interest	no gain if company successful
first call on assets if company liquidates	

If you cannot get to the annual general or other meetings, use your proxy voting card which will have been sent to you with the statement of the company's account and the chairman's report. (These are your 'Report and Accounts'.) Shareholders are generally a lethargic lot, occasionally spurred to action by some ginger group of shareholders who mail them with criticism of the Board and its actions or ask for support to unseat the Board or one of its members.

Preference shares

This special class of a company's shares gives the holder first call on a company's realized assets if the company goes into liquidation. The interest on a preference share is fixed, unlike the dividend (the interest) on an ordinary share, which may go up or down according to the company's fortunes. Thus the 'prefs' may get a better or a worse income, but some people like predictability of their income and, in the old days when interest rates showed little variation, these

were very popular. Now there are still some good deals to be had but the experts can spot them while few of the rest of us can.

Preference share prices do fluctuate, in line with interest rates; they become in demand when interest rates are falling, so the buying and selling prices rise. When interest rates rise, and the income from the prefs looks less good, demand falls and the price does also. The preference share with a low interest rate will probably have a low buying and selling price.

Cumulative preference shares

Sometimes a company does so badly that it fails even to pay the fixed interest on the preference shares. Cumulative preference shareholders get the accumulated interest paid to them when the company recovers.

If a company goes into liquidation, the preference shareholders are paid back before the ordinary shareholders, though they have to come after the holders of loan stock or debentures. There may be no cumulative

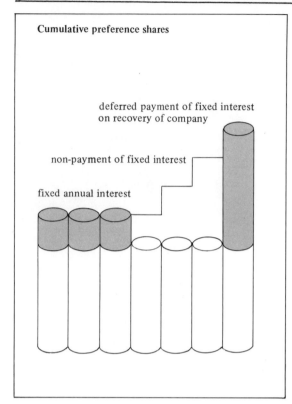

Cumulative preference shares

deferred payment of fixed interest
on recovery of company

non-payment of fixed interest

fixed annual interest

prefs to buy, of course. But, if there are, they are safer — though no company expects to go broke. The very fact that cumulative preference stock existed would indicate to me not to buy the prefs. But, as I've already said, always leave such things to the experts.

Stock
Having just used this word in the singular makes this a good place to explain that it is the stake or holding in a company. If you own shares, you have a stock in the company. However, they leave out the 'a' and say you have stock. Hence stocks and shares mean the same thing.

Loan stock or debentures
These mean much the same thing and carry similar rights — mainly the right to be repaid before any other shareholders (even preference shareholders) in the event of the company going broke and having to sell all its assets and also a sure dividend. If the sale of assets

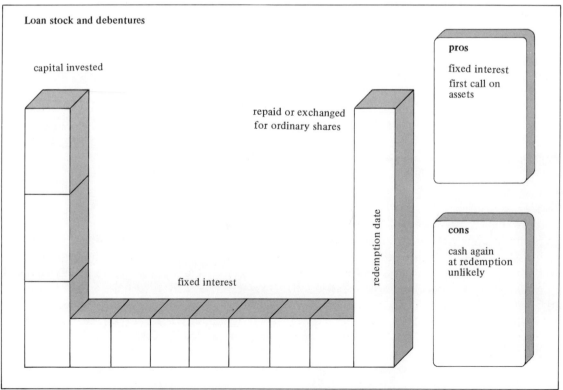

Loan stock and debentures

capital invested

repaid or exchanged
for ordinary shares

redemption date

fixed interest

pros

fixed interest
first call on
assets

cons

cash again
at redemption
unlikely

realizes less than the sum of loans repayable to loan stock and debenture holders, then the payout will be done on a percentage basis according to each holding.

Both loan and debenture stock carry fixed rates of annual interest which is usually paid to you twice yearly and both will have a final redemption date in the event of the company continuing in business. At such a date, the holder will normally get an option to be repaid the debt or to exchange his holding for ordinary shares in the company. Both kinds of stock are usually sold in large 'parcels' of £100 or more and interest is then paid twice a year.

Loan stock does not normally have any security attached to the agreement, while a debenture would have something like the factory, offices, plant or machinery. Banks, for example, sell loan stock and very safe it is, not needing the security of buildings because of the large sums of money and realizeable investments the banks must hold by law – and that is apart from the unlikelihood of our big clearing banks ever going broke.

Though such stock does not give a capital cash gain on repayment, the market price does fluctuate according to supply and demand and to interest rates, as with preference shares. Thus it is possible to buy and sell loan stock or debentures at profit.

Employee shares

A good many companies run special schemes of shares for employees, usually called something like 'Employee Profit-linked Shares'. These are exactly the same as shares, whether the employer company is public or private, but there are certain firm restrictions, imposed by Government. You may not be able to buy them until you have been with the company continuously for a definite period; you will have to hold them for a minimum term; they are for you, and you alone, so that you cannot transfer or sell them except to the company; and they are subject to your being employed with the company, although

there may be provisions for holding them after you leave, if you retire early and that kind of thing. Should the company be a private company and eventually float, your own shares are still in a special class of their own. Some companies give free shares. There are tax advantages when you come to sell the shares on retirement, if you have held them for a minimum period. Though all such shares are closely similar, each company can vary some of the rules subject to specific legal requirements, and there is little point in my giving a detailed example. If your company has such a scheme, it will see that you get a full explanation and there will always be some executive ready to explain more fully. My advice is always to buy such shares. Of course, being profit-linked, they may do badly in some years and really well in others. But you can pay for them out of your income, by deduction from your salary, instead of having to find lump sums.

New shares

These are often called 'new issues'. When a company's shares become freely bought and sold in the Stock Exchange, the company has 'floated' or 'gone public'; the shares are therefore listed or 'quoted'. The shares floated are new shares for which members of the public apply through forms published in newspaper and periodical advertisements by the company's stockbrokers and/or merchant bankers and financial advisers. Any newly floated company will have a register of existing shareholders (see under 'register' later in this chapter). The shares may all be in the hands of the founders and partners plus a few employees (maybe all the employees, now that the Government allows employees profit-linked shares). The register may include friends of the company or it may not, and the list might be short or long.

While the company trades prior to flotation, it is a private company. It holds proper shareholders' meetings and generally conforms to the laws and procedures of proper Board meetings, paying dividends if they can and wish to and so forth. But its doings, though properly detailed and returned to the files at Companies House every year (where they are open to scrutiny by anyone who calls and pays the fee) are not public, as with floated companies.

Eventually, the time comes when the founders want to turn their own shares into hard cash. They have probably been very short of cash all the time it was invested in the company and they now want to take some of the proceeds out of the company, subject to the relevant taxation of course. They still need money for the company — in fact, they need more for expansion of some kind, for new factories or offices, products or whatever. So they float off the capital as shares, getting money for some of their own personal shares as well as more for the new shares in the company from the public keen to invest in their profits so far and promises of profit ahead. We have already seen how the company and its advisers decide how many shares to sell simply by splitting up the capital employed in the business into equal shares at — say — 100p each.

It is worth repeating that the new shares will almost certainly not be issued at 100p, but at a valuation per share assessed by experts that might be much higher. Their value will be on the register before flotation, whether the company has been recently valued for that purpose by accountants and financial advisers or whether the valuation has naturally been 'visible' over a number of years via private or 'unquoted' share deals.

The prospectus

A prospectus is then prepared to attract share-buyers. It must by law contain everything possible about the past and present performance of the company as well as seriously considered projections for the future. It shows exactly how many shares the directors, partners or founders hold, how many shares are to be sold, and every detail will have the signed approval of the accountants and lawyers, who will have spent many days and weeks studying the figures and asking innumerable questions of the directors. Their own reputations depend upon how well they do their job of verification and, quite apart from the strict codes of practice that bind accounting and legal firms, their own commercial reputations are too important to put at risk by doing this particular job carelessly. Eventually a market price for the share is calculated and goes into the prospectus and application forms, together with data about the earnings per share, dividend and so forth (see later in this chapter).

Occasionally a share will be placed by 'going to tender'. In other words, all possible data will be given to potential buyers, who will then decide for themselves what they think the share is worth and will send their tenders in with their applications, hoping that the price they offer is close enough to the price eventually agreed to permit of an allocation. Obviously, this is a clever method and has been highly successful, but it is so bewildering to all but the knowledgeable and sophisticated shareholder that it is rarely used. The advantage to the company and issuing house is that the price at which the new shares come to be sold will be the 'true' market price, based on the demand for the shares, and they might realize more money for the new shares than had they played safe and set their own price. However, the confusion for so many smaller shareholders might prove to be a disadvantage, resulting in limited applications for the shares, which might defeat the original object of getting a high price. This is, in a way, something like an auction sale with the same sort of risks and benefits attendant on it.

If you want to tender because you like the company, there will be stockbrokers who can advise you, either directly or through your bank. Often, there will be some guidance in the prospectus like 'not less than . . .'

As a rule, the offer for sale is made by an issuing house (such as a merchant bank) which also underwrites the issue. That means that the issuing house will buy all the unsold shares, if any. They handle the applications, which have to be in by a certain date, stated clearly on the forms. Dealings begin on another date, also clearly stated and not to be confused.

The applications may not all succeed. An issue might be oversubscribed, meaning that people have applied for more shares than the number on sale. The allocation may then be made in various ways. More often than not, lots are drawn and the unlucky applicants get their money back — sometimes they merely find their own cheques returned, or the issuing house may bank all cheques and then repay by writing their own cheques. If the latter bounce, they would not get an allocation. A company may state it will cash cheques to discourage stags (see Chapter 6) but its nuisance value and administration cost may not be worth the action, and most applicants will merely get their own cheques back again.

Sometimes, applicants may get a percentage of their applications — such as one-tenth, so that they get 250 shares if they applied for 2,500. At other times, all small applications (say, under 2,000 shares, but shareholders will be told at the time) may be met and proportionate allocations may be made to those who asked for larger holdings.

An oversubscribed issue is a successful one, and lucky applicants will see their share price rise immediately, meaning instant profit. Since there is no stamp duty on new shares, and very few expenses, because you are buying directly and not through those wholesalers, the stockbrokers and jobbers, the profits are bound to be nicely clear of expenses. If the issue is undersubscribed, then the underwriters give the company the difference, as it were, and hold the shares as an investment — they must have believed in the company to handle the issue, so spare no tears for them. They win more often than they lose.

As I said, dealings start a few days after allocation. Never be in a hurry to sell new shares once the price has risen. The public enthusiasm means a healthy future more often than not. Then follow your share price in the newspaper columns. There is one great 'plus' about buying new shares. Stockbrokers will not normally handle small sums for new private clients, so that buying new shares is often a good way into the market, since you may be able to buy as few as 50 shares whose price can vary.

Placings

A descriptive word, which means that parcels of shares are placed with financial houses of some kind rather than floated on the open market. This is a cheaper way of doing things because it saves all the heavy costs of professional services — advertising and so forth — which beset the new issues. Placed shares have no Stock Exchange quotation but are often bought and sold privately. A placing might be made when the company's directors need more money, but less than they would attract by going public; they hang on to their independence and privacy a little longer. Also, many companies at various stages of their existence need money but not as much as a large new issue would provide, and a placing would suit them very well.

Rights issues

These are issues of new shares to existing shareholders only on a proportionate basis. The company may want to raise a limited amount of extra capital or a goodly sum. It offers one new share for three, seven, ten or whatever old shares. You will normally hear them spoken of without the extra words simply as a 'one for ten rights' and so on. The new shares will have a lower price tag to make them attractive and, though only existing shareholders have the right to buy, they may sell their rights, usually for rather less than the actual rights value. Suppose

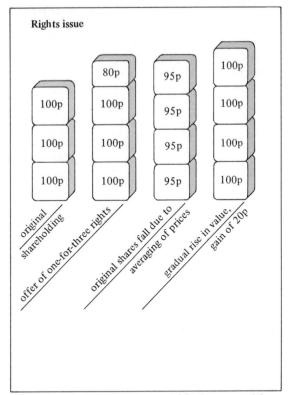

Rights issue

original shareholding

offer of one-for-three rights

original shares fall due to averaging of prices

gradual rise in value, gain of 20p

you have the right to buy 100 shares at 80p each but just haven't the necessary £80 or don't wish to increase your holding in that particular company, you may sell the rights to the 100 cheaper shares (we will assume the actual price of the old, ordinary shares is about 100p). What you get will be governed by market demand, but you will not get £80 or anything approaching it. You sell your rights through your broker. But you will make a small profit on selling your rights. There may, however, be a snag, which is that the market price of your old ordinary shares will fall. It works like this. Let us say that one new share is issued for every three existing shares and let us assume the existing share price to be 100p. In theory, the four shares dealt in after the rights issue has been taken up will equal between them 3 x 100p + 1 x 80p. Thus four shares will have cost 380p, making each share worth 95p. When the rights come on to the free market, the shares will probably be marked by the jobbers at 95p in the middle. So the price of the old shares has fallen, as it were.

History shows that most share prices move fairly rapidly after a rights issue, moving close to the old share price, so that you may very likely soon find yourself, if you bought the rights issue, with four shares worth a total of 400p for which you paid 380p (leaving out any brokerage, etc). Now there is no brokerage or stamp duty on rights issue shares either, so the 80p is really rather cheap. Obviously, if the company's future prosperity is suspect, then there will be few people taking up the rights (or if times are generally bad and money is short). In that case, the rights will often be sold, making the rights share price lower and thus, using our equation again, making the eventual price per share lower and probably proving very slow to equalize with the old share price.

Take up rights if you can afford to do so, making your average purchase price per share lower — it often pays in the way I have just explained, as the shares tend to find a higher level anyway.

If you have an enormous and significant holding, giving you strong voting power and a say in the company's affairs, you should certainly take up the rights; if you don't, you will effectively reduce your holding, or, as they say, 'dilute your equity'. For most of us, the dilution is immaterial, but the principle holds good. In any case, never ignore communications from the company in which you own shares or their financial representatives but ask, ask, ask if you do not understand what you receive. Never risk throwing away paper rights that may be worth money.

Capitalization issues

Often called 'bonus' or 'scrip' issues, sometimes even 'free issues'. All the last three descriptions are misleading, since the shares are not free at all though the announcement may look that way. The company will think the share price looks unpopularly expensive, and will therefore decide that it should have 100,000 issued shares of 100p each

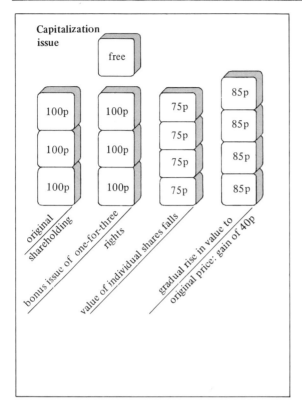

Capitalization issue

free

100p 100p 75p 85p

100p 100p 75p 85p

100p 100p 75p 85p

original shareholding

bonus issue of one-for-three rights

value of individual shares falls

gradual rise in value to original price: gain of 40p

issue (much more often known by the shorter names I gave even if they are mildly misleading).

It would announce, for example, that every holder of three shares would get one 'free' share, and you would hear talk of a 'one-for-three'. Now that did not actually mean a free share because, if you have three shares worth 100p each on the market and you get a free share, you are actually going to be holding four shares worth one-quarter of 300p each, namely 74p each. The company has not, as it were, issued more capital but merely reconstructed its capital and altered the value of the shares a little. As I say, the actual figures would not be that simple because such simplicity would not warrant such action but it makes the thing rather clearer.

Again, history shows that new, lower-cost shares are popular and, if the company is doing well, the price does tend to climb quite a bit, not to the old level but nearer to it. So you might very rapidly have four shares each worth 85p, which means you make a quick profit of 40p on the original three shares since you will have incurred no buying costs of any kind to get the extra share. You are probably going to be even more pleased about your bonus issue when the dividend comes along because the dividend will be announced on a per-share basis so that you get the extra income for your extra new shares. That is if the company is doing well. If not, the dividend may well be adjusted to match the extra shares on the market, being lowered a little per share so that the company's dividend payout will be the same as it would have been before the issue, only spread over a greater number of shares. Such issues are usually made by companies in a state of prosperity anyway, so it is never as bad as I might have made it sound here. In fact, history indicates that the term 'bonus issue' is fairly close to the market. 'Free issue' is not. 'Scrip issue' can mean anything you want it to. There are also 'share splits', all very much the same thing.

rather than 50,000 at 200p. In fact, it is bringing its employed capital and its reserves close together but that is basically internal accounting and we need not go into that. Emphasizing that I am using simple figures to simplify the explanation and that no company is really likely to be dealing in such small numbers of shares as 50,000 and 100,000, I would also add that 'top-heavy' share prices are not likely to make the shares unattractive these days but that was much of the theory behind the capitalization issues of old.

In the days when the nominal or par value of a share was anything from a shilling (in old money before decimalization) to five shillings, prices of £1 per shilling or florin share were thought to be so expensive for small investors that they would not buy them. Also companies were expanding at such a rate during the 'fifties and 'sixties that the numbers of shares was a false representation of the company structure. So the company would make a capitalization

Dividends

The dividend is that proportion of company profits that the company, via its Board of Directors, decides to distribute to ordinary shareholders. It is probably paid in two parts, not necessarily equal – in fact rarely equal – per year, so that you get some dividend income every six months. Though historically expressed as a percentage of the nominal value of the shares, almost all companies today also state the actual cash value in pence of the dividend per share. So, if, say, the profits to be distributed are £140,000, and there are a million shares, the dividend per share will be 14p for the year (probably not 7p each six months, but an unequal figure).

Now, if the nominal value of your share is 100p, the yield of your dividend is *not* in this case 14 per cent. It is 7 per cent. The simple equation goes thus, the 'yield' being what you get, what your share yields:

$$\frac{\text{Nominal value of share} \times \text{yield}}{\text{Market price of share}} = \text{dividend}$$

Thus, using our 100p share standing at 200p in the market, we get

$$\frac{100 \times 14}{200} = 7 \text{ (per cent in this case).}$$

As I have said, the dividend is payable equally on voting and non-voting shares (the latter being called 'A' shares as a rule). The 'A' shares will have a lower price in the market, so the yield on them is better. You must decide whether you want income or capital growth from your investment; 'A' shares give better income, but, as I said before, they are far too unpopular to last long and there are fewer every year. However, companies like the Savoy Hotels group (which includes the Savoy, the Connaught, Claridges and other big luxury hotels) has saved itself from being taken over by the fact that would-be buyers cannot get sufficient voting stock. Good or bad? Not so good for shareholders but fine for British tradition and the tourists love

that. Dividends are, as we have seen in Chapter 2, taxable as unearned income.

That, of course, presupposes that you always receive a dividend. If your company does badly, the directors quite simply will 'pass' the dividend and you will get nothing that half-year, year, maybe up to two or more years. When the company does well again, it will restore the dividend. It does not pay you any arrears on your ordinary shares, merely starts paying again.

When you buy shares near the dividend date, you either buy them with the dividend due or after the dividend. That means that you buy them with the seller retaining the right to receive the next dividend, which will have been announced but is not yet due and payable; you are then buying 'ex-dividend', usually spelled 'XD' in the financial columns, and referred to as 'X-Div'. To buy with the dividend rights, you buy 'cum-dividend'.

How to read the prices

Study the prices columns of the *Financial Times*, shown here, and you will find, first, the high and low prices of the current year; then the name of the shares under the relevant industrial or commercial heading; the current day's price; the up or down change on the previous trading day; the dividend rate; the times company profits cover the dividend; in the eighth column, the current yield gross of tax. Finally you get the price-earnings ratio. It will also note if the shares are 'X' or 'Cum-D'.

The register

Every company is compelled to keep or have kept a register of shareholders and the number of shares they hold. A shareholder's name will not filter through to the register at once since it takes time to close the Account, as we have seen in Chapter 6, and then to sign the appropriate transfer form, by which means the name gets back to the company registrar – which may be a professional company. Your papers may come

124½	80	Slough Ests	102		Q10					
£238	£167	Do.10%Conv.'90	£204		Q8.0					
£120	£103	Do.8%Conv.91-94	£103		3.96	4.1	1.5	24.0	67½	
410	284	Stock Conversn.	386	−10	♦5.0	1.8	1.1	69.4	69	
635	252	Sunley (B) Inv	625	−10	t033c	1.7	7.0	10.0	136	10
56½	29	Swire Props. $HK1	79	−2	h0.61	2.1	1.1	64.8	89	
89	49	Town Centre	20½	−1½	0.01				103	
25	14	Town & City 10p	20½		4.96	1.5	5.1	16.3	90½	
162	122	Trafford Park	139		0.42	3.2	2.0	19.0	92	
34	22	U.K. Property	29½	−5	5.62	445	1.8	67.2	35	
445	310	Utd. Real Prop	440	−1	t2.97	1.6	2.0	43.2	74	
225	129	Warner Estate	211	−5	7.64	1.4	2.5	42.3	120	10
470	340	Warnford Inv. 20p	440	−1	1.5	♦	6.4	♦	177	133
40	26½	W'stmin. & C'ty P.	33½xd	−1					268	202
53	26	W'minster P. 20p	37	−1					86	69
73	40	Winston Ests.	53	−2	t1.42	2.0	3.8	19.0	52	44

SHIPPING

380	293	Brit. & Com. 50p	358		10.59	2.9	4.2	11.6	70	
252	184	Common Bros. 50p	252		th1.14	11.0	0.7	13.3	53	
245	125	Fisher (J)	240		t9.12	2.5	5.2	(8.3)	40	
308	218	Furness Withy £1	253	−3	t5.1	7.1	2.5	6.6	40	
325	98	Hunting Gibsn. £1	295xd		td1.9	0.7	—	(61.4)	83	
48½	38½	Jacobs (J.I.) 20p	44½		h0.6	—	2.2	—	185	
41	21	Lon. O'Seas. Frtrs.	38½		t6.84	—	4.5	—	168	
222	125	Lyle Shipping	220		t1.0	—	—	‡	103	
245	215	Man. Liners 20p	230	+12	—	—	—	—	200	
36½	17½	Mersey Dk. Units	23	−½	—	—	—	—	162	
214	127	Milford Docks £1	214	−1	23.43	5.0	2.3	14.5	104	
117	89½	Ocean Transport	103½	−1½	8.38	0.7	11.6	(22)	104	
119	71	P. & O. Defd. £1	112	−4	6.54	1.3	8.6	(113)	133	
150	64	Reardon Sm. 50p	105		0.1	—	0.1	—	112	
88	32½	Do. 'A' 50p	69		0.1	—	0.2	—	103	
94½	58	Runciman (W.)	88	+1	3.75	—	6.2	—	97½	

SHOES AND LEATHER

41	23	Allebone 10p	27	+1	1.33	2.7	—	(5.7)	68	
70	52	Booth (Intn'l)	66		4.69	2.2	10.2	5.3	95	
70	59	Footwear Invs.	59		d5.04	3.5	12.2	♦	123	
78	91½	Garnar Scotblair	95		t5.0	3.5	7.5	4.2	107½	
104	48	Headlam, Sims 5p	59		1.7	6.7	4.1	4.8	145	
70	71	Hiltons 20p	71d	−11	th3.63	5.3	7.3	♦	68	
105	71	K Shoes	71	−1	th2.0	3.3	4.0	6.0	73	
77	52½	Lambert Hth. 20p	51		t3.5	3.6	9.8	4.8	98	
59	47	Newbold & Burt'n.	58		th2.48	3.5	6.1	6.7	114	
62	40	Oliver (G) 'A'	118	−2	t2.14	5.9	2.6	5.5	95	
122	50		55	+1	t3.09	2.5	8.2	5.5	96	

from somewhere totally different from the company itself. The register gives the name of the holder or his nominee (many investors and companies buy in nominee names to conceal their personal interest from as many people as possible though the Inland Revenue knows who buys).

The Financial Times index

You will read or hear (on radio, etc.) of the *Financial Times* index. The detailed explanation of this is complicated so let me say, as briefly as possible, that it is a continuing measurement of the prices of the thirty shares most representative as a sample of the Stock Exchange's share dealings. Shares are taken from different sectors of commerce and interest, and are changed if a company gets taken over or goes out of business.

The companies are normally major ones and bankruptcy cases among them are highly unlikely — but even giants get swallowed in takeovers, so there have been changes. The prices of the shares are averaged and it is reckoned that these market fluctuations give the best indication of general movements. In America, a similar index run by the *Wall Street Journal* is called the 'Dow-Jones index' (or, more familiarly, as just the 'Dow-Jones'). The F.T. index, quoted twice a day, is no more than a sensitive barometer and should not frighten or encourage you. It shows how the wind is blowing, how the market reacts to Government or other policies; it can fluctuate very rapidly, though it tends to show a trend.

Blue chips

So British nowadays that everybody forgets we stole the phrase from America. A 'blue chip' is a top-quality ordinary share, that's all, and it stems from the fact that highest gambling chips in the United States are coloured blue. Do not confuse them with 'high fliers' which are almost the reverse — risky stocks for the adventurous and gamblers. I.C.I. (Imperial Chemical Industries) is one of Britain's blue chips. Its price is ultra-sensitive to market and Government action, to adverse or favourable Budgets. Quite honestly, many say that the I.C.I. price is in itself a market index and almost as reliable as the F.T. index.

Conglomerates

A conglomerate is a large family of smaller companies, the latter usually acquired one by one either through takeover bids (of which more very shortly) or by mutual agreement to buy and sell. By definition, a conglomerate owns a lot of different businesses with little logical connection. It is intriguing to know who buys what and who owns whom, and I would heartily recommend an hour or two at your local library looking through the large volume called just that *Who Owns Whom*. Here you can trace all the interlocking companies by looking up in two ways. On the one hand, you can look up the company in which you plan to buy shares and see all the subsidiary companies it owns. Or you can look up a company in which you would like to own shares and find that it belongs to a 'parent' company whose name might be less familiar to you, or at least more unexpected. Then look up the parent, and you will discover the company structure. It is interesting as well as instructive.

The 'in' word for parent companies is 'conglomerates'. They used to be called, in Britain, 'holding companies' which does describe them better than the American word, but the latter is the one that has stuck. The independence (called 'autonomy' in business parlance) of the subsidiaries varies greatly from one company to another, but the theory is that costs for every member company of a conglomerate can be saved by centralizing such functions as accounting, property, finance, computer use or installation, etc. In fact, small is now thought to be beautiful. Thus decentralization has recently become the name of the game, making each operation its own profit centre, giving the 'local' management and staff their own incentives and apportioning praise and blame where it is earned. Since so many companies are conglomerates, it is difficult to avoid investing in them, but they have their drawbacks to investors. You might think that conglomerates are particularly safe investments since, being diversified, they are less vulnerable; you would often be proved wrong.

The company you particularly like might be booming away, selling its products exceptionally well and making big profits. But its success might be offset by the relative failure of a sister or brother company (the 'sex' of a company is a matter of tradition or personal preference, so say what you please). Let us look at Sears Holdings, mainly because I shall be writing about it next under takeover bids. Sears was owned, and initially managed, by the late Sir Charles Clore, pioneer in Britain of the takeover bid. Look it up in *Who Owns Whom* and you will find that it owns the giant British Shoe Corporation, which comprises Lilley and

Skinner, Dolcis, Saxone, Freeman Hardy & Willis, Trueform and a host of manufacturing shoe companies as well as these retail chains. It also owns Selfridges of London and the Miss Selfridge chain plus a number of other stores in other cities under the name of Lewis's, not to be confused with the John Lewis Partnership. It also owns Mappin and Webb and Garrard, the prestigious Crown Jewellers in Regent Street, as well as many other jewellers under famous names and on varying price levels. Add to that, among other things, the William Hill betting and gaming business, a number of large engineering divisions (many making textile machinery), financial concerns, property development companies and motor vehicle sales companies.

Say the shoe business does a bomb one year but taxes squeeze the rich or tourists so that jewellery sales do badly; then the whole group's profit results might be affected by that unfortunate division. When you look up a company's report and accounts, you will be able to see what proportion of turnover and profits comes from what enterprise or group of enterprises and you will be able to see if one of the company's divisions has had a bad or good effect on the entire group or whether the result has been cushioned. As I said, this cushioning cuts two ways, concealing the good as well as the bad. Some subsidiary divisions announce their own profits and turnover publicly after giving them to the parent Board (which keeps a continuing watchful eye anyway) but most do not and none of them can sell their shares, which are owned by the conglomerate.

But the top companies are mainly good performers, not to be avoided. Look up I.C.I., Unilever, Reckitt and Colman, or Fison's and you will find masses of familiar household names amid the lists of companies under those top umbrellas. It not only teaches you a little about your company but also about business. Quite apart from that, it makes very fascinating reading. Just

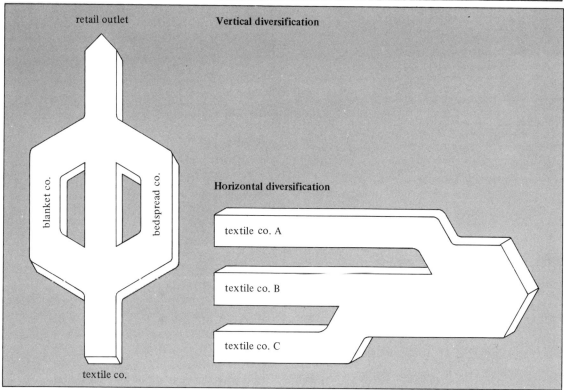

retail outlet

Vertical diversification

blanket co.

bedspread co.

textile co.

Horizontal diversification

textile co. A

textile co. B

textile co. C

as the annual reports can, if they are worded simply enough, which rather few are.

Takeover bids and mergers

Why companies do it

A takeover bid is made by one company for the shares of another in an effort to buy it, to take it over. In fact, the takeover bid is not always an aggressive action, though it has connotations of attacker and defender, and is given a lot of journalistic space. When a takeover bid is friendly and the 'victim' company's directors approve it publicly, the word most often used is 'merger'. There is a subtle difference between the two words but there is technically very little difference in the end.

There are several reasons for one company wanting to buy another. The first is logic, less and less brought into play these days. Suppose you have a textiles firm making woven or knitted fabrics; it may find logic in buying a bedspread or blanket company,

or even a clothing company — that is called vertical diversification, meaning that the first company can then trade with its new acquisition as it is next in the chain of trade. Further vertical diversification would be to buy the shops that sell bedspreads, blankets or clothing. You may also hear the phrase 'vertical merger'.

But Company X might look longingly at Company Y because it is making the *same* things — say lace — and there seem to be obvious advantages in having a larger share of the textiles market, serving more and bigger customers with more products. That would be a 'horizontal' diversification or merger. The advantages could be pooled production and accounting costs, bigger and longer production runs of certain textiles that reduce the unit price, assured customer lists, exports, new plant and equipment in one company to take over from the old in another, that kind of thing.

Strictly speaking, neither of these two merger situations lead to the 'conglomerate' but the first step has been taken and logic tends to disappear while both sorts of merger, if successful, spur the companies involved to takeovers that convert them into conglomerates.

Then there is the conglomerate type of takeover or merger, where Company X wants more earnings and believes it has the management qualities to monitor and advise or run more companies; their earnings come with them into the ever-growing fold of the parent. I have already expressed certain doubts about conglomerates as a whole category, though not about the individual companies mentioned. Logic rarely applies to the acquisitiveness of conglomerates. Obviously there are other reasons for merging – the age and wish to retire of the management of Company Y, willing to sell to the younger management Company X, or vice versa. Company X might merely want to own, rather than compete in open market with a rival concern; sometimes a company might take such action to make itself too big to be swallowed up by another.

Then again, a company might not have been 'using' its assets. Instead of having spent its cash on new machinery, for instance, the company might still have the cash available, which makes it covetable. If another company takes it over, that cash can easily be withdrawn. Or, it might not have revalued its properties and, with inflation what it is, these might be valued in the company's books far too low; the company would then seem worth less than its true value, the share price would be depressed, and the company would be highly vulnerable to a bid.

Or, the company might not have realized its full potential in terms of sales or development of new products. Company X might believe it could quickly recover its purchase price and then make fast profits.

An uncontested bid
The bid approach may well be friendly. If there is reason to believe that Company Y's directors will welcome a bid for the shares at a good bit above the market price and will be willing to recommend them to their share-

holders, then Company X's directors will discuss it with Y executives, the financial advisers will be brought in and various valuations will be made so that a bid or offer price may be agreed; that price is offered and publicly distributed by X to all shareholders by post, together with as full an explanation as possible of the reasons and the logic for the merger and its future prospects.

The directors of Company X must try to get the best possible price for their company and are bound to explain why they think it a good price. It is, in the end, up to the shareholders to take the final decision which must be made at a meeting of the shareholders – if they can stir themselves from their usual lethargy to vote for or against, either by going to the meetings or by using the proxy voting cards sent with the relevant data. Such bids may succeed the first time without undue publicity, essentially if the price is right. The bid may be defended and, if the shareholders think the bid price too low, they must protest in every way possible, even writing to the press, who will probably already have started making such comments anyway. If your company is in the throes of a bid, read the financial columns very carefully, even taking the trouble to go to the local library if you begrudge buying the costlier financial journals and periodicals.

A golden rule is that you should never sell your shares right away. There may be a risk in not doing so, of course, if the bid fails and the bidder goes away, leaving the share price to tumble back to where it was before the higher-price bid was announced. But more of that after we take a look at a contested bid, which is never called a merger, even if it ends up that way.

A contested bid
Sir Charles Clore made the first major takeover bid to the public when, without any consultation with the directors of Freeman Hardy and Willis, he offered its shareholders a healthy cash premium on their

share price. They accepted in droves, and did very well, whether they accepted Sears Holdings shares or the cash value of the bid. Clore bought a chain of shops with abysmal book values by then-current property value definitions, since nobody had revalued the properties or written up their value in the balance sheet. Clore started a major vogue for takeover bids of this aggressive kind and it woke directors up; they were forced to look further than the 'pending tray' to the changes in the world about them, the movements in prices and values, and need for forward thinking and sophisticated accounting. An army of small shareholders can lose or save a company by the way it votes in bids.

You the shareholder
As a shareholder, you may be offered straight cash for your shares at so much per share or the shares of the new company in exchange for yours in the old (based on the value per share of the bid) or a mixture of both. In rare cases there are other options. Read the postal forms that will be sent to you carefully, for you have a choice.

I said you should never sell right away. You should also not accept the bid at once. The reason is that another company might wake up to the attractions of Company Y and make a better offer for it than Company X. Equally, Company Y might decide to defend itself by bringing into the open all sorts of promises and projects it had failed to mention or to exploit until the bid, and these might force a higher offer out of Smith. One way and another, the bid offer may rise several times, meaning that each price is higher than the last. If X is set on getting hold of Y, it may even offer more than the shares are really worth, sure that it can make them worth more in the longer term. It is said still in the City that shareholder loyalty is worth no more than a shilling (and the term lives on since decimalization). Well, if you have 300 shares, you have 300 shillings each time someone tries to buy your loyalty. If it happens four

times, you have made 300 by 4 shillings (5p now) which amounts to £15 above the bid price, which was probably higher than your shares anyway. So wait and watch.

Don't leave it too long. The initial offer will give you an acceptance date which may become extended (you will be notified, and it will be reported in the press and in the contending companies' advertisements). Be ready to sell or to accept, according to whether you want to realize your investment or whether you fancy shares in the new company. Your capital gains tax position might affect your decision. Your CGT will not actually be computed and payable until you sell your new X shares so it may be a good idea simply to transfer them.

What it costs
As I write, I am not in a position to be very specific about the cost of buying shares because the system is under investigation by the Restrictive Practices Court, which may well mean a number of changes, either voluntary or enforced, in both method of buying and commission structures.

At present, all brokers charge pretty much the same commissions, which work on a sliding scale, making it more expensive to buy shares with lower values. Reasonable enough, since the costs are much the same for the broker whether he does a large or a small transaction (in value terms, that is, not necessarily numbers of shares). But there may well be a feeling that, because all charges are so similar, the element of competition to hold down prices is missing. Brokers can and often do give advice, which is not always good but always aims to be. They can often get hold of shares that are difficult to buy. They are useful people and there are many arguments against the job being taken over largely by computers. However, it is becoming so very difficult for anyone to buy shares with small sums, such as £500, that the investing public is driven to unit trusts, building societies and such when they might like to buy shares, a stake in British industry.

Furthermore, it is felt to be socially desirable that share ownership should be as widely spread as possible, that we would all work much harder for the eventual wealth of our nation if we had a goodly stake in our industries, so it is probably advisable to do anything that might encourage share owner-ship by the less wealthy (always remem-bering that risks are attached for the buyer, and as long as buyers are made aware of them). The Government is talking about tax concessions to make share-buying attractive.

Whatever the changes taking place, you may be sure that it will cost money to buy and to sell shares. When you buy, imme-diately add the cost to your purchase price and make a mental note that you will again pay costs on a similar basis when you sell − they may even be higher because the shares may have gone up in value (and com-mission is based on value). Incidentally, it is cheaper to buy Government shares (gilt-edged stock, etc.) than ordinary equities. The charges will be itemized on your con-tract note, which arrives as soon as the Post Office can get it to you after the shares are bought. It may be helpful to work out the cost per share by dividing the broker's charges by the number of shares, then adding the cost per share on to the price you paid. That way you know how much you need to sell at to break even or make a profit. Remember always that there is the spread between buying and selling prices and you will need to make that up too.

Then there are other official costs, not subject to the Restrictive Practices Court investigations. First, the stamp duty, more properly called 'transfer stamp duty'. This is officially levied at the rate of 2 per cent or £2 per every £100 of shares you buy. How-ever, it is not worked out at a straight 2 per cent. You pay 40p on every £20 worth of shares up to £300; then £1 per every £50 or part of £50 thereafter. So the cost of stamp duty should also be broken down and added to the price per share to arrive at the break-even sale price. Once you know that, you will find you will always remember it. The extra minimal charges for contract stamp, from 10p to a maximum of 60p, are not worth worrying about. You pay no stamp duty on selling so you can also forget about that once you have made the first calculation on buying.

As I write, total costs come to something like 4 per cent on £500, or £20 to buy £500 of shares. Not high, and I am not suggesting that it could fall after the court's findings, or not at that level anyway. There might be higher level adjustments. The present minimum charge of £7 may remain, could even be higher. As I said, the work involved on small deals is much the same as on larger ones.

How to find a broker

This is a real hurdle because stockbrokers make so little on small bargains that most of them honestly discourage, even refuse them, except from existing valued clients or from clients who usually make larger deals. It is not even very easy to spend as little as £5,000. But write to the Stock Exchange and ask for lists, stressing that you are a small buyer (if that is the case). Ring up those on the lists and ask hopefully. If you find them unresponsive, your way in is through new issues, which advertise in the financial sections of newspapers and periodicals. Then you can apply for small numbers of shares, without incurring any buying costs. When the Government sold off some of its holding in British Petroleum shares at the end of 1979, it allowed applications for as few as 75 shares (at 363p each of which 150p was payable on application and the rest three months later). Also you can usually buy with small sums through your bank. They do not charge extra for the service except in some special circumstances and, because your small order combines with many other small orders through the same bank, brokers deal happily in such transactions. In any case, banks are good customers, so small deals are accepted from them. Not all branches handle the work, but all banks do.

Never forget that you will have to return to the Inland Revenue both dividend income and your capital gains on selling. Dividend income over £5,000 per annum is taxed at unearned income rate. There is appropriate space on the tax form for this. Your broker or bank will automatically return the stamp duty, as legal firms do with houses, so the taxman will know about your purchase anyway. Be glad, as I've already said, if you qualify to pay capital gains tax when you sell However, you can offset any losses you make by selling stocks against the profits you make, as far as tax goes.

Government stock or gilt-edged

I have deliberately kept shares of this kind until the end of the chapter because they differ in so many ways from ordinary equities and other company shares. The cost of buying differs and the tax differs too. They also have a fixed price, being sold in £100 units and they come under four main categories. Before coming to those, let me start with the major difference: you are buying into the Government when you buy gilt-edged but you are not buying shares as you do in a company, hoping that it will make a profit. (As you are probably aware, the Government doesn't make much of a profit.) You are buying the Government's promise to pay you, at the time of redemption, exactly what you paid for the units; but, in between, you are buying an absolutely surefire, certain dividend. If the Government fares badly, you can be sure it will simply 'print' more money to meet the dividend. So, while you may not actually be heading for a capital gain, you will never suffer from a passed dividend but get your income, regular as the proverbial clockwork, twice a year. And you may be able to buy a £100 unit for less than £100, depending on current interest rates (see below).

Your Government stock, the piece of paper which says you own it, is a series of I.O.U.s, part of the National Debt. There are about 80 or more different kinds of

Government stock always available, some new ones coming in to take place of those that are about to mature. The Government, unlike a company, will not make a profit. Its 'earnings' come from such things as income tax, customs and excise and other taxes and duties which, believe me, do not help to balance its Budget. It also invests in companies, some of which – like B.P. (British Petroleum) – can be profitable. But it also invests in duds like British Leyland.

The Government does not invest purely for profit, but altruistically, for the good of the nation and its people. The motor-car industry not only employs so many thousands of people but it also sustains hundreds of companies which make parts for cars. hundreds of others that sell them and even more hundreds that sell petrol and carry out servicing and repairs. Think about it – the car is the backbone of our industry, even accounting for a large sector of the insurance industry. Kill the car, and you kill off millions of jobs and livelihoods. Right, you say, there will always be foreign and imported cars and indeed these are proving more popular than British cars. True, but foreign cars are usually made abroad, using foreign parts and spares, so that only the retailers, service centres and insurers would continue to thrive on imported cars. We must have cars in Britain if we possibly can.

General Motors and Ford, both major American companies, have enormous factories and manufacturing capacity over here and they buy parts in Britain so they really amount pretty much to British-made cars, supporting British industry. The main drawback about them, from an economist's point of view, is that the profits may not be reinvested in Britain or British industry but may be siphoned back to America to the parent companies, thus affecting what are called our 'invisibles' in the balance of payments arithmetic (see Chapter 10). However, since the pound sterling has been freed from exchange controls and our own currency moves freely to invest abroad, which was once strictly limited, the theory is that we can sustain the strength of sterling and the demand for it by making the pound attractively strong vis-à-vis foreign currencies. Thus companies want to earn pounds and they may therefore reinvest in our country. The quid pro quo is confusing and the explanations are even more so since the variations in interest rates and the laws of supply and demand utterly confuse even the cognoscenti. I will reveal a little of the mystique in the section on 'How the System Works'. To do it in any detail would need an entire book and even then one has to take a great deal on trust, without explanation.

That digression was long, but it was intended to show that the Government's investment policies cannot necessarily be aimed at profitability but must also look after the people. Thus the Government's earnings from industry will be worthless, if one regards them from the point of view of a shareholder in the Government. It will also invest – does invest – in nationalized industries in a sort of way since it makes up deficits incurred by such industries going into loss.

Not that nationalized industries always lose money. Prices are charged to the customer more or less on the basis of breaking even after accounting for the necessary cost of new plant and equipment, of progress – if need be to meet popular demand – expansions. The Government approach varies according to whether it is essentially left wing or right wing, but the end result is pretty much the same. We, the consumers, still have to bear the rising costs. Either the nationalized industries get heavy Government subsidies from left-wing parties, enabling them to keep their prices down, and the taxpayer has to be stung with higher tax to help out higher Government spending (to say nothing of how many more industries get nationalized in left-wing periods). Or a right-wing Government gets tough about spending and subsidizing so we

pay higher prices (albeit with lower taxation to give us more money in the pocket).

More digression, but it is important to see what the Government has to do with its money and how it either spends less or even makes some. The Conservative Government returned in May 1979 was faced with the drastic need to cut public spending, already mooted by the predecessor Labour Government which had just embarked on that slippery slope but which must have been almost thankful to hand the task over since it is the kind of thing that makes Government very unpopular with everyone and not just those who believe in more expenditure on education, health or highways. Some of the ways to raise money included selling off shares held by the Government in oil, aeronautics and other industries which had been so propped up by Government funds that they were largely owned by the Government. Other methods were to axe several Government agencies and departments plus the administration that spawned other costs. So now you have a glimpse of how the Government prints money to lend or to spend, and borrows it back from us in the form of stock we buy; of how it takes in income from some sources, though never enough; and of how it tries as hard as possible to hold the National Debt in some measure of control (see Chapter 10).

Buying gilts

The Government sells through its own broker and its sales are also handled by the Bank of England. It is much easier to buy gilts (always sold in £100 units) than to buy equities and you can even buy many of them through the Post Office. The cost is also lower for equities. The Government is itself a big buyer and seller of its own stock, and as such helps to create the supply and demand situation, thus influencing prices. If it wants to attract public money, the Government can 'ease' the price by such manipulation, making the stock attractive.

In the main, however, the prices of gilts
— which is what they are always called —
reflect the interest levels. When interest
rates look all set to fall, gilts will rise because
the yield at Government interest rates will
be attractive. High interest rates mean gilts
will lose value in the marketplace; to change
the situation the Government might start
buying in to harden the price. If prices rise,
the Government can then sell to bring them
down. Very roughly, something like a third
of the entire turnover of the Stock Exchange
is accounted for by dealings in gilts — well
over £105 billion in 1979, for instance.

Some of the stocks have been in existence
for ever — the word stock or stocks is used
when you speak of Government. You will
have read or heard of 2½ per cent Consols
in such epics as *The Forsyte Saga* or other
histories and novels of the Victorian era,
and these still exist. War Loan, British
Transport and such are also old names
which no longer have much to do with wars
or transport but there they are. The majority of newcomers are called something like
Treasury or Exchequer.

Now turn to the financial pages of a newspaper, like the one reproduced here from
a day picked at random from the *Financial
Times*. The heading is 'British Funds' which,
in the *Daily Mail*, becomes the more familiar
'British Stocks'. You will notice that there
are four different categories with differing
lives of from five, fifteen, over fifteen years
to 'undated'. The first are the short-dated
stocks or, as the F.T. describes them, the
'shorts'. These are due for redemption
within five years of the date of purchase, are
unlikely to change much in value at all even
in the open market because values move
towards redemption prices as the date
draws nearer, and the date with these is
close anyway. This final redemption price,
not too far away to be badly eroded by
inflation, makes them nice, safe stocks. But
you are not likely to make any capital gain.

Then we come to the 'middles'; the F.T.
doesn't call them this, but others do. These
are the five- to fifteen-year stocks, the

BRITISH FUNDS — Financial Times listing showing 'Shorts' (Lives up to Five Years), 'Five to Fifteen Years' and 'Over Fifteen Years' sections, with columns for 1979 High/Low, Stock, Price £, + or −, and Yield (Interest/Redemption).

medium-term or medium-dated stocks. They fluctuate more in price than the shorts, according to whether the Government's measures are popular or unpopular, but you probably get better redemption profits on them, which are tax-free, by the way.

The long-term or long-dated stocks are more sensitive to the moving levels of interest rates in the way I have already mentioned and are subject to many price fluctuations.

Finally the undated stocks that will never be redeemed. Prices are totally sensitive to interest rates and there really is no value in owning or buying these except for the sake of income. Because the prices are terribly low, the yield is very good indeed since it is declared on £100. For instance, look at Treasury 2½ per cent, which happened to be at £20 on the day this column was published. The yield on that day was therefor 12.62 per cent, which is very nice. The interest is usually paid gross, so remember to keep enough money in the bank to meet the tax due on it, which will vary according to your total income. Do not run away with the misconception that the Government will ever redeem the stock. I have seen staunch British types buying War Loan as it fell, convinced that the Government would honour an unwritten debt. It never has and the poor people have had to console themselves with good yields which, when War Loan prices fell to £18, went above 19 per cent. Very good too, though the yield now is less favourable. The Government does honour its promise to pay the interest.

Take a closer look at the individual names of the funds, and you will see a date or dates immediately after the name of the fund itself, which indicates the redemption date; in some cases, you will see more than one date which gives the Government a band of time in which to choose the best moment for the redemption of your stock at £100. The date Government will choose depends largely on what is happening to interest rates. It might prefer to redeem than to be paying unduly high rates for the next couple of years, for instance.

Study the 'Treasury 14 per cent', to be redeemed in 1982. At the time this table was published, it was in much demand and the High and Low prices of 1979 in the first and second columns were both above the redemption price because the interim interest rates and yield were so tempting. Had you bought in November 1979, when the table was published, you would have paid £100 and 5/8ths of £1, meaning £100.62½p per £100 parcel of stock (see the fourth column). The price had dropped by ¼ (25p) on the preceding day (see fifth column). The yield at that time was very near the declared interest, the actual market price being so close to the par value that it was 13.91 per cent. The yield at the redemption date is in the final column. Now you can work out what you will get for that stock over the period left for it to run. Its price will no longer fluctuate very much as the redemption date is about two years from publication so the interest yield will not fall unduly (or rise either). In your final year you get an adjusted interest according to the date of redemption, in this case 13.66 per cent. With a minimum of £26 interest to come and the redemption price in hand, you can see that this is a pretty good investment, especially as it is so safe. You may hear the expression 'coupon' in the context of gilts. The coupon is simply the declared percentage of interest to be paid on the original value of the share. Your algebraic but simple formula for the yield is:

$$\text{Yield} = \frac{\text{Par value x Coupon (percentage interest)}}{\text{Price}}$$

Much like the dividend formula on ordinary shares. Let us look at another stock in the list, the Exchequer 10 per cent 1983. The price in this printed list was 89. Par value is always 100, so we get:

$$\text{Yield} = \frac{100 \times 10}{89} = \frac{1,000}{89} = 11.23 \text{ per cent}$$

I deliberately took an easy sum so let us get our calculators and go back to the harder original one, the Treasury 14 per cent, and work back to the F.T.'s published figure:

$$\text{Yield} = \frac{100 \times 14}{100.625 \ (\pounds 100\frac{5}{8}\text{ths})} = 13.91$$

which means the F.T. got it right after all. Not that I was actually holding my breath though misprints do take place and are always corrected amid the F.T. prices.

The way of working out the actual redemption yield is rather more complicated but I think I have now shown that the F.T. can get it right (as will other newspapers that publish such data) so it is worth looking it all up from time to time.

Tax on stocks

At the moment, gilts are free of CGT if held more than a year, but some dated stocks might be taxable. Unearned income tax rates apply on interest received and you pay, as already said, according to your own tax rates. My brief advice is that Government stocks have much to recommend them because you know exactly what you are getting and you can sleep peacefully at night – or whenever it is that you do sleep. But do not forget the snags of inflation, the fact that £100 is never worth £100 next year. You may be able to trade profitably, by buying when prices are depressed. You may merely want the high yields. You can buy and sell gilts like ordinary shares, the buying costs are low and there is no stamp duty. You can get a list at any time from: The Director, Bonds and Stock Office, Lytham St Annes, Lancashire FY0 1YN. You can buy by spending £1 for every parcel worth £250 at nominal prices (not market prices, remember) and a further 50p for every subsequent £125 at nominal prices.

Even so, finding the right collection of gilts is very important, and it needs very precise experience and knowledge of markets. There are experts who can do it wonderfully, covering the investment with endowment insurance policies so that your capital is intact, and juggling the actual jigsaw of purchased stocks so that you can get either income or capital growth, whichever suits you, and even a judicious mixture of both. I know of none that will deal in sums of under £5,000 for these special schemes. But you can buy gilts at any time and can hardly go wrong if you are waiting to plan your investment portfolio at some future time and want somewhere safe to put your money in the meantime where you can be sure to be able to draw it without loss.

Local authorities

You can also buy shares in local government, naturally enough; they are often very good value. Many a city or borough has resorted to this method of raising money after seeing the national Government's success. Obviously, a country's credit is certain, since it can itself control the money supply that feeds its coffers; local authorities, without that advantage, have to be more generous to tempt buyers into what are less secure stocks. In fact, cities do not seem to go broke, though they get very near it, and the story of how New York was bailed out just short of bankruptcy is an intriguing one, but too long for us here.

The type of loan is the same as that of the Government, but with a rather higher return for the shareholder. The reason for their apparently 'weak' credit rating should not deter or worry you. Since local authority income comes from rates, rents, grants from various Government departments for housing, education and so on, their income is variable according to the dictates of Government, the amenities and desirability of their areas, and the assiduity of the ratepayers, who can prevent their council from having to borrow expensively if they pay on time, thus helping to hold their rates steadier. In fact, Government is being rather tough with local authorities at present, curtailing all kinds of supplementary grants but the British Government has never let a local authority go quite broke, as has happened in America.

There are a number of variations on the Government theme, such as the offer of stock below par of the nominal value in order to offer some capital gain at redemption. Or there are conditions that allow for higher rates of interest to lenders who leave their money invested over a longer period. And so on. Mostly, these can prove to be a very good investment, and they really are pretty safe.

Chapter Eight

Unit Trusts
and Building Society Deposits

One way of buying shares, and a way that almost anyone can afford if they have a little spare money, is through unit trusts. These have sometimes been called the 'poor man's investment trusts' and, indeed, there is some reason. Unit trusts might better be called the beginner's investment in stocks and shares. What happens is that a group of investment experts, of professionals in the money markets, take your money and the funds of hundreds or thousands of other people, lump the cash together into one huge investment sum, and then invest it for you. You might never otherwise be able to buy shares, because you have no broker and insufficient cash. You therefore buy unit trusts, and let experts manage the portfolio of which you hold a small percentage (or large if you are happy with their performance).

Now you have no influence over what these experts do, and you are entirely in their hands. But you have a little choice because, by and large, most unit trusts tend to specialize in certain areas. For instance, one trust will invest mainly to yield high income; another will be investing largely in European stocks or funds; a third will concentrate on the retail market; and so on. Effectively, they use a pool of money to which you contribute. They take the whole portfolio and divide it into units just as a company divides its capital into shares. You buy so many units, which means you have a tiny percentage of every share in that trust's portfolio. You will have a list of the shares in your trust, so you can follow prices.

The law and trustees

Unit trusts are very strictly governed by law, especially because they are available for purchase by so many people who have little money to spare and whose investments must be protected. To some extent, the law tries to protect those whose funds and knowledge are limited, allowing the wealthier to look after themselves, to get proper professional advice or to learn the business. That has to be right and fair. I am not necessarily an addict of over-protection for the consumer, believing that each individual ought to learn by his own mistakes and try not to make them by doing a little careful research and study before embarking on the unknown. But that is perhaps a rather harsh, survival-of-the-fittest law, and I grew up in an age where consumer protection was fairly non-existent. Certainly the modern laws on unit trusts are commendable. Money means too much to people. The less you have, the more valuable and important it is.

Buying unit trusts

You must first look for unit trusts that are authorized by the Board of Trade (as it then was) Act of 1958 for the Prevention of Fraud. There are other trusts, but avoid them. You can always ask if a unit trust is a member, though most will proudly state their authorization on their literature. They must operate only under a trust deed. They also operate under a trustee, which may be a bank, a finance house that banks or an insurance company.

They must also be a part of a parent group with a fully paid-up capital (meaning that the money is readily available because the capital is paid up, not just entered on paper and therefore notional; notional capital is not readily negotiable into hard cash in cases of possible emergency). The truism of money is that, if one is rich, one almost never meets crises or emergencies, hence the kind of double protection of the trust's paid-up capital. Its wealth is a sort of natural protection against disaster. Now the trustee is not necessarily the firm that chooses the shares, nor manages the investment portfolio. Barclay's Bank Unicorn, for example, will be managed by the Unicorn management, though Barclays act as trustees, as guardians who watch the rules being observed at all times and monitor the performance of their trusts, checking prices and operations all the time, much as auditors run their eyes over company accounts through the year and not just at the year end. The trustees must also make sure that the unit trust has a healthy reserve so that, in the unlikely event of unmitigated crisis, there is something to keep them going. Otherwise, they might be forced to sell their holdings at a loss and the unit-holders would also lose. Everything possible is done to protect the unit-holder.

The unit trust itself must have a paid-up capital of £50,000 (over and above the trustee's £500,000). That keeps out the frauds and the weaklings, financially speaking. By and large, advertising claims are under watchful control and, though some of the claims may sound enticing, they are rarely too extravagant. Never forget, however, that advertisements can lie a little by omission. A company may blow its trumpet loudly about the glowing success of last year without referring to the bad performance of the year before which, after all, set the lower performance base on which the vaunted progress, the percentage increase being advertised, is based. If you want to buy unit trusts, I do thoroughly recommend really excellent magazines called *Planned*

Savings and *Money Management,* which plot the performances of all the trusts continuously so that you can trace them over a long period and back the one you prefer.

How to find them
You will find that most unit trusts belong to large groups, many of whose names will be as familiar as those of the High Street banks. The *Financial Times, The Times* and *Daily Telegraph* have lists of all the trusts and their prices on Saturdays, together with features on the current markets, on the new trusts, on the outlook as far as they, the financial commentators, can tell you. The magazines just mentioned are worth taking regularly for this kind of information.

As I said, the names are usually familiar – Barclays Unicorn, Allied Hambro (Hambro being a merchant bank with insurance company offshoots), Hill Samuel Trust Managers (another merchant bank), T.S.B. Trust Company (Trustee Savings Bank), National Westminster, Norwich Union and so on almost ad infinitum, it seems. The address of each is listed in the papers I have mentioned and can always be found in the London telephone directory at your local library if there are none in your local directory (but not all unit trust managements are in London by any means). Unit trusts are bought directly from the companies. There are at least 350 trusts operating in Britain, which makes it all rather bewildering. Some of the largest, the oldest (and incidentally with excellent performance records) may not have such familiar names like 'Save and Prosper' (held by trustee Bank of Scotland and Royal Bank of Scotland) or M & G Securities (an insurance group called M & G Holdings is quoted on the Stock Exchange). I thought it might help to take a profile of one of these (with some reference to the others where differences arise) to clarify the kind of structure of the larger trusts – these two being the largest. As I write, the best performing trusts are linked to banks and merchant banks rather than insurance.

How they work

Each trust has many smaller trusts within it. Save and Prosper, for example, had nineteen when we printed this book, and might have added another since. These sub-divisions are generally called 'funds'. And, in Save and Prosper's case, the funds are divided into three groups with different investment objectives.

Starting with the funds aimed at producing income, these are again sub-divided into two groups. The first invests in high-yield stocks to give high income, very good for the low-income families who pay little tax and excellent for the elderly. Since prices of shares, and therefore the capital value of one's investment, can fluctuate so much and there is always an element of risk, there is much to be said for high-income units, but they are not suitable for people already earning good money and paying high levels of tax. The second sub-division is to give increasing income. Initially, the income from such trusts is low, but it grows as the years go by. By the same token, the capital is at least maintained in the early years and probably also later. The names of the actual funds in each sector are (for high income) High Return Unit Trust and Income Units; (for increasing income) High-Yield Units and Scotyields (Scotbits being a division of the Save and Prosper Group, giving part of its name to several funds).

Then come the funds of the type with which the movement, originally an American idea, started at the beginning of the 1930s. These are, in Save and Prosper's own words, 'the broadly-based funds invested worldwide by the investment managers who think they know where money is to be made'. For example they might have moved fast in foreign markets — for they are buying and selling all the time to take advantage of special opportunities, when sterling was liberated at the end of 1979, when it was permitted to invest freely abroad without the restrictions that limited the sterling sums to invest overseas. These broad-based funds have no special income value or promises.

Of course the dividends are divided up and you get a proportion of the total according to the size of your holding. Here you are hoping for capital growth, and the names for the funds are Capital Units, Investment Trust Units or Universal Growth Fund. That, I must emphasize, is on the Save and Prosper list; the M & G list, or any other, is quite different; though, as much as possible, the names of the funds will try to imply their objectives.

Back to Save and Prosper. The third broad category covers funds that concentrate on specific investment situations. Some might invest in certain geographical areas like Scotland or Japan, America or South-East Asia, Europe or Britain. Most investors would choose a sprinkling of these funds because to choose one would be to put all your eggs in one basket, never a good investment policy — sometimes successful, but only with luck. Start with Britain, if only for the reason that you can follow the separate fortunes of the shares in your fund's portfolio and that not only adds interest but actually teaches you much in case you buy stocks and shares directly one day.

Some companies, such as M & G and Hambros, do what they call 'Recovery Funds', which can be great fun and, in the case of Hambro's, they have had spectacular success. The idea is that you invest in ailing companies that they believe are going to recover. The merchant banking side, called in to 'doctor' ailing companies, to deal with special situations, to float companies and to handle all the complicated financial machinery of a merchant bank, is probably well placed to recognize recovery situations and to forecast those that might do well; it will avoid those whose future is likely already to be so mortgaged that recovery is either unlikely or a long way off (though such companies are sometimes saved by takeovers and, after absorption into other conglomerates, can still prove rewarding).

M & G is what financial experts might call highly sophisticated, with many highly specialized funds. They run 24 funds aimed

at the areas outlined for Save and Prosper
but with two extra categories, these being:
(a) funds giving a balance between growth
and income, a combination of the two
which is good for people of many ages and
in many income groups; and (b) specialist
funds for charities and pensions schemes.
Thus you can see that you have some choice
as to the kind of investment you make
though not in the actual individual investments you make.

So, to summarize, you get:

(1) *Professional management*, which costs
you a little though not very much by
normal City standards (brokers give
advice free but it is not always expert
or even professional). We shall see the
costs later in this chapter.

(2) *A good, wise spread of investment*. This
has both benefits and disadvantages,
rather on the lines of buying into con-
golmerates. The good investments
cushion the bad ones, the bad ones
take the gloss off the booming ones.
You can be lucky and get few baddies.
But at least the risk is lower than buying
stocks and shares off your own bat.

(3) *Opportunity*. You could never take
advantage of special situations, of
sudden opportunities in the investment
market on your own unless you had
knowledge, time, a daily study of
economics, markets and trends to say
nothing of various Government policies
here and abroad. To begin with, the
size of your investment is too small and
the costs of switching in and out of
this or that too great. To go on with,
you would have problems finding the
currency for foreign investments at
short notice – even with sterling free
and your bank able to hold accounts
for you in foreign currency, as the
trusts do. Trusts can 'manage' currency, guard against the inevitable fluctuations and invest worldwide for you.

(4) *Market Data* is not at your fingertips
as a private investor, but the experts
who manage your funds are constantly

watching and listening. Backed by
research departments, computers and
all the fast aids to modern knowledge,
they can act on information that you
probably would not get. Mark you, I
do wonder periodically whether good
old hunch isn't being lost by all this
science, but at least science is fairly
safe; though hunch may be more
profitable. You note that I keep
stressing the safety. It is one of the
distinct advantages of unit trusts, to
offset the disadvantages (one of which
I have just mentioned, the inability to
boom away if baddies in the portfolio
hold back the winners).

(5) *Tax advantages* which, to keep this
part of the list from becoming too
long, I shall talk about later in this
chapter.

(6) *Lower buying costs* than for stocks and
shares, and I also propose to deal with
that in greater detail shortly.

(7) *Low risk*, which I think I have already
emphasized.

(8) *Easy to buy and sell*. The best investment for anyone is the one he can
actually buy and afford. You can start
with very little money in unit trusts, of
which more also in this chapter.

(9) *No trouble*, because most of the work
is done for you by the fund managers,
and you have the minimum of paper-
work to worry about. You can follow
the prices of your units in the papers I
have mentioned. Your managers will
give you reports (usually twice a year
but some annually) which include very
detailed accounts of the performance
to date and some indication of the
prospects. These are easy to understand
and you need never worry about what
to do with rights issues, bonus issues
and such (see Chapter 7 on stocks and
shares).

(10) *Versatility*. Because there are so many
funds in different specialized areas that
you can match the right fund to your
special circumstances.

(11) *Availability*. In life we have too often to like what we can get rather than get what we like. As with loans, the availability of investment is perhaps the most decisive factor as to whether we should take it or not.

How to choose a fund

I have already mentioned *Planned Savings* and *Money Management* magazines as the best reference works on the subject for anyone. But it is also the case that fund manager are very helpful and really will answer your letters. Just work out what you require of an investment and that, in the experience of the experts, is the most difficult thing to persuade people to do. That is where we hope this book may help, to clarify your own thoughts and objectives on what you want your money to do for you.

For example, you may wish your son to go to private school or you may hope he will get to university. Write to a fund manager or unit trust headquarters and say something like: 'My son is three years old and I am quite happy for him to go to the local state school until he is older but would like a public school/university/special training when he is 13/18/?. I can afford to invest so much this year and probably a minimum of £XXX every year though I think this could be increased annually, especially as my income is growing and my prospects of promotion are good. I do not need any income now, do not expect to need any capital suddenly (though I do have little in reserve for emergencies) and I would like your advice.'

I am not suggesting for one moment that you will get a long, detailed personal reply because that kind of service costs so much money that it could not be afforded out of the charges for unit trust management, which are kept as low as possible compatible with expertise. But you will at least be sent the forms for the kind of funds to buy. Send copies of this letter (there are photostat machines dotted all over the country in little instantprint shops, railway or tube stations, etc.) to several trusts, to the ones with the best performances, as tracked in *Planned Savings* or *Money Management* magazines, noting that these vary from one year to another as a rule.

I cannot repeat too often that each person must crystallize his or her own objectives because the experts can only help if you help yourself. No doctor can diagnose an ailment unless he knows where the aches and pains are, what the symptoms are. The same is true of money advisers and, since each need is different, and investments tend to be rather general, the personal diagnosis is very, very important to get started on the right path.

How much do I need?

Obviously that varies from one fund to another, but the minimum is likely to be £250 for the initial investment, to which you can add smaller sums as you go (from about £50). There will be higher minimums, all clearly stated on the application forms, up to several thousand pounds. The actual prices of the units are based on the value of the securities in that particular fund's portfolio and are assessed in line with a special formula dictated by the Department of Trade and Industry. Many funds can be bought out of income with small monthly sums paid by banker's order.

The spread – the difference between buying and selling prices – is usually very much bigger with unit trusts than with stocks and shares. Although in this case it is not the jobber who takes the difference, but the unit trust company. That is because the legal permitted formula allows some of the cost incurred by the managers, the dealing costs, and initial professional costs to be added to the purchase price. The law governs very strictly what costs may be fed into this 'spread', which naturally widens it. But it does mean that, when you sell, the costs are paid and it is a little easier to compute what your gain (or loss?) might be merely by glancing at the buying and selling prices in the relevant journals.

The cost

Unit trust managers make their charges in two different ways, or minor variants of these two ways. There may on the one hand be an initial charge – let's take 5 per cent, though it might be less (the total charges over a long period being restricted by law to a permitted maximum). This could be charged as a one-off at the front of your purchase, called a front-end charge; or it could be charged on an annual basis. The majority seem to like a combination of the two, with a front-end charge amounting to about two-thirds of the total plus a very small annual charge. Charges in Britain are lower than in other countries and really considerably lower than in America; there is a chance that they might rise a little. But that, I think, is a good idea. If realistic charges were allowed for management of existing trusts, there would need to be less effort devoted to spawning new trusts to get new money in. At present, since the unit trusts get an attractive amount of front-end charges, it is obvious that they want to start new funds to bring in new money with a good element of front-end cash flow.

As I see it, that merely increases the income of advertising agents, financial brokers and such, without necessarily improving the fortunes of the unit trust managements in the long-term. Thus unit-holders might not get the full benefit. Under the Conservative Government, which is encouraging an uncontrolled prices free-for-all and therefore stimulating competition, we may get different charging systems, though the restrictive legal ceiling will still apply. I think this would only be advantageous to unit-holders, even if the annual charge went up a bit. It is perfectly OK to spend a little more money if you get far greater value for it and I think there really are too many unit trust funds about at the moment – a confusing, bewildering array of them.

How to buy

Directly from the unit trust managements as listed in the magazines I've mentioned. They can be bought through stockbrokers, banks and other financial agents, but why? You can telephone for application forms or write for advice along the lines I have given.

Dividends

Usually referred to as income in this sector, since the distribution may not always rely solely on dividends but also on other cash realizations within the fund. This may be distributed twice a year (or once in some cases), but it may also be reinvested in the funds, being added to the invested sum already there. The dividends, whether reinvested or taken (and there is either a choice or a prior agreement to reinvest; you have some freedom of choice), are subject to tax; and, when you get your tax credit note (meaning that the tax has been paid at standard rate and you are getting a net amount) you must remember that you may have a further liability to tax if you pay at higher than the standard rates, or if your income from unit trusts or stocks is more than £5,000 per annum.

If your tax is at standard rate, you have nothing more to pay since the unit trust company has already paid it.

Capital gains tax on units

Here you get distinct advantages. The unit trust itself pays tax at a reduced rate on capital gains when it 'realizes' an investment, because that investment is really only partially realized; the cash is not taken because the investment is switched from one investment straight into another. Currently, the capital gains payable by unit trusts is 10 per cent so you, the unit-holder, get a credit note for 10 per cent; therefore when you pay CGT on the sale of your unit trusts, you pay the tax less 10 per cent (which currently means you pay 20 per cent instead of 30 per cent). Therefore, up to £3,000 of gain may be tax-free: the first £1,000 is tax-free anyway and the 15% on £2,000 comes to £300. But you have a credit of 10% of £3,000, which comes to £300. As I write, there are still hopes that CGT will be changed in 1980 to taper off, so that long-held investments attract less CGT on realization than short-held investments so these figures might change a little. Unit trusts, being companies, also pay corporation tax on their profits like any other company but these are not built into your units so do not worry.

Insurance links

Unit trusts linked to insurance companies have, in the recent past, performed rather less well than those attached to banks and merchant banks (Hambro's falling between two stools since the Hambro insurance company is the one that holds unit trusts and has shown remarkable expertise). But you will see offered unit-linked insurances and vice versa. There could be distinct advantages in some of these, even if the capital growth on the units is less dramatic than on other units, because you get at the moment tax relief on the premiums paid into the life-endowment policy, which is invested in the purchase of units. There is still the Damoclean sword hanging over the insurance industry, since the Government stated its intention to remove tax reliefs on premiums, but that will take some time yet, I think. The magazines, *Planned Savings* and *Money Management*, are very clear on this kind of issue and, since the position is rather fluid, subject to change, I would recommend a study of one or the other plus the Saturday serious papers and their financial columns.

How to sell

Selling is easy. You have a certificate and you simply renounce it by filling in the form on the back of it and sending it off to your unit trust management (I believe in sending such missives by registered post or, if humanly possible, in delivering them one day when passing in the car or on foot). If the certificate is lost or destroyed, you have to fill in an indemnity form which takes time, and delays your getting the money from the sale; I would suggest keeping the certificates at the bank if you are not methodical and tidy about documents. While most managers pay promptly on receipt of the certificate, they are legally entitled not to pay until Settlement Day (see Chapter 6 on the Stock Exchange).

Discounts

Very occasionally, there is an initial discount offer for a new unit trust for a limited period, clearly set out (often headlined) in the advertisements. Worth considering, of course, but never take up any investment merely because it is cheap unless it suits your book (or should I say portfolio?). Nothing is cheap unless it is right for you. That puce dress with the long skirt at the sales, or the trousers with the flared bottoms – they are probably in the sale because they suit nobody. You would never be so foolish as to buy them, would you? Well, don't buy investments because they carry a money-off tag. Buy them because they fit into your scheme of financial life and for no other reason.

As savings

Though I shall deal with savings later on, I think it worth emphasizing that unit trusts can be good savings schemes because, to some extent, they can be bought out of income. You can put in monthly sums, or periodic small sums whenever you have cash to spare to add to your investment. That is impossible with stocks and shares. Thus you can turn income into capital. If you are likely never to have much capital but often some spare cash, buy a fund that allows for regular top-ups of small sums.

Investment trusts

I have placed these here because too many people think of them as rather like unit trusts. In one way that is true, but they are actually companies of the kind described under Stocks and Shares (Chapter 7) with authorized and issued capital, new issues, rights issues and the rest. Their business is investment, not necessarily in stocks and shares. They do manage the pool of shareholder's money as unit trust managements do, and they enjoy similar tax advantages. They are subject to strict laws and are in constant argument with the Inland Revenue, but they are often very good investments, even when they are high fliers (which is the time to watch them and be prepared to sell before they reach the peak, being satisfied with some gain rather than hanging on for total gain).

They can come unstuck very fast — Slater Walker, to quote only one memorable example. But there are some excellent ones. However, they are not easy to buy and sell and you need large investment sums, unlike unit trusts. Strictly speaking, they do not belong in this chapter, which deals with investments that are easy to make with smallish sums; I include them to clear up the confusion with unit trusts.

Building societies

The safe, safe investment. The boring investment, the essential investment. The poor investment. All these things are said about investments with building societies and all of them are half-truths, but half-truths only.

We have already seen one side of the operations of building societies in the chapter on housing. But, apart from being the nation's great lenders, they are the great borrowers too. They borrow from investors who save with the building societies. You may wonder why I haven't listed these societies under the chapter on savings but, with savings and investments so clearly linked as to be almost indivisible, and because building societies are technically selling shares in themselves, I thought we would discuss them under this chapter on easy investments. Easy and safe.

Their structure

Building societies must have assets of more than £2.5 million, of which 7½ per cent must be in liquid funds, meaning that the funds are either in cash or immediately realizeable for cash at current market values up to the extent of 7½ per cent. They are bound to hold reserves — ready to use at once and therefore also in fast-realizeable investments, or in cash on deposit and attracting interest — of at least 2½ per cent of total assets. The very large societies, worth more than a billion pounds (£1,000 million) are allowed to drop their reserve funds to 1.25 per cent on the basis that they will have more than ample reserves to meet crises.

They live and operate under the Trustee and Investments Act of 1971 and you should really invest in societies of trustee status (names and addresses from the Building Societies Association, 34 Park Street, London W1Y 4AL). There may be some without trustee status that appeal to you because you may be looking for a home in a particular area and wish to be investing in a local society to be sure of getting a loan. (As I said in Chapter 3, mortgages are more available to savers with building societies.) Go ahead. These days you are hardly in danger since, even without trustee status, the affairs of building societies are controlled by strict laws and you are unlikely to find any cowboys, but do make quite, quite sure that they are reputable societies, not just some local wide boy who has managed to contrive the word 'society' or a phrase such as 'home society' into the name of his company.

Now the reason for the trustee rules is simple enough. In City parlance, building societies lend long and borrow short, always said to be the short cut to disaster. It means that they have to lend money for long periods into the future, but can only borrow money for short periods. While investors like to be able to draw out their building society cash or sell their shares at very short notice, the society can offset its risks by investing some of its lending money in short-dated Government stock and local authority loans (see Chapter 7). It can invest in other things. That 7½ per cent of liquid funds plus the 2½ per cent reserve funds is not lying idle, but is earning money. Also, people put money in almost as fast as they draw it out, so the level of investments may stay much the same. In other words, they are not lending all that they borrow all the time. In any case, they are extremely careful about the people to whom they lend, even on housing, and many, many home borrowers move and repay well within the 20, 30 or 40 years.

You will also notice that the society pays less interest to its depositors than it charges to borrowers for mortgages on homes in the same way as banks charge more to lend than they give on deposit. Interest rates change rather slowly as do mortgage rates, but you will see regular announcements, monthly at least, about any changes, and also about whether the inflow of funds is worse or better than the outflow. If the inflow is poor, then money for mortgages will be short. If the reverse (rather rare, by the way), then there will be a temporary easement of mortgage money supply because there may be a queue to satisfy.

Why invest in a building society? Because:

1. Your money is absolutely safe.
2. It costs you nothing.
3. It is easy — branches are everywhere.
4. It pays interest.
5. There may be tax advantages for standard-rate taxpayers (more of this shortly)
6. You have a wide choice of investment or savings schemes as so many companies cover so much differing ground and there is almost always one to suit you.
7. You can get some or all of your money out easily enough although it may pay more to leave it in for longer.
8. Their schemes compare pretty favourably with many, many others.
9. You can start with as little as you like — even £1 if you must, though surely you can manage more.
10. You can add to your investment as often or as rarely as you like with as much or as little as you have or wish to save.
11. You will find it much easier to get a mortgage when you want one, though that does not mean you should stay away from society investments merely because you already have one.

What kind of investment in a building society?

This may be harder to understand because the number of different schemes with different names are seemingly legion. Personally, I deplore the way most societies resort to incomprehensible financial jargon for their schemes, and think they could well take a leaf out of the Government's book and describe their offers and schemes far more succinctly. Basically they all offer much the same thing anyway. Whatever they call it, whether a bond, a share, a scheme, or whatever, they are paying you interest on your deposited money. The longer you promise to leave your money in, the better the interest rates might be, worked on a progressive scale for the time it's in.

If, on the other hand, you have a fixed interest scheme with your chosen society, keep an eye on the rates announced on new offers and switch your deposits or investment to take advantage of higher rates as they come on offer. Or you may find some that offer escalator provisions, meaning that you automatically get the bumping up of interest rates. Whichever you do, you will benefit from leaving the money there for four or five years rather than one or two.

Furthermore, you can get some extra 'bonus' out of agreeing to invest a specific monthly sum, anything between £1 (maybe even less) to £100 (maybe more) monthly and consistently. Such an investment could get you 1 to 1½ per cent above the normal rate over the same period.

As I said, the differences are slight but they are there and, for the most part, the pros and cons are clearly and lucidly set out in the leaflets. Look up your local yellow pages and get leaflets from each society in the area, or read the advertisements and apply for more leaflets from societies that may not have a branch near you. Compare the schemes — it will mean quite a bit of study — and then decide what to do. It really isn't difficult and the assistants at branch offices are generally more than helpful. If they aren't, ask to see the manager or his deputy. You are the boss. You have they money they want. See that you get service and advice.

Bondshares

Several building societies are offering Bonds or Bondshares, for which you pay large lump sums from about a hundred pounds and upwards for a minimum investment. The return is better than if you put your money in driblet-wise. For more about bonds see page 95.

Tax

The interest on building society investments is paid to you after deduction of tax at standard rate. Many will talk loosely of the interest being tax-free. Not so. You merely owe no tax on your interest as you receive it, the tax having been paid — those leaflets will lay it all out clearly for you. In general, you can improve on building society rates, though they are competing with better schemes all the time.

If you do not pay tax at standard rate, if you are a low-income earner, you cannot claim back the tax already paid by the society, which is assessed on an estimated average of what investors might pay if each was individually taxed and paid individually, though obviously the present system is cheaper for most and far less trouble. But, and it must be remembered, the low-income, low-tax person cannot reclaim the tax he would not have paid. Thus building society deposits are not necessarily the right investment for such people unless they are saving for the specific purpose of wanting a mortgage one day. That would make it worthwhile, because I think it will become harder than ever to borrow from building societies without being a depositor. I also think that is the fair way to do it, except in the case of really high-interest mortgages which would help subsidize the low-interest ones, a case of the richer helping the poorer.

Standard-rate taxpayers obviously get saved a lot of trouble, though they have to return the income from their society investments on their annual tax form. For them, building societies usually represent a good, high-yielding and safe investment. Higher-rate tax payers will have to pay extra tax, over and above what the society has already paid. They are assessed on the gross interest. Of course, the 30 per cent paid by the society is deducted from the gross you would normally owe because it has been paid so you are not paying tax twice but only the difference between 30 per cent and — say — 40 per cent if that is your top tax rate. People who pay no tax should go for deposit accounts at banks or finance houses (see Chapter 5 on savings).

One of the older forms of investment in Britain, building society investments are still among the most popular. Smaller societies may be paying marginally higher interest to attract funds that usually pour into the giant, heavily advertised concerns. But the trend is towards size and towards allowing societies more freedom of operation in financial and overseas markets. Our system of home loans is the best in the world, our mortgages enviable and our potential market in Europe large. I would expect to see some very, very attractive investment offers to come from building societies.

Chapter Nine

Personal

You may be working for the Civil Service, I.C.I., British Rail, the hapless British Leyland or Smith & Jones around the corner. But, whoever your employer is, you work for yourself and your family. Remember that and use your earnings accordingly. Use your money to buy you contentment and security, fun and warmth, food and lodging. That means you must be as free to spend as to save as long as you can afford both. Spending is much, much more fun if you are already saving, buying your home and so forth. If you manage your money.

The day that you are born is the day you become eligible for sickness, injury, disablement or death. The day that you marry is the day you become eligible for divorce. Life is like that. The depression of disaster and divorce do nothing to spoil the thrill of your birth for your family or the joys of marriage for you and your beloved.

Nor should they. But I bring out the points to emphasize that life is not all joy and happiness. That you should manage your life — which means your money — to cushion you against the bad patches. As I have already said in the Introduction, misery is not lessened by a secure financial background but it is just a little easier to bear because security takes away one of the terrible emotions of disaster: fear. Fear that you cannot manage when ill, disabled or alone. And money management can reduce fear quite markedly.

The basic philosophy of money management is to be selfish. Yes, selfish. You must provide for yourself and, if you have depen-dents, for them too, though you will never be able to buy them as much security as you can for yourself. But you can try. When I say selfish, I mean remain an individual and think of yourself as being one all through life. When you start work, begin providing for your retirement because, as I've already said, it is so much cheaper then, and remains cheaper all your life, giving you a chance to boost the benefits as you earn more and as you draw nearer to retirement. Start, then, before you have dependents and you will be able to do that much more for them as you acquire them.

Now that we have learned about some of the ways of spending and making money, let's take a cradle to grave approach to our personal financial management as well as at some rather less traditional or normal ideas about investment or money-making.

Up to school age

Obviously, you have nothing but carefree enjoyment of your home and your pocket money for most of these years. The pocket money will never be enough and it might pay to come to some arrangement with parents to wash the cars or paint the fence, to do jobs that are not normal, everyday contributions to the family life and which all children should do — and be raised to do since their reluctance or laziness is all too often bred in them by parents who never train them to co-operate.

Child earnings

You will find reference to these in Chapter 2 on Tax. So all I will repeat here is that, if the earnings come to more than the tax-free allowance permitted for every individual in the land, then your parents or you (if you are old enough) must see to it that your earnings are returned to the Inland Revenue. And parents, do not forget to draw your child allowances. They are rightfully yours, and you no longer get tax allowance on your income to help with the children's costs, except in certain cases.

How children earn

Babies and very young children have few ways of earning except by modelling or acting. Some babies collect quite a bit this way and so do children, either from press advertising, television commercials, or parts in TV, screen or theatre entertainment. A competitive field, believe it or not, but there are specialist agencies who deal in babies, the young and even in pets — my own Dalmation earned some modelling money.

Children also do earn more as they grow older. There are paper rounds, for instance, or Saturday deliveries for the butcher or for other traders. There are mushroom farms, fruit farms and such that employ pickers and packers. As they grow older (and, for their own sakes, preferably after taking O levels) children can do Saturday jobs in retail stores looking for extra weekend help. The pay for a single day is good.

Children (if I can still call them children after they have taken their O level exams) also run disco groups. Usually, they have to buy the equipment on hire purchase, with parental guarantee, but they get their money back when booked for local parties; in some cases, they can lay out capital to hire a local hall and run their own discos, charging admittance and providing some snacks, on the basis of people bringing their own drinks. The equipment can cost any-thing from about £300 upwards, but needs to include the record deck and amplifier, the light-shows, and the speakers, plus the odd drum or percussion equipment. Main-tenance includes new discs as they appear in the top twenty, running a small van, however beat-up, to get the equipment to the site or hiring it (or having benevolent parents to chauffeur or lend the car, but never depend on that).

Drawbacks to child earnings

These are social, of course. You never get the girlfriends or boyfriends unless you can dance at the discos though an occasional boy or girl will stop dancing to chat up the enslaved couple who run it. You need to work in partnership. In almost any decent job, your social life is likely to suffer, so, if it is important to you, think about that one. If you have a paper round, you will have to go to bed earlier than anyone else. Your Saturday or Sunday jobs will mean no free time when everyone else is footloose. On the other hand, you will have more money for your entertainment, for your clothes or whatever turns you on. You can earn quite a bit without paying tax and it is wonderful training for life.

When not to work

When exams are looming and you despera-tely need time to study. OK, some families need their student children to earn some-thing but there are student grants and other financial help. Take it whenever poss-ible. Never sacrifice the future for the affluent present. It will not be worthwhile. If, on the other hand, you are one of those bright people who never needs to revise but who knows everything, you might have freedom to earn. But watch it even then. Fatigue can dull the best brains.

School leavers

The lucky, lucky ones are those that know exactly what they want to do and get on with the necessary further education, training, apprenticeship or whatever to achieve their goals: artists, engineers, draughtsmen, agricultural or building fanatics, economists, sociologists and so forth. But oh, how many, many youngsters have no idea what they want. Here, let me suggest they forget tradition and try for training that goes with their best subjects. For instance, there is a dearth of women in statistical, research, stockbroking and other jobs that need a smattering of mathematics and economics. The future could be good and most of those jobs fit very well with marriage and childbirth, since they can be suspended and then, with brief refresher courses, picked up again. They do not necessarily depend on promotion. The law, accountancy and personnel administration are a few other possibilities. Girls shun such jobs because, they think, they seem unfeminine and the boys prefer girls in the social or artistic classes.

Boys are as bound to tradition as girls and, though less as time goes by, to snob values that are unimportant. Boys do not believe in taking up cooking and catering as often as they might and there are plenty of shop-keeping and shop management opportunities they might look at. Woodworking and carpentry, pottery and art, building and highways – all jobs in which unemployment is low. In my limited experience there is too little imagination among career advisers. Parents and children must use their own. If only they would get together to discuss it more often; at the moment parents tend to leave it to the schools and schools to the parents. Poor youngsters.

Every school leaver, even if he goes straight into a factory, ought to be encouraged to take up some speciality and to become proficient in it. The engineer apprentice might take evening classes in woodwork or jewellery making. The sociologist in pottery. Anything. There are several good reasons. One is having a second string in case your chosen job is not the right one. The second string may also be wrong but, if it is different from the trainee job, at least

doing it will help greatly to clarify the youngster's mind. Another is that the youngster will meet people of different ages under equal circumstances, get into conversation with them and learn a good deal about himself in the process. Too often, the young have only parents, teachers and family friends among the older age groups, and everyone knows their ideas are worthless to the young because familiarity breeds contempt.

In any case, it is a good thing to meet people with whom you are not at college, to broaden your horizons. University does this very well, and evening classes may be neither desirable nor possible. But for those who start their jobs young, it is a very good idea. And, for those who do not find socializing easy, it is an even better one.

Everybody, in my view, should learn to type. Not just women but everybody, and it is on most school or college curricula. There are so many, many jobs in which the ability to type is a great boon, even a help to advancement, whether you are male or female. There are times when you need a stop-gap job and when temporary typing could be of real help. Most importantly, the machines of the future, of the electronic age, depend much on the keyboard. Microchip machines, electronic marvels, will take over many jobs, but skill in putting the data into those machines to tell them what to do is based on being able to keyboard, to learn skilled fingering. En passant, I can tell you that, if I had learned to type early instead of having to teach myself late in life, I would have finished this book in half the time with a lot less backache, shoulder ache, muscle ache and extra work for those who helped me.

Starting work

Assuming you are over 18 when you start work — though you might have been getting a wage or salary to take intensive training in a job — you are now a financial adult. You can take out insurance, buy a home, do anything you can afford. Please do not hurry. Doing the wrong thing is every bit as foolish as doing nothing. You may be earning too little to put your money into a building society and enjoy the tax advantages. You should nevertheless open a building society account of some kind, even if you put very little into it. Talk to your bank manager about the special plans for students (see Chapter 1). Talk to him about building society deposits. The reason for the latter is that you will inevitably want a building society loan for your home one day and savers will get preferential treatment. A small savings scheme is a good idea anyway.

As you grow up

It is really never too soon to start an insurance scheme. So let's look at a rough order of what you might do as your earnings come in:

1. Start a building society account to deposit any spare cash.
2. Start some insurance/savings/endowment scheme (study a good many, then decide). Make sure the scheme is not too long-term because benefits change with the years, usually for the better, and you don't want to be stuck in one that lags well behind inflation. No insurance scheme can actually keep pace but they don't do badly, especially when they are linked to investments, like unit trusts for instance.
3. Look at some unit trusts. These days, since the exchange control was dropped, they are benefiting from the ease and low cost of investing overseas and their funds (see Chapter 8) are often linked to insurance schemes so that you have both a savings and capital growth scheme together with some insurance protection.
4. Buy a home. Do that as soon as you know you are likely to be staying put in one place for some time and you are ready to leave the family home. It really is never too soon as long as you can earn enough to get the mortgage necessary for one.

Small studio flats in or near the town, ruined cottages (becoming scarcer), nearly derelict town houses in older parts of towns and cities may be within your reach. But buy as soon as the mortgage can be had.

If you move, you will have a house to sell but, because of the costs involved in buying and selling homes, I hope you don't have to move too soon. If you marry, you can sell or go on living there if the place will hold two people. A good many couples in love nowadays buy a home jointly. Fine, as long as the legal contract is done by a solicitor. But very complicated if and when the split comes, as one partner may not be able to buy out or take over the other partner's share. Still the home will undoubtedly have gone up in price so maybe they can sell, split the proceeds and start again with capital that they probably never had in the first place.

If possible, buy your own place and let the loved in. Do not charge rent (your owner-occupied home is subject to Capital Gains Tax if you let it or had a temporary tenant for part of it). Let him or her buy the food and drink while you provide the home but no rent, please. Though I must repeat the CGT is levied only after deduction of all costs like mortgage repayments, interest, rates and such over the years of ownership, so . . . .

But buy that home as soon as you can. Your income thus buys capital, and capital growth that stays more or less in parallel with inflation. And insure the contents of your home.

5. Think about a pension scheme (if over 20) if your employer hasn't one.
6. Never commit yourself to more fixed cost than you can afford even for good savings.

At 25 or over

Assuming you have done all that I have already mentioned, and taken out a pension scheme, see about boosting it a bit, taking out some kind of life-endowment policy that is not linked to your home and that provides benefit if you are unable to work through injury or accident, prolonged illness, etc. Your employer will probably have a sickness or disability scheme to save you taking out an expensive one. But it may pay you certain sums for, say, a maximum of six months' illness; the State supplementary earnings-related benefit also lasts only six months. To include in your insurance something that takes over after six months and gives you a small weekly income would cost very little indeed. Look into it.

Do not forget to raise the insurance cover on your home and its contents in line with inflation, because you must consider the replacement costs in the event of loss. This is something you should look at regularly, all through life. The insurance company usually sends reminders along with its demands for premiums every year; in the case of the insurance of the building, you might not need to change the value, since the building society may arrange it for you (though you have to pay the premiums). Keep an eye on that, and make quite sure you are well covered.

If you want to educate children privately, look at a school fees insurance scheme.

From 30 to 45

You may be perpetually broke, with children to feed, clothe and educate. For private education, there are insurance plans. Or you can have a series of endowment policies to mature at different times.

If you are doing especially well at work, you may now have some pocket money, as it were, some spare money to invest because you have your home, insurance and pension all arranged.

There are some golden rules about investment. The first is that, before you decide what investment, you must diagnose your character and your needs thoroughly. You give yourself a tough, inquisitorial session

and, armed with the answers, you can go to see various advisers and find out what you want or need. The sort or questions you should ask yourself are:

(a) What is your temperament? Are you worried about taking risks? Are you a gambler type? Do you like a bit of excitement with your money?

(b) Have you really got spare capital or income? I mean, could you face a crisis that involved more money or could you face a drop in income? Remember, if you make a capital investment, you might be forced to sell when prices have slumped. Or, if you make an investment out of income, you might not get as much benefit if you discontinue before the contractual date. Whatever you plan, be sure you can maintain your commitment.

(c) If investing capital, might you need to get at the money quickly, or can you really spare it for some time?

(d) Always remember that the higher the risk, the greater the chance of gain (and vice versa, irrevocably). Just as an example, when the production company wanted money for 'Evita' and advertised for sums of £1,000 per investor, the investors might have lost the £1,000 very fast if the show had flopped within weeks. In fact they got their £1,000 back in about seven months and then sat back to enjoy about £150 per month income for a long time as the bookings ran into 'full house' night after night. Yet look at the flops – the list is very long of shows that have closed in weeks. Those that make money out of being 'angels' (backing shows) need to back them on a sustained basis, averaging their risks and returns from a series of shows.

If you buy stocks and shares, you are less likely to lose the lot and, in any case, there is some relief from Capital Gains Tax up to an annual maximum, while income from backing a show is taxable at income tax rates, and then as unearned income, on top of other earnings. Also, you may offset losses from shares in any one year against gains in that year or the year after while you cannot offset losses of money invested in show business.

(e) What is your age? Are you looking for short-term or long-term investment? And do you need to protect your capital for your heirs? Do you want to?

(f) Do you want income or capital growth? To get a mixture of the two you will get smaller capital growth or lower income. You can invest for maximum income or (you hope) for maximum growth.

(g) Do you know something about your chosen investment? Meaning, will you know more or less when to sell and cut your losses or when you have notched up sufficient gain to be satisfied and so sell at perhaps less profit that you might have made if you had stayed in, but a good profit none the less.

(h) Are you enjoying your investment, bored by it or frightened by it?

By the time you've answered all those questions, you should know whether you want to be an angel (difficult but possible through one or two companies; if you know an impresario; or read advertisements in *The Stage*, the weekly newspaper of the business); an antiques specialist; a collector of jewellery, cigarette cards, stamps, matchboxes or bottle tops. Remember, if investing in things, that it is much easier to buy them than to find buyers when you want to sell. You may buy directly, at junk shops (whose owners know more and more about values, thus offering fewer real bargains), privately or at auction sales. If you go to the latter, watch the dealers (it is not difficult to find out who they are if you go to many sales and see the same faces at most of them). When they stop, tread carefully. Don't go too high above them.

Antiques and things

You may buy in a shop or through a dealer.

Once you leave a shop, whether you buy a diamond ring or a grandfather clock, your purchase is probably worth exactly half what you have just paid for it in terms of sale or realization value. Built into the cost of your purchase are the dealer's overheads of rates, light, heat, staff, even VAT in some cases, the cost of keeping goods in stock which ties up his available capital and then some money for himself. Half is what you might get if you went back to the same dealer with similar goods (although he might buy back your recent purchase for a small consideration if he's nice and you're lucky).

That's a fair guide, but of course you might be a skilful or lucky buyer. Now you have to keep the goods, if you did buy through a shop, until you can get your money back or find a private buyer who will pay more or less what you paid.

Keeping the goods is, in theory, keeping your own capital tied up, unrealized until you can sell. That doesn't matter in the least if you get great pleasure out of wearing the diamond ring or watching the grandfather clock. That's a pleasure and, indeed, that's why you should buy what you understand and enjoy, because the investment in pleasure is so great. But, besides locking up your capital, the ring or clock also cost you money in annual insurance premiums. You have an investment that costs money, yields no income and will one day (you hope) give you capital profit. Good luck, and I hope you make it. With inflation so rampant, the re-sale price of your ring or clock will have been catching up very fast with the purchase price and passing it, so you should be all right. Suppose inflation slows down? If you cannot make a profit, at least be happy. Buy always what pleases you.

Gambling

When you are maturing or mature and have some spare money, you might like gambling. Football pools may be something you started young, with a small weekly stake — not a bad idea despite the appalling odds stacked against you. Easier if you send off a cheque for the three, six or twelve months all at once, filling in a fixed line of numbers and then being able to forget all about the things for a long period unless you decide to change the numbers.

Playing roulette, craps, blackjack or any of the casino games is for the rich. Bingo is for the social-minded, the gregarious types, often a very good centre for the elderly without the risk of losses being too much. Horse-racing can be cheap or expensive, fun or boring, depending on your nature. Greyhounds, lotteries and the rest are less fascinating, but each has its own appeal to someone. There is absolutely nothing wrong with gambling as long as you can stop, know when to stop and don't get bitten by this dangerous bug. But, always, do what makes you happy. Don't gamble for its own sake but as an adjunct to an evening out, a social occasion. Or try premium bonds where at least you don't lose your stake. There is the advantage with gambling that any rewards are tax-free.

Holidays

You are probably freer to enjoy these now that the children are older and you have a little more spare cash. I advise holiday insurance, holiday medical insurance, and then have a good time.

Luxuries

You can afford them now and, if you don't buy some, you may regret it later on so go on, spoil yourself.

Future retirement

No, you are only 45 and you are not yet ready to retire (you hope against hope that your employer thinks likewise). But you should be looking at your potential retirement income and thinking of topping it up

perhaps. You may have an endowment policy maturing soon. It could be invested for retirement, or partly so, with some kind of deferred fund; or in a bond that gives later growth and thus investment again later on for income. By now, you should have a pretty good idea of what inflation has done to the provisions you and your employer have already made, so you can see a trend for the future. Take advice from a professional or sound broker about your insurance and review your investments now.

45 to retirement

Now you should probably again be revising that portfolio you looked at a year or so back. You are beginning to secure home and income for the future. This is a consolidating period, a period when you will probably be very active about your capital and your portfolio in the early part but moving slowly in the latter part. Your earnings are probably high, so your tax is high. You want to get a bit of safety. Perhaps you should consider some building society bonds with tax advantages and some growth bonds with ditto? Some gilt-edged investments and some more insurance cover while you are still fit and young enough to warrant decently reasonable premiums? If you invest in with-profits endowment insurance that will provide the sum you invested in gilts, you can enjoy the high income from the gilts, which will pay for the premiums; the premium in turn protects the capital invested in gilts maturing at the end of, say, ten years. The gilts income pays the premium for you and gives you some spending money and your capital is there plus some more for a new investment plan when you are 55 or 60. A good way of doing things about this time, but get a real professional at the job, like Warren Financial Services, 117 High Street, Epsom, Surrey. They specialize in split-second timing and very precise arithmetic, buying gilts at exactly the right price, getting a

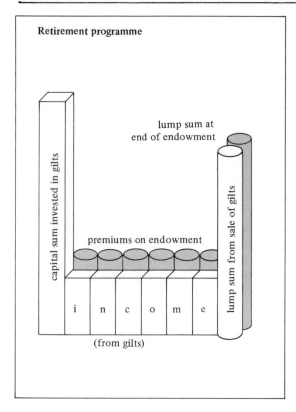

Retirement programme

lump sum at end of endowment

capital sum invested in gilts

premiums on endowment

lump sum from sale of gilts

i n c o m e

(from gilts)

bit of reduction on the insurance premiums and setting it all out very carefully for you to understand (but you do need a £10,000 minimum investment). Terrific at all ages but ripe for this age.

Retirement

Well covered in the pensions and insurance chapters but you can now buy retirement certificates linked to the retail prices index and showing healthy gains (tax-free); save some tax (with age allowance); get all sorts of cut-price concessions for travel, entertainment and so forth; work less; and like it. Do try to like it rather than resent it. You may also be able to move to a smaller or cheaper home, thus unlocking some of your capital to invest for greater comfort.

Death

Your financial worries and joys are over. I hope you enjoyed both of them, the worries being less than the joys.

There are some things you ought to do which haven't been entirely covered in these chapters and one of the first, I am afraid, is that you should make a will. This is essential.

The will

That should be made the moment you have any money at all. It can always be very simple and you can buy will forms, ready printed, that will often be enough if you are leaving everything you own at time of death to your mother, father, both equally, or people of that kind. You fall in love and, without marriage, may wish to leave at least something to the loved one. Not as simple as the first will but probably still possible on the will form. When you marry, simple enough. Everything to him or her, with maybe a little something for the children. Legally, if you do not make a will, every-thing will go to your nearest relative — spouse, child or parent.

If you want your children to have, say, £1,000 each tax-free (free of capital transfer tax, that is), you may be all in the clear as long as you haven't already given away your permitted sums in CTT during your lifetime.

If you have already given away all that you are allowed, you can still say they must have £1,000 each free of CTT. In such a case, the estate will be valued with those £1,000 bequests added in and assessed before they are distributed. The children will each get £1,000 and not pay tax on that, but the estate will pay tax on the money. As wills become more complicated, with children, step-children, ex-wives or husbands, ex-mistresses or lovers, grandchildren, step-grandchildren and all, the will must be properly done by legal experts. Your bank may charge less for the job than your lawyer and they will still use experts. A bank manager told me that his clients suffer more agonies of suspense while inadequate or confused wills are sorted out and the bequests get eaten away by legal fees than at any other time. You will not want to leave that kind of in-heritance to those you love.

You will need an executor. If your relatives are intelligent and prepared to do the work, go ahead and choose one. If not, try the bank (the charges are not small but could save the inheritors a bit of money). Better to use a firm, legal, banking or otherwise, than an individual who may die, go to live abroad or just disappear from the family tree. But, for goodness sake, make the will. You can at least give your money to the people you choose rather than think of it going to some relative you dislike. You can save them money, too, by making a simple, proper, legal will. It is never, never too early to do this. People hate to face it but it is very, very important.

Divorce, separation, etc.

The tax position has already been covered in Chapter 2. My own views about the need for each partner to maintain personal independence are also known. I offer a further reason for this, over and above all financial considerations. You fall in love as two individuals. Don't try to merge or submerge in the other's personality. Stay freshly individual. Men and women do not leave as often out of lust for a new bedmate as for the stimulus of a new and interesting companion (the bed comes after they get to be fascinated with each other's company). Any psychiatrist will tell you that one. Her youth, his maturity, these attractions to your spouse may be superficial. The rivals may just be interesting individuals, not bogged down in family and home affairs. Of course there are plenty of other reasons, some sad, like illness or disability, and some less so.

Whatever the cause, try to forget it unless you really think you can cure it. No good just curing the symptoms, like restlessness and his or her love affair with her or him (or even with him and him or her and her). The affair might get nipped in the bud. The cause, whoever's fault, is much harder to uproot. Unless cured it may simply lead to another affair, another diversion from the path of companionship or marriage and it may have nothing to do with extra-marital love or sex. If you cannot cure the cause, do something about splitting up.

If it is all terribly simple, with no children, neither party wanting anything from the other either financially or in any other way, then go for a do-it-yourself divorce, which is £25 for filing it (but that might rise as you read this). There will be other costs involved but small and few. If there is the slightest issue on which you might argue, get legal advice. You may be able to get the legal advice on what to do and then, if you can agree amicably to the professional's suggestions, you can still do it yourself. Basically, in a divorce, the marital funds are pooled, probably sold up and realized, and then redistributed. The more legal fees are involved, the less there is to share and there are no rules about who pays for it all.

If there is any question of maintenance for the ex-spouse, for children or for both, then use the law. But, as far as you possibly can, be reasonable and agree when the other side is reasonable. Vindictiveness is expensive, profiting only the lawyers.

As much as possible, get together to agree on things before the lawyers start arguing as middlemen between you. Then both of you can each instruct your lawyers quite simply and cut out a large number of professional man-hours, thus savings hundreds, perhaps even thousands of pounds in legal costs. There usually is a fair share-out basis. Try to find it and try to conform to it with dignity. In any case, amicability pays because there will have to be future contact over the children, if any, or other joint holdings. The friendliness is all too often killed by early bitterness and it does pay to try to preserve it at all costs. Listen to your solicitor. But, in doing so, remember that he will be advising you on the maximum advantages you can get. Your spouse's solicitor can advise his client too, and also on maximum advantages. So there must be a degree of give and take. The right settlement is probably a compromise.

If you leave the lawyers to fight it out, you will lose a lot of money.

When you get a settlement, legalize it in court. Not only because the tax problems are simpler but because the more dependent party is more protected.

The home may have to be sold and shared. But, if the departing party is going to start a new home with someone else, there may just be a chance that the home may stay with the parent that keeps the children and some other financial adjustment made. In any case, both husband and wife are going to have to drop their standards, to live in cheaper homes with smaller incomes. Trying to maintain standards is impossible (and expensive). The time has gone when a woman must expect financial security for ever in return for a few, or many, years of marriage. She may not get security even if he has the money and may still find herself on supplementary benefits of some kind.

Agreements can involve continuing payments from one side to the other; a lump-sum settlement (which may be the house, either free and clear of mortgage, with the mortgage for the wife to pay or with the ex-spouse continuing to pay the mortgage until cleared). I know one lady who, in 1974 (when house values were comparatively slumped) chose to keep the whole house, to take over the mortgage and his insurance premiums as well as his arrears of income tax (fairly substantial but she was earning). He would then pay her nothing at all. He thought he was well off. His income has become a pension that barely meets his needs. Her house, then valued at £25,000, sold for £102,000 in 1979. Suppose she had fought for the share of his income (and pension as he retired). He would have been penurious, it is true, and so he is better off. But she did very well out of the deal.

The home
The old thing about the home being in her name matters no longer. It will still in the eyes of the law be shared, even if not in joint names. Some account is taken of what each party put into the home. Maybe he paid the mortgage, but she bought the food and worked there, redecorated the place, cooked for him, cleaned for him and such. All that can be more or less measured. Where there are children, the court takes an emotional and social view and the wage-earner must continue to support the children and the person who looks after them. If a break-up can be avoided, it is for the children's sake.

Matrimonial assets
Wedding presents are joint property as are the essential furnishings (the latter often being granted to the parent who has the children even if the home is sold). Personal belongings, such as antique chairs, paintings or other things belong to the person who took them into the marriage or bought them afterwards. A wife is allowed to buy things out of the housekeeping money, as long as the family has not gone short, and to consider them as her own. I am afraid that it really does pay to decide who owns what from the time it enters the home. I know two couples with separate insurance policies for their own valuables. They are very happy together and divorce could not be further from their minds but they are, in that respect at least, ready for it.

Maintenance
Keep records, whether you give or receive. I believe in paying by banker's draft to the bank so that documentary evidence is always there, always official, always easy to prove. Keep in touch. It may sound impossible but one woman I met recently told, as a joke, how she couldn't understand why her maintenance cheque never arrived (he paid it directly to her) until she also realized that she had never told him of her change of address. Do not be afraid of going to court over recalcitrant spouses who 'overlook' payments. If your payments do not keep up with inflation, you can apply to the court to have them raised. Do not be ashamed of

going to social security.

If in doubt, see the Citizens Advice Bureau. They will always be ready with advice and they can probably also give addresses of the local branches of associations for one-parent families, of which there are now a goodly number. Their advice is good. The associations also have files full of experience, advice and case histories on homes, maintenance, finance, children, tax and everything else. Most single-parent family associations also hold social functions at low cost to bring the lonely together. This could be doubtful help. The sad and lonely often dwell so much on their troubles that they pile the agony on for each other. Escape from the lonely might be better.

Living and loving without marriage

Many couples do this and the decision has to be purely personal. There may be something about it that keeps people on their toes. There may be some resentment too if one party feels that he/she is worth bedding but not wedding. Trial marriage may not be a bad idea but it may be terrible, taking all the romance out of the orange-blossom atmosphere. One couple, who had lived together for four years, told me how their parents were nagging about marriage for them both. Why, said he, should they bother so much about it? After all, it was only a piece of paper. I said, perhaps acidly, that − if it really was only a piece of paper − why were they so scared of it? When they married, they told me I had started them thinking about it. Thank goodness that, after another four years, they are still happy. Imagine the responsibility of my remark.

I'm not moralizing. All I will say is that it is even more important for loving couples without marriage to keep records of who owns what. Common-law wives and husbands do have legal rights these days but it is much easier not to have to call in the law without

ready proof. In homosexual relationships, legalizing possessions is equally important.

The car

I don't have to tell you about insuring the car because somebody will, from the moment you buy one. If they don't, just try having an accident and see what happens. To drive without insurance is to drive illegally. Your insurance will cost you anything from around £70 (with a no-claims bonus and on a small, cheap car) up to hundreds of pounds a year. It depends on:

(a) Your age and the ages of any other drivers of the car. Bad to be young or old. Middling is best.
(b) How many drivers are insured to drive the same car.
(c) The records of the drivers, their driving histories, their accidents.
(d) The profession of the driver(s). Journalists and actors are poor risks, accountants good. Crazy, isn't it, when you think of your sober journalist friends and your crazy accountant in that madhouse of an office? But professions do count. They may put the car at risk.
(e) The value of your car and what repairs and replacements would cost.
(f) The make and kind of car. Sports cars are expensive to insure, sedate saloons less so.
(g) Where you keep it − in the street, in a garage, in a public place, in private or where?
(h) Where you live and drive, in country or city. They dislike London, the insurers.
(i) Whether you are British; and if not, why not? and what are you? The French are crazy drivers, as far as the insurers are concerned.

You will find that the lowest insurance premium is probably for a non-drinking housewife or teacher in mid thirties, without a single accident in the past, who drives a Mini to and from school and the shops in the West Country. A London actor or journalist, in his/her twenties with a sports car is in for a high premium. If you use the car to carry goods or for business, make quite sure that you are insured while you are doing either. Premiums cost less if you agree to pay the first £25, £50 or £100 of damage.

How to get the insurance
Through the Automobile Association (A.A.), a broker, and maybe your bank (not all can do the policies but some do) or an insurance broker. Get several estimates, always. Costs vary.

Claims
Always notify your insurance agent, broker or company at once if you have an accident, even if you do not plan to claim. Even if not your fault, notify your insurance company at once, because the other man's company will come on to you in time. If your fault, still notify even if you have less than £25, £50 or £100 of damages. If at all serious, tell the local police. Your claim form will always ask if the police were notified.

Buying the car
One of the most difficult things you will do and you may well make mistakes. Be sure in advance what you can afford and don't exceed it. See if you can afford repayments if buying on hire purchase. If buying second-hand, go only to reputable dealers, who will at least give a three-month guarantee. Don't be pushed into a purchase. Think about spending up to £30 or so (depending on the car, distance and all) for a check by the A.A. or Royal Automobile Club (R.A.C.). Ask for the M.O.T. certificate. Take a test drive. Look at the speedometer and hope the reading has not been fiddled; then see if the car has been flogged to death in a short time (it should have averaged less than 10,000 miles per year of its life). Look at the tyres. Ask how long since the last M.O.T.

If buying a new car, still go to a reputable dealer. Ask carefully what is included in the price and if there are any hidden extras.

Test drive it.

Think about the running costs. Do not run away with the idea that small cars with small engines are always the cheapest — lack of power can add to the costs per mile. Write to the Department of Energy for the official leaflet on fuel consumption and note how a small engine can be pretty thirsty for petrol. It may also wear less well. The Department of Energy's special 'cars' address is: Thames House South, Millbank, London SW1.

Trading standards
You will have a local trading standards office whose address you can get through your local Town Hall. There you can pick up leaflets published by the Office of Fair Trading on shoppers' rights on electrical goods, furniture, shows, laundries and also notes on how to cope (legally) with door-to-door salesmen, credit Acts and such. You can save money by shopping wisely, so do have a look at the booklets.

Travel
If you don't read advertisements but do travel, check for cheaper ways of doing it. Don't just buy a ticket to ride without seeing if returns are cheaper (probably at certain hours), youth or age has benefits (usually with a proper annual card, paid for but still worth having), and so on. I had to tell my own mother, when she was coming from Jersey, that British Airways had special return concessions for flying for O.A.P.s. Yet they did advertise it.

Coaches are perhaps used less than they should be. Usually very comfortable and, with an excellent national network, they can take you anywhere for much, much less than British Rail can. A bit slower, yes, but comfortable. Not so cheap on short runs, for which British Rail does cheap day returns, but great on long distances.

Don't buy season tickets without working out how often you are going to use them and comparing the cost of use with the cost of the ticket. With holidays, days off and such-like you may be overpaying.

Borrowing

Please, please don't, except from banks or respectable finance houses (and then ask the bank for advice and do heed it). If you plan to instal double-glazing or have a home extension, ask the relevant bureau or association about the offered contracts or take them to your bank (worth a small fee). Never, never sign anything that you cannot read in detail and understand thoroughly. If the salesman will not leave the contract with you while you seek advice on it, you are better off without him. Get your hire purchase and your services through respectable firms with reputations. Never be coerced. For your fair rights in a hire purchase deal see Chapter 2.

The Consumer Credit Act is for your protection. It isn't marvellous, but it's not bad and it's the best we've got. There are loopholes, so be very careful about how you borrow. It is a good rule never to apply for postal loans. I know there are many good companies who advertise them, but there are plenty of knaves so just keep away. And make sure you do have insurance cover on your loans in case you fall ill or die and leave debt legacy to your loved ones. If the lender doesn't want or offer insurance cover, run a mile. His rates will be high.

Go to your bank or to a finance house like United Dominions Trust, Lombard, etc. They may irritate you with their questions and seem nit-picking, but that's for you protection too. On the whole, if the bank won't lend to you, you are a bad credit risk and you should not borrow for your own sake.

But, if the bank admits you are OK but it has no funds, then try a finance house. Only in person, not in writing.

Mistrust everyone. Even if you are normally the trusting type, ask questions that

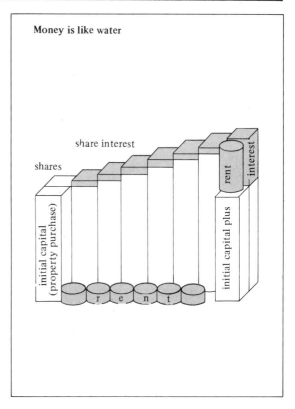

Money is like water

prove your mistrust and watch the foe retreat while the 'friend' tries patiently to explain. It is your money they are after. Either they must pay for the privilege of getting it or they must lend on reasonable terms, if it's borrowing you want.

Money is like water

Yes, it is. Not only does it go like water, but it finds a natural level. You can only 'buy' so much money with money. But there is a value for money that is not only national, endemic to Britain, but universal.

Take an example. A man has a certain sum of money — let's day £10,000. If he puts it into a capital growth investment he will get, over ten years, roughly the same in capital growth that he would get if he put it out to earn income. In other words, the ten-year income would add up to much the same as capital growth at the end of ten years (even taking taxation into account, unless there are special tax cases). If he invests the £10,000 in property, he would expect the total rental income for the period to roughly equal the capital increase he would have gained in, say, a good share, or also to equal the interest he would have got on deposit. Over the last twenty years, property has done better than expectations.

That's what a good investment is, something that gives you the proper level of return, while keeping your money safe. Of course there are variations — see the foregoing chapters, based on whether you want the money now or later, and whether you give it all now, in small instalments or later.

But money has a level. Bad investments are those that fall below it. Good ones are not necessarily ones that rise above it, for the latter may involve risk, such as buying shares that could go down but luckily do not.

I promise you, a first-class deal is simply a good deal, one that everyone can get. Please don't cry for the moon, for the man who offers you the moon is either a fool or fraud.

Your money is yours. Keep it. Spend it. And love it.

Chapter Ten

The World of Money

'Tony, you got Bahrein on? Good, then tomorrow June 22nd 9/32nds Fiji . . . OK?'

'Swiss . . . trente-deux . . . three million pour six mois . . . OK?'

'John, got anything in a one-year at 508/507 through seller's name?'

'Can do, trying to pay you out of arbitrage, try to get 48, see if I can get anything out of the sterling room . . . OK?'

'She'll give you the sterling and take the Eurodollars . . . OK?'

The language of money, picked in short staccato phrases from the confused babel of voices in a foreign-exchange dealings room, is the language of money being shifted around the world in millions of somebody's currency, on loan for six months, or to be repaid in six weeks. Unilever here in Britain may be buying raw foods from abroad to make into the familiar packs we buy here, and need to pay in foreign currency; they come into the foreign-exchange market for dollars, francs, yen or marks.

A bank may be short of marks, yen, francs or dollars, and call the dealers to get its requirements. Or a local authority like the Wolverhampton or Newcastle Council may want a loan until the rates come in, so the money brokers, in the room next to the foreign business, phone round to raise it. A Bahrein company may want sterling, or a New York firm may need marks. And, just as tourists shop around for the best exchang rates for their money, so these large organizations ring up the dealers to shop around for the best rates for them and the dealers shout the odds back and forth, as it were.

Indeed, the dealing rooms are very much like bookmakers' rooms, with overworked, overheated young men, their ties loosened and their shirtsleeves rolled up, yelling at each other and talking coolly but rapidly into the speakers before them on desks that are really modern electronic switchboards connecting them by instant telephone to the rest of the world. Bells do not ring but lights flash constantly as callers come in or the buttons marked 'Bank of Santander' of 'Chicago' are punched for instant connection. The odd phrases, the curious terse language shifts millions from Tokyo to Detroit, from Singapore to Rio de Janeiro and the 'OK' seals the deal, so that the dealer can shout for his colleagues to hear and stop duplicated dealings, 'I've done a deal.'

All the dealings are done on trust, subject to confirmation at leisure, after the bustle of the telephoned transactions. Actual money never changes hands. Nobody warehouses money as coins or notes in these foreign-exchange companies, but the dealers know where available cash, in almost any currency, lies in wait to be loaned or exchanged. Their direct lines to the banks and other money sources ensure that they can buy fast, perhaps before the rate moves up a fraction, when one currency is growing stronger every minute; that fraction, multiplied by millions, can mean a great deal of money to the principals involved.

Let's be honest. Dealings on the foreign-exchange market are not simply for practical purposes, not simply for people to trade round the world. There are many

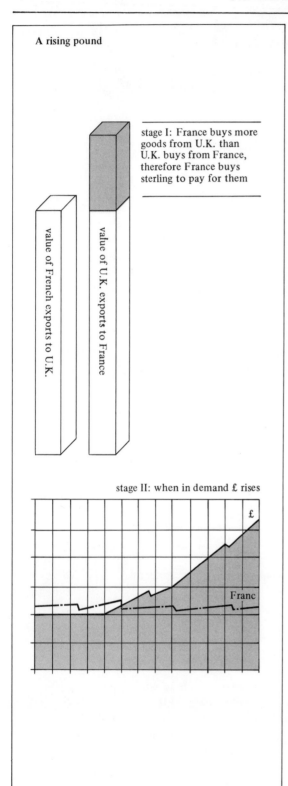

A rising pound

stage I: France buys more goods from U.K. than U.K. buys from France, therefore France buys sterling to pay for them

value of French exports to U.K.

value of U.K. exports to France

stage II: when in demand £ rises

£

Franc

speculators who, if they think a currency is falling or rising against either their own currency or one of which they have large holdings, will buy or sell in order to make a quick profit on the changing values of the currencies vis-à-vis each other. Fortunes have been made, and lost, that way. Generally speaking, a country's currency is strong if its trade is prosperous and its Government policies trusted. If it is selling a good deal of its internal production abroad, the currency stays strong. Should Britain, for instance, be selling a far higher value of goods to France than vice versa, then France would need pounds to pay for the goods and would buy sterling. When it is in demand, the value of sterling rises against the value of the French francs. As the pound strengthens visibly, other countries try to buy it before it goes up further, thus making sure they get their sterling needs at a lower rate when they come to pay for their British goods. This self-perpetuating spiral goes on until something happens to reverse it, to discourage the buying of pounds and to stimulate the buying of marks or guilders or French francs.

While trade is one way of shifting money about the world, tourism is another – Spain and Italy benefit tremendously from the foreign currencies poured into their countries by tourists, and tourism has saved Greece from terrible slumps in the last thirty or forty years. Earnings from tourism are among a country's 'invisible exports', a term you will often read or hear. Invisible exports also include the sale of know-how or services abroad – like consultancies on how to build hospitals or make cars, sales of financial investments and that kind of thing. The term is logical, meaning that you cannot actually see and touch what is exported.

Foreign investment is a prime mover of capital around the world today but, in the early days of money, capital moved only with people.

How it began

Among the earliest recorded currencies are cattle and iron bars, pieces of iron and such. The cattle were favoured because they were more portable than heavy iron, being able to tread their own way with their traders, finding food and water on the way, while iron had to be loaded and carried, involving slow journeys and many carriers. In the Far East, because of the lack of food and water over huge tracts of land, cattle were not used for exchange; beautiful shells from the coasts (not those ugly oyster shells that might contain the pearls we value today) became a coveted currency. Rice and crude local clothes were the inlanders' currency until they discovered that the earth could yield sparkling stones and metals as lovely as the coastal shells. As man found gems beneath the earth's crust, he began to dig even more deeply to find better ones, larger and more brilliant. Then, because of the labour, time and even danger involved in finding them, such gems became endowed with even greater value.

One advantage of the gems was that they were dug up in varying sizes, so that it was easy enough to vary the 'coinage' by assessing the different sizes and weights at different values. Even so, there were disadvantages, so that people began to look for metals that could be cut into convenient sizes and weights. Copper was the prime material for early crude coins of the type we now use, silver and gold followed.

The portable coin made trading much simpler than mere barter and exchange. The man who made tables could not take them very far in search of the man who made hunting-knives (if those were what he wanted in exchange), while the knife-maker might not want a table at all. The symbol with specific value, the iron bar, ox or piece of copper, became the trading token And that's all money really is, a token. Today, of course, the tokens take many shapes, from scraps of paper as cheques to plastic cards (credit cards).

Whether values were marked on the early pieces of metal is doubtful, but regular traders memorized the values and there was a kind of local agreement on what the symbols were worth, which was not difficult when trade was carried on in relatively small, local geographical areas only. As traders moved further afield, looking for more than tables, hunting knives or hides, the trading tokens began to be more like our present-day coins. In the 12th century B.C., copper was fashioned into something like our modern coinage, presumably rounded to avoid the scratching or wear on cloth of square coins with pointed corners. In India, values were scratched on to the surfaces.

The Eastern system spread so that, by 700 B.C., Greeks and Romans were clearly marking values on their silver and, to decorate or identify the pieces, they also began to mark the coins with the heads of gods. Apollo was the favourite and, around 400 B.C., Apollo coins were in demand all over the limited trading world. Alexander the Great was probably the first ruler to insist upon having his image on coins, about 300 B.C., and other rulers subsequently followed that particular megolamaniac's example, a custom which survives today as rulers' heads decorate most of the world's coins.

In Britain, we lagged behind, because we did so little overseas trade. We were still lugging heavy iron bars about the country in 55 B.C., though people in agricultural areas dealt more happily and conveniently in corn and cattle. The Romans under Caesar taught us how to make coins, the main metals then being gold and silver. It is often said today that one of the tragedies of Jesus Christ's betrayal was that he was sold for a mere handful of silver, but the truth is that thirty pieces of silver was a fat fee in those days, probably the equivalent of many thousands of pounds today.

While coins of precious metals were useful, the country needed to have actual stocks of the precious metals that could be fashioned into them. This need developed into what came to be known as the 'gold standard' (there was a silver standard but it never really acquired the importance of the gold standard). For as long as it was the basis of our printing notes or minting coins, the gold standard simply meant that the Government printed and minted no more money than equalled the value of the gold it owned.

Greedy and crooked men, who have always existed, discovered lead and other base metals, and they also discovered ways of mixing gold with such base metals so that coin looked gold, was the same size as the golden coin it imitated, and yet had nothing like the value of gold contained in it though the 'true' value (indicated in terms of the value of gold) was still printed on the coin face. Thus more coins could be made from the hoard of gold and some went to great lengths, coating lead with thin layers of silver and gold. This was called 'debasing the coinage' and one of the worst culprits was the extravagant, much-married, lascivious Henry VIII, whose expenses bid fair to bankrupt the country when the Government alleged it could raise no more from taxing the people and traders.

Henry's actions led to traders mistrusting coins, so that they began to hoard pure silver and gold, using it for trade instead of the country's coin which, because nobody wanted it, became even more worthless. British trade slumped because ships would not bring goods to our shore in exchange for the debased coinage; in turn that meant we could not load outgoing ships with our goods to earn foreign coins. Our hoards of gold and silver were either kept, unused, or sent secretly out of the country for the few goods our own manufacturers needed to continue in business. It was not until the reign of Queen Elizabeth I that crisis was averted. Her financial adviser, one Sir Thomas Gresham, became famous for the dictum that 'Bad money drives out good,' which many attribute to another Gresham altogether. However, Gresham and his contemporary financial geniuses advised that we go out to the world to trade, and sailors like Sir

Francis Drake and Sir Walter Raleigh did just that, subsidized in their explorations by State money, so that the State was gambling on their merchant adventuring.

Letters of credit, payable in silver and gold, became gradually fashionable, as they were safer to carry; thieves and pirates could not cash them, since the names of payees were clearly written on the letters and attested by witnesses. Trust in Queen Elizabeth's Government made such letters acceptable. The system survives today. The trade stimulated by the Queen's reign put Britain on to the world maps among traders, and also improved the value of the coinage.

Strange currencies persisted for many years. In 1642, tobacco was declared legal tender by some American states. Tobacco remained legal currency for some 200 years in Virginia and for about 150 years in Maryland although it crumbled and lost its value. The expression that you were 'smoking money' was literally true in America, where the phrase was born. People had to keep their tobacco moist in vaults or holes in the ground until something could be found to take its place, and it acquired terrific values as the demand for coin in exchange for tobacco grew.

Paper money of various kinds had long been in existence in 1690, but the paper had been rather more like our present-day cheques, promises to pay a named bearer or payee. That year the Government of the State of Massachusetts launched an attack in 1690 on a Quebec fortress expected to yield rich treasures, but the fortress proved impregnable, the attack failed and the State had no money for its soldiers. Proper government notes were printed by the Massachusetts Bay Company and given to the soldiers to be redeemed as the people of the State paid their taxes. Since the notes were used by soldiers to pay for their living needs, the people of Massachusetts in turn used them to pay the taxes, which put the local government into a terrible state and made a nonsense of the whole thing. But the incident showed

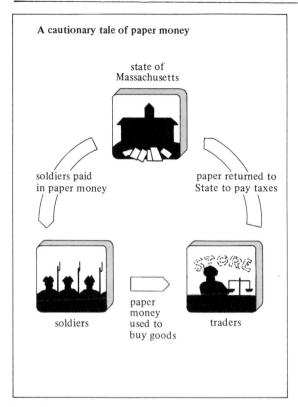

A cautionary tale of paper money

state of Massachusetts

soldiers paid in paper money

paper returned to State to pay taxes

soldiers

paper money used to buy goods

STORE

traders

how foolish it was merely to print notes without some substantial backing. And that lesson was still true some 250 years later when everybody started just to print money once more.

The gold standard

The world's solution, or at least the solution of the sophisticated trading world, was the gold standard; economists advocated it, people who never really knew the value of their country's coin and paper welcomed it. It didn't matter too much while countries were largely self-sufficient and few people travelled, because their own money in their own country had some kind of stability. One could still buy the same weight of carrots from the local shop because the local shop got enough money for the carrots to buy their onions. But, when goods had to be imported and to be bought in foreign currencies, any coinage that was mistrusted as being unbacked by gold was at a disadvantage. It could be exchanged for

less of foreign currencies than if backed by gold reserves.

And that brings us back to the beginning of this chapter, the need for foreign-exchange brokers to help the money go round the world. The fact that a gold standard was adopted by many did not mean that coins were made of gold or silver. Indeed, they mostly were not, despite golden sovereigns, eagles (American) and Louis (French), etc. While there were for a long time gold and silver coins, there were also coins of mixed metals, of various alloys and, of course, copper, the oldest coin metal we know. It meant that the total of the face values of all the coins or paper money must not be greater than the value of a country's gold reserves.

Though the gold standard was accepted, there were many lobbyists for a silver standard when it looked as if the world's gold supplies might run out. The growing world population needed more and more money and, as their living standards gradually improved with the growth of international trade, shortage of the available money actually led to some hardships, forcing many companies to trade down to the available money rather than up to their customer demand. Fortunately, more gold lay in the earth to be discovered and a gold standard crisis was averted by gold rushes in the Klondike, the Yukon and, most importantly, in South Africa. All have been so immortalized by fiction and Hollywood that gold fever needs little elaboration from me.

When gold ran low

Periodic gold shortages did not inhibit governments from finding other ways to meet the demand for money and payments, and they began to merely issue certificates guaranteeing payment or even print bank-notes. Any banknotes or coins issued over and above the value of a country's gold reserves became known as a 'fiduciary issue', from a Latin word meaning that the issue was based entirely on trust, in this case of the relevant governments. Britain's first fiduciary issue was as long ago as 1844, by special Royal Charter. The Bank of England was then permitted by the Government to print £14 million, such notes and coin to be backed by the Government's promise to accept them as legal tender. Our entire money issue is now fiduciary although our Government does buy and hold gold reserves among other special investments. But we shall learn more about that when we look at how the Bank of England manages our Government accounts.

Fixing the world gold prices

The world's gold prices are now fixed twice a day, every trading day, in London and in Zurich, Switzerland. In London, at 10.30 a.m. and at 3 p.m. each day, five men assemble in the gold-fixing room at Rothschild's, the world's leading centre for gold trading since the Napoleonic wars and a merchant bank founded in 1804.

The five men who assemble at tables over-looked by portraits and an ornate old wall clock are representatives of London's five bullion dealers, Rothschild (the host), Sharps Pixley, Moccatta and Goldsmid, Samuel Montagu and Johnson Matthey. The chairman of the fixing, from Rothschild, quotes a price, based on the dealings of the hours since the last price-fixing. That price is instantly passed back to the dealing rooms where, in turn, worldwide customers are alerted. The customers report back their requirements, buying and selling, on Good Delivery Bars (roughly 12.5 kg. of gold each).

The fixers state the requirements and the price is adjusted according to supply and demand. If there is no unanimous agreement, the whole process starts again, with the price reported back, the requirements again noted and so on back to the fixers. At all times, the fixers' prices are public knowledge as are the world's gold requirements, and modern communications have speeded the process sharply.

Each fixer has before him a miniature Union Jack on a stick. As each agrees the proposed price, he topples his tiny flag. When all five flags are down, the price is fixed. The world accepts the London fixing. The spread between buying and selling prices in gold is very narrow indeed.

The Fed

Fascinatingly, the gold does not physically move from buyer to seller but is moved from one shelf to another in the vast vaults where stocks of the world's gold lie – Fort Knox, Bank of England, anywhere. A vast hoard, more than in Fort Knox, lies beneath the 'Fed', the Federal Reserve Bank in New York where racks are loaded with bullion. As the intricate dealings are completed, burly porters load their trolleys, moving gold from Switzerland to England, from America to Japan, or Hong Kong to Russia. That's what the skill and intricacy of the money men boils down to, a team of husky porters.

In 1979, the United States Treasury 'lost' 5,200 ounces of gold or failed to account for its whereabouts. Long investigation showed that one employee had walked out with 600 ounces (he was imprisoned). Simple book-keeping errors accounted for another 500 ounces. But the Treasury had simply to write off 4,100 ounces (then worth more than $1.2 million) as lost, stolen, or wrongly entered in the books. Well, easy come, easy go.

Currencies

As long as Britain prospers and looks like continuing to do so, it matters not a bit that we have no gold, merely Government promises. Other countries know that we can trade abroad, that we shall have a ready supply of foreign currencies or be able to get them in order to pay for our imports, and that sterling is in good fettle because our goods are in demand. As far as possible, a government tries to protect its country's currency against falling too far below a certain level, which it can do by various rather sophisticated means, even by buying its own currency in the market and storing it so that the currency becomes in short supply – the value being geared to the ancient and modern laws of supply and demand.

If they wanted to, a consortium of countries could ruin another country or smaller consortium by selling, selling, selling the currency of the victim(s) so that its value fell badly; but such things only happen in novels, because there are never enough countries that trust each other to form a really strong consortium. Also, there is a perpetual fear of reprisals. Fear holds more people and nations together in the money market than it separates. Trust is the essence of the financial world, mainly because mistrust ruins one's credit, and so everybody plays the game according to the rules. No country is self-sufficient. Every country needs others and, in trade, their currencies.

When a country wants to trade abroad aggressively, but finds its own currency out of favour, it may devalue. The theory is that, if sterling, for example, looks cheap against the dollar, Americans will buy our goods since they become cheap to buy (since Americans can buy more sterling for their dollars). The theory is often upset by the fact that our manufacturers either make undesirable or sub-standard goods or fail to deliver them on time or in other ways fail to capture foreign customers. The hardest currency in the world is making good-value merchandise, selling it effectively and delivering it on time. Because their currencies have been strong for so long, West German, Swiss, Dutch and Japanese goods have often been very expensive compared with British counterparts. But the exports of those countries stayed high because the customers wanted their quality, versatility, service and prompt deliveries. Value is not buying cheap, but buying what you want and getting it when you want it.

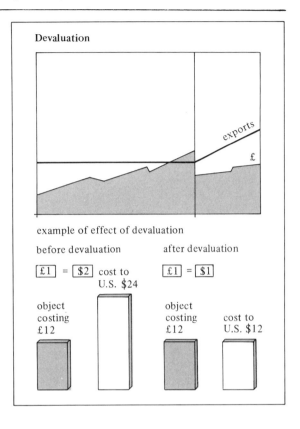

Devaluation

example of effect of devaluation

before devaluation | after devaluation
£1 = $2 cost to U.S. $24 | £1 = $1
object costing £12 | object costing £12 | cost to U.S. $12

The Snake

You may have heard or read of 'the Snake', now killed off as unworkable. It was a much-discussed policy among many countries with the object of keeping currency rates steady one against the other by mutual agreements. It did not work because it was administered by politicians who, because they never trust each other, engendered little trust from their own trading concerns let alone foreign traders. Political moves and government monetary policies could so react on various currencies that gamblers tried to speculate in currencies on what they suspected to be imminent government action. Whether they won or lost is immaterial. The point is that there ensued such hectic foreign-exchange trading activity that rates began to see-saw like crazy, thus defeating the object of the exercise.

European Monetary Agreement

Otherwise known as the European Payments
Union, this was set up in 1950 to act as a
kind of central bank for Europe, a clearing
house for its member countries. It is a complicated organization that keeps trade
accounts for all its members and sets deficits
off against surpluses so that each country's
net balance is clearly on record. Methods
and systems alter frequently enough but the
basis remains the same and it more or less
works, incorporating many mutual international agreements to hold European
currencies fairly stable. Even so, many
financiers would tell you that they would
rather gamble on the tea-leaves than on
what any government and its politicians
reveal or promise.

The I.M.F.

At the heart of the money-go-round is the
International Monetary Fund, the I.M.F.
It began life as an agency of the United
Nations Organization in 1944, with the aim
of improving international trade by making
payments between nations quicker and
simpler. Because it tries to make the currency
of any of its member countries readily
convertible into other currencies, it contributes much to the stability of exchange
rates, and greatly helps those countries
whose coinage is not widely acceptable,
is not easily convertible, thus hindering
that country's ability to trade. Money often
moves in spirals, and this was no exception.
The I.M.F. helped convertibility and made
trade easier for the initially handicapped
countries. As they traded, their currencies
strengthened, became in greater demand and
became convertible.

The I.M.F. is based on international agreements by all members and is not therefore
subject to the vagaries of politicians, which
makes it totally unlike the defunct Snake.
It also arranges loans to members with
balance of payment problems (i.e. those
countries that owe abroad more than they

are earning by their exports, visible and
invisible). The gap between owing more
for imports and receiving less for exports is
an adverse balance of trade, a problem. The
reverse is desirable, just as though countries
were people who like their income to exceed
their outgoings.

The I.M.F. policy is that it means weakness to the whole chain of members to allow
any one country to fall too low in the inter-
trade relationship, that it is necessary to
keep every link in the chain strong if possible.
So it lends to the impecunious, demanding
in return financial policies that put the
borrowing country on its feet as soon as
possible, so that a sensible, good-housekeeping
policy is instituted. Britain has had to borrow
often and Chancellor Denis Healey's cap-in-
hand visit was the last famous one in 1978,
when we got a good deal of stick for being
lazy, unproductive, over-cushioned and not
ready to face our own internal responsibilities. Cuts in public spending, started by
Healey's masters, the Labour Government,
and intensified by the Thatcher Conservative
Government, were part of the many efforts
to keep our budgets in some kind of order,
to reduce our various overdrafts. The many
ways of saving money, raising more and
and generally trying to reduce the debt found
favour with the I.M.F., which was willing
to lend. As you can see, it is rather the same
for individuals. Your credit is good when you
don't need money and anyone would then
lend to you. When you are desperate, when
you need it, the lenders vanish or make
excuses. Of course the Government has to
repay loans to the I.M.F. as and when it can
and subject to certain agreements, from the
money it raises in Britain and from foreign
investments. We have always repaid, and our
credit-worthiness remains.

What we now need is to produce more
goods faster and to sell them widely. Our
annual rate of growth of production has been
falling disastrously since the turn of the
century and, somehow, we seem unable to
raise it again.

The Bank of England

The Bank of England is Britain's central bank, the keeper of the Government's bank account, the seller of Government stocks (the same as shares but always called 'stock' in this context), the printer and provider of our banknotes, the guardian of sterling, the adviser to the world on how to bank and the main link between us and the rest of the financial world.

Besides all that, it is one of the most imposing and lovely historic buildings in this country, a great fortress bounded by four busy City of London streets. The windowless outer stone walls look as though they surround a stronghold, but their hardness is softened by the tall, fluted, graceful pillars that flank the entrance opposite the pillared Royal Exchange. The outer shell was built between 1798 and 1828 under the designing supervision of Sir John Soane, a familiar name to lovers of British architectural history and stately homes of England. The inner building, designed by Sir Herbert Baker, was started at the beginning of the 1920s but, because of the need to continue both work and security while the work went on, it was not finished until just before the 1939 war.

The entrance is wonderful. Beneath the pillared high ceilings are floors of deep grey set with jewel-coloured mosaics of scenes that capture the eye and symbolize the Bank. The main scene on which your feet tread as you enter the large hall is that of St George fighting his fire-breathing dragon, flanked by cornucopia that represent, one assumes, the Bank's wealth. The slate-grey floors carry their many and varied mosaic patterns right through the corridors of the ground floor to the bronze-pillared stone staircase that leads to the first-floor 'banking parlours', as they still call them, leading off thickly-carpeted corridors that lend silence to this part of the building.

Here, heavily-framed paintings of former Bank directors line the walls against which stand antiques polished and maintained with loving care. Longcase clocks, an impressive grandfather and an elegant grandmother, join other clocks and ornaments. Outside the Court Room, where the Court of Directors meet, is a Chippendale desk of incredible solidity yet graceful lines, more or less oval with recesses for the knees of four conferring people.

In one of the parlours hangs what must be one of Britain's finest chandeliers, a huge, sparkling pendant of hundreds of fine crystals, catching the light from the open courtyard, a huge gem that would grace any ballroom. The Court Room itself is a large room with a gallery at one end and doors at each corner. A nice touch is that the two doors at the corners, which would normally lead out onto the courtyard a floor below, are false but they were brought up when the room was rebuilt on the first floor after a long history on the garden courtyard floor.

The high ceiling is fine, painted in fresh colours highlighted with gold, the carpet beneath being especially woven to repeat, as though to reflect, the circular motifs. On the wall above the gallery is a curved slot in which a pointer moves towards the various points of the compass indicated above the curving groove. It is directly connected to the weather-vane on the roof, still there though the directors now make their decisions on much more scientific and precise data than the strength and direction of the winds. But, for an island race, it was essential for those who governed our finances to know whether ships could make port safely and on time.

There are seven floors with three vault floors below. Below them all is the operations room or rooms, where the electricity generator runs, lighting, heating and protecting the Bank and its inmates. It was one of the first buildings ever to instal such a facility, which remains partly because it saves money — and this is a truly cost-conscious organization — but also because it is so reliable, an essential quality when so many computers and security systems must run without risk of stoppage. The Bank even has its own artesian wells from which it draws all its own water supplies. Truly an island fortress.

The Old Lady

The Bank was established in 1694 under an Act of Parliament and Charter with a capital of £1.2 million, then a very large sum. At first privately owned, it was nationalized in 1946 which, amusingly, is a simple re-assembly of the figures that comprise the starting date. It is run by a Governor and Deputy Governor, each appointed for five years, with sixteen directors – all are appointed by the reigning sovereign and any four can become fulltime executive directors.

In the beginning, when it was a bank for industry, commerce and private customers, it was not without problems. Rival bankers, already issuing their own banknotes, resented a strong rival and Tory politicians were suspicious of this body with such high official blessing yet without the history and longevity of the normal establishment organizations. A severe shortage of money in Britain led, in 1696 (two years after the Bank began) to a revaluation of our coins, a kind of internal reconstruction of the value of money, which was confusing, to say the least. And, since confusion breeds uncertainty, there were money worries.

However, through the eighteenth century Britain prospered despite clouds on the economic horizon like the Jacobite rebellion that sought to put the Stuarts back on the throne so that the threat of civil war hung uneasily over our trade affairs. In 1720, the South Sea Bubble burst. The South Sea Company had grown so fast and generated so much trade that it had attracted many investors, not least the Bank of England and many of its depositors. The Bank struggled to maintain its funds and credit-worthiness when the South Sea Company collapsed, owing all the investors a great deal of money.

It was, as the solidly entrenched pillar of the established, often connected with Government and thus attracted some of the hate against Government. In 1709 rioters

attacked as a result of unpopular political policies; later, during the Gordon Riots, the Bank was again in danger from angry men led by Lord George Gordon who wanted publicly to protest against an Act of Parliament that eased the then hard lot of Roman Catholics. Luckily, the rioters first stormed Newgate Prison and took a day of rest during which the secret of the attack on the Bank leaked out. When they arrived to invade, a corps of horse and foot guards had arrived to defend the Bank. For nearly two centuries after that night, until 1973, guards came from the barracks at Knightsbridge to defend the Bank. Since 1973, it has run its own security system.

In the latter part of the nineteenth century, mainly to speed the expansion of the issue of notes and their distribution, the Bank opened branches in 14 towns or cities of which 7 remain in Birmingham, Bristol, Leeds, Liverpool, Manchester, Newcastle and Southampton. The Bank had been given the sole right in England and Wales to print and distribute banknotes, a landmark in the Bank's history proving its proper official status and standing with the Government.

The nickname of the Bank, 'The Old Lady of Threadneedle Street', is thought to have originated from a cartoon by one James Gillray during the Napoleonic wars. The wars were bleeding the Government funds and Pitt the Younger was pleading for money. Gillray's cartoon showed Pitt trying to wrest the Bank's hoard of gold from an old lady sitting on a locked chest guarding it with her life. Though the main entrance is no longer on Threadneedle Street, that is still one of the Bank's bordering streets and the official address.

Though the Bank still transacts ordinary banking business, the number of private customers decreases year by year, probably because of the greater convenience of local High Street clearing banks. The Bank would not now accept new private accounts, though staff bank accounts are serviced and they use the grand Drawing Office, as the banking hall is still called.

What the Old Lady does

1. She is the central bank of the nation and Government's banker (but not the Queen's, as so many people believe – the Queen banks at Coutts, part of the National Westminster Group).

   The Government needs much the same services we all expect from our own local banks but a lot more besides. The Bank looks after the accounts of Her Majesty's Exchequer (hence the ministerial title of 'Chancellor of the Exchequer') and the National Loans Fund, to which all Government income finds its way and from which payments are made after being authorized by Government. Various Government departments also bank there, though they are not forced to do so.

   She is also the bank to all the other banks, yours and mine and to a great many overseas banks.

   She is banker to many of the nationalized industries – though they are free to bank where they like and often run more than one account.

   As Government banker, the Old Lady has the job of receiving, paying out and transferring Government funds. She might also invest Government funds to make them grow or, if the investment be something like British Leyland, diminish. The Government must authorize all that it spends and such accounts are carefully monitored by and have to be accounted for to the Comptroller General; he then has to present properly audited accounts to Parliament which, in turn, must justify them to the electorate (if the latter ever tries to understand them, though they are announced in the Budget and clearly set out in specialist financial newspapers).

2. The Bank takes care of the Government's cash needs by borrowing or lending. Short-, medium- or long-term borrowing is done through the gilt-edged market (see Chapter 7). The Government effectively sells shares in itself and its operations, thus borrowing from shareholders the money it needs to finance such operations. The Government's promise to repay the loans at fixed dates is sacrosanct, as are the promises to meet annual agreed interest. The Bank's other sources of income are, naturally, income tax, duties, indirect taxes, that kind of thing. The Government also invests, as we have seen, in good or bad investments, depending on the country's needs (see Chapter 7: Stocks and Shares).

3. The Bank manages these Government stocks (they are always called 'stocks' in the context of Government shares), which form the bulk of what is called the National Debt, that debt being what the Government owes on the stock it has sold through the Bank of England. The registers of all the names of all stockholders are kept on storage discs and updated every day, with alterations processed by computer. The Bank also acts as Registrar for nationalized industries' shares and other borrowers from Government as well as lenders to Government.

   The Government pays dividends on the stock it sells, usually called interest and usually fixed (see Chapter 7).

4. The Bank also runs the Exchange Equalization Account, governing all exchange control regulations; these determine how much we may buy of foreign currency or spend abroad of British sterling. In 1979, exchange control was dropped, partly on the advice of the Bank itself because sterling seemed strong enough to find its own way around the world without being cossetted, protected and virtually imprisoned in England.

   If exchange controls are again imposed, and we again become restricted to how much we can spend abroad or how much sterling we can exchange for foreign currency, the Bank will again control it. The job may be non-existent, but the responsibility has not been taken away if ever needed again.

5. And the Bank is financial consultant

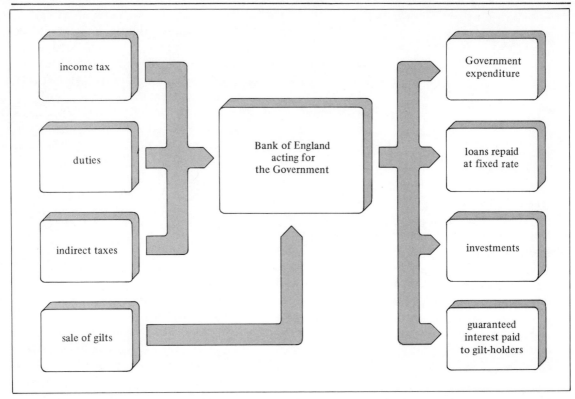

and adviser to the Government.

Issuing banknotes

The Bank of England runs the design, all stages of production and printing and the final distribution of banknotes. Since the end of the nineteenth century, all private banknote printing has been stopped in England and Wales, though Scotland, Ireland, Isle of Man and the Channel Isles continue to be allowed the privilege of their own banks' notes though such notes are not legal tender (legal tender being the notes and coin that *must* be accepted as payment of debt). The notes are, however, accepted by custom, especially by banks, though often refused by shops.

British banknotes are the best in the world, yet the cheapest to make. The paper is made by Portals, a famous Hampshire-based firm also noted for its water-treatment skills (the River Test runs through its grounds and is a testing ground for many water-cleansing and improvement systems). The special paper is watermarked and so produced as to contain all kinds of security markings or ingredients that are very difficult to copy — forgery, an occupational pastime in America, is so rare here as to be virtually non-existent because British paper could change fairly often. A metallic thread runs through it, also difficult to copy, and the mixture may also change. Counterfeiters beware.

The paper then goes to Loughton, Essex, for printing. More than 8 million notes are printed daily, on average. That's 8 million actual notes, the value being much greater since they can be of any value, from £1 upwards. Each note costs roughly 1p to produce, which sounds cheap enough until you realize that means £80,000 a day production cost. Old notes come back after being 'garbled', being sorted out by experienced staff in the many banks that use notes. Garbling takes out the notes that are about to fall apart, which are then bundled, returned to Loughton and burned in the furnaces there to provide central heating and hot water. In fact, notes are the only

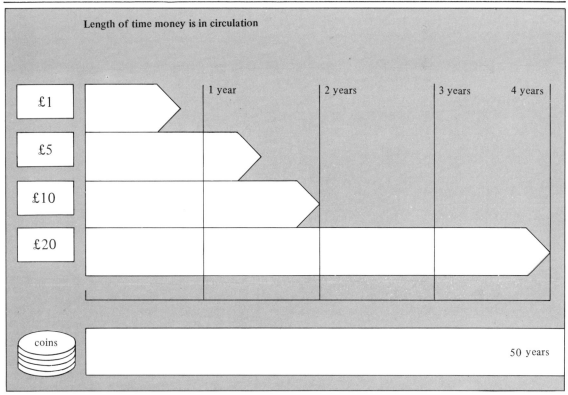

Length of time money is in circulation

	1 year	2 years	3 years	4 years
£1				
£5				
£10				
£20				

coins — 50 years

fuel burned at Loughton, which makes it nearly as self-sufficient as The Old Lady in Threadneedle Street herself.

A £1 note lasts about 10 months, while a £5 note runs to about 18 months, a £10 note 2 years and a £20 goes on in reasonable condition for 4 years. This could change if more credit cards are used, reducing the handling of notes, but the life expectation has remained pretty consistent even through rising inflation when you might expect to see fivers and tenners getting more and more use. Coins are made by the Royal Mint and each has an approximate life of about 50 years. Many still have the fluted, milled rims that were designed to prevent people filing away the edges of gold or silver. The filing would no longer be of any value to anyone but the milled edges remain. By the same token, all but the new £1 notes still bear their serial number twice, printed on each side of the note.

The original object was to defeat highwaymen and footpads. Notes were torn in half and carried to London by separate coaches and teams, to be matched only at the secret place of destination, thus making paper money at least not worth stealing.

We use few notes around January, and the demand rises slightly and slowly towards Easter, where we have the first low peak. Then there is a short decline, but demand starts to pick up again in late May, moving gradually upwards through the tourist, holiday and summer season, rising to the highest peak on or near December 21st, depending on how the shopping days fall. Thus, though production is about 8 million notes daily, the distribution varies to meet demand, and not all the £9,600 million pounds' worth of money allowed to be issued is always in circulation.

At times, if demand should run ahead of production and stocks of new notes, banks will be asked to make their garbling of old notes a trifle less selective just to keep enough in circulation. At such times, you get 'reissued' notes, no new ones from your local banks. Customers grumble but these are better than none.

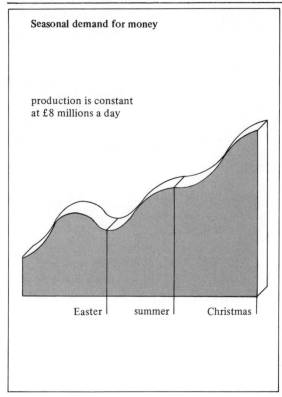

Seasonal demand for money

production is constant
at £8 millions a day

Easter | summer | Christmas

Fiduciary issue

I have already described this as the issue of notes not backed by gold reserves held by the issuing government; the issue is always fixed by the Government, and the permitted issue in 1844 was £14 million, when we needed that much over and above the value of our gold reserves. The amount climbed gradually until 1928 when a £260 million limit was set, subject to periodic review by Parliament. Britain came off the gold standard in 1919, climbed back on again in 1925 and finally came off for good and all in 1931.

By 1935 all but a small token amount of the annual money issue was fiduciary. In 1979, notes to the value of £9,600 million were issued. The way the Government, the Treasury and those that look after our finances actually settle the amount of money we need is not simple enough to explain here; but, in the simplest terms, they give an order to print however much is in demand. When I tell you that the 1945 total was £1,300, you can see we now need nearly 7½ times as much money as we did in 1945.

How the Bank of England controls the money supply.

Because the availability of credit is really 'money', the Bank of England can squeeze the amount of money around by limiting or discouraging borrowing. One of the ways of discouraging borrowing is to raise interest rates (which also has the beneficial effect of encouraging people to save, and foreigners to put their money on deposit in England). The Bank of England can also limit the amount of money banks are allowed to lend. When she is trying to limit credit, the Bank is using her 'corset'.

The Banking Act April 1979

The slump of 1974 is indelibly scarred on the memories of many; property prices plummeted and fringe banks crashed because so many of them were invested in property or had depositors who were and who were forced into disastrous, money-losing sales of their office blocks and residential developments. The bankruptcies were mostly averted by the Bank of England's 'lifeboat', the popular term to describe the Bank's rescue operations; they underpinned loans from clearing banks to troubled borrowers.

The Bank is far from profligate and those kept afloat by the lifeboat had to prove their capacity for recovery; companies had to reform, and review and often change their management structures. The Old Lady helped only those she judged sound, and many are now on firm, dry and profitable land.

Companies were not the only victims and many private people lost money: one good result was the 1979 Banking Act, which became law in October of that year. It requires that any and every organization taking deposits be specially authorized, be forced to seek specific permission from the Bank of England and be subject to their vetting and continued close scrutiny.

The Old Lady has two lists of deposit-takers: in one are the familiar, recognized banks who give the wide services we all know and use; then there is a second tier of licensed deposit-takers that give fewer but specialized services and these include hire-purchase companies and such.

All must have adequate capital and liquidity in the form of realizeable assets which can rapidly be converted to cash, as well as some hard cash reserves. There is now little excuse for anyone giving money to a financial firm for any dubious scheme because anyone can write to the Bank of England to query the standing of the firm with which they plan to do business, deposit their money or enter into hire-purchase agreement. The Bank will not disclose the firm's financial details but will confirm whether or not it is on one of the authorized lists. Alas, consumers are too often their own worst enemies, tempted by glowing advertisements promising apparently rich rewards and it is still incredible how many people trustingly send cheques to all sorts of dubious concerns. Since such concerns are still likely to exist and to advertise, it is well worth checking on at least their solvency. The Bank, a principal adviser to Government on monetary policy, is also our friend.

What is money?

In Britain we as individuals rarely discuss it, are even shy about it and entirely reluctant to understand it or its use — the Americans are much more sophisticated about the whole financial world. Oddly, our increasing openness and frankness in regard to sex and its deviations have not extended to money, about which we still have Victorian attitudes. It is considered in rather bad taste to talk about your earnings and investments unless they happen to be either spectacularly high or low. We complain about money a lot, too, but we rarely express joy in that context and it is genuinely thought to be rather blue-stocking to know anything much about it at all. Women are especially resistant; I was recently interviewing a number of girls about to take their A levels, none of whom were taking any kind of financial or economic subject.

This worried me because there are so many good jobs in the money world that women could enjoy and in which they could earn well, taking time off to have their babies without losing their positions or earning powers since the analytical, stockbroking and other money jobs rarely need more than a refresher course to get back to after absence. The girls were more or less unanimous that money was stuffy, blue-stocking, deadly unattractive and likely to repel boyfriends. I was also taken aback that, in this day and age, youngsters still seem to think that men manage money and women, even with their greater earning powers and better opportunities, are still dependants.

Money is, as we saw from the start, a symbol. It is not just cash (or what the Americans call 'the poor man's credit card'). It is coin, paper, cheques, plastic cards, bonds, stocks and shares, mortgages, anything. There is no answer to why one currency should be worth more than another, or why gold should be more valuable than the same weight in silver. Or, if there is an answer, it lies in the old, old law of supply and demand. If all the pebbles in the world were pounded into sand, then men and nations would fight over gravel and stones as they do over gold. If one company is doing so well that everyone wants its shares, then the share price rises. If a country is exporting like mad and getting rich, its currency is in great demand and gathers strength so that the mark, the yen, Swiss franc or whatever can buy more dollars or pounds per unit of its own currency.

Money is also what the Government prosaically calls 'chattels', belongings like fine paintings, rare Oriental carpets, Ming china and *objets d'art* or fine wines. It is in fact anything negotiable, anything that can readily be converted back into those coins and pieces of paper we think of as money but which in the financial word are regarded only as cash symbols of part of the available money supply. There are some anecdotes to signify the City's attitude to cash, its dislike of cash, not paper. One is the story of the merchant banker who rang the chairman of a company for whom he had arranged a takeover. 'I have good news and bad news,' said the banker. 'We can buy Company A for £7 million instead of £8 million as I had feared. The bad news is that we have to find £250,000 in cash.' That may be apocryphal but it is true that, when a director of Warburg's, the top merchant bank which at that time was masterminding the takeover of a huge publishing empire by the Mirror Newspapers group (now Reed International), rose from a meeting which had decided to raise the offer price above its initial offer, he said, 'That settles it. We go up £5 million.' He left, only to return to the boardroom a few moments later to ask, 'Can anyone lend me five bob (now 25p) for the taxi fare back to the City?'

They say Royalty never carries cash. And, if the rash of credit cards from chain stores and supermarkets is any guide, we shall soon be as close to a cashless society in Britain as they are in America where, they say, you need only enough cash for taxis and tipping.

We have been slow to trust cashless transactions but banks are enthusiastic about discouraging cash and encouraging cheques and cards not because we are thereby tempted to spend more, as the cynics insist, but because it cuts down risks of theft and loss as well as the cost of security. A facility for credit does tempt us to spend more, and it should thus energize us all to learn more about money so that, being familiar with it, we can better control it.

Credit cards are a serious worry to the Government, however, who are less able to curb our spending. It was never very difficult to apply the corset on money supplies and to pull the whalebone tightly. It is extremely difficult to curb credit spending. That is, how ever, the Government's special problem. More and more, our money will be electronic symbols, little flashes of light, flitting, like Tinker Bell across a Christmas theatre, from one bank to another, one town to another, one country to another as it so often does already. We shall buy our groceries with

cards, and those little electronic flashes will debit our accounts as fast as we can spend the money (equally speeding up the input of our funds).

Already banking hours are becoming things of the past as far as withdrawals are concerned and bank customers are more and more keyboarding their money needs from machines implanted in the banks' outer walls, such machines being able to give the current state of the person's account on a tiny paper printout as well as being able to yield banknotes. National Westminster was one of the pioneers of outer-wall withdrawals when it introduced the 'ten-pounders' (because each keyboard operation yielded £10). It is replacing the old ten-pounders with modern service tills that pay out £100, £200 or whatever your particular credit limit is, plus data on your current account.

Lloyds, which originally installed its Cashpoint machines inside the banks, is now stepping up the number of outsiders while Barclaybank equipment is coming into more and more shopping streets (Midland Bank, a late starter compared with the others, is now automating fast). Soon, these service tills or cashpoints will not only be in the bank walls but at factory gates, near cinemas and shops, at any convenient place, and there could be competition for wall sites – how soon I cannot predict but it will come and people will be able to draw cash almost anywhere (always subject to credit limits).

Equally, we shall probably be using Eurocheques before long, to say nothing of Eurocards so that we can vend ourselves cash anywhere in the European community and even in fringe countries. The saving of costs on security, on what are euphemistically termed leakages, of large-scale thefts and even of lives, make the plastic cards and the keyboard inevitable substitutes for money. Not, maybe, as much fun to gloat over a plastic card as a bundle of banknotes but much, much safer. Governments, worldwide, will print as much money as their peoples need. Inflation will climb on.

Money to the older generations is something which now seems to have endless noughts tagged on to the end of it; they may recall what could be done with 6d when they were little. Up to the first wartime budget of 1940, the old sixpenny piece (now 2½p) could buy half a pint of beer, a packet of five cigarettes, a box of matches and a sausage roll or tiny pie, and on some of these get change of either ¼d or ½d, depending on the type of beer or your appetite for pie or sausage roll. The fact remains that, despite what looks to us like (and is) rampant inflation, salaries and wages have risen faster over the years than inflation — never catching up, but narrowing the gap slightly. A bottle of whisky, in the context of today's average earnings, is cheaper than when it was 12 old shillings (60p). Beer costs more and so does housing, as do cars. It is one of the sadnesses that many necessities also do, but one of the better things that at least we have a more caring State.

As inflation continues, we may in the future choose to do what the French did in the 'fifties, and knock a nought off our currency, introducing new pounds as they introduced new francs. Thus, in time, the pound could become 10p, the 10p piece 1p and we might have New Pounds just to stop the whole thing becoming unwieldy, and having to hand over several pounds for a short train ride or a few litres of petrol.

What is money? Believe me, I cannot tell you more than that it is something of which we all, however poor or rich, want more. But money does not have fully to be understood to be enjoyed, manipulated to our own desires and ends and used to enrich our lives. The main thing is not to be blasé. Even if you eat caviar, don't lose that slight thrill that comes with acquiring something that gives pleasure to you and yours, that old feeling of still getting a kick from a 2p lollipop stick, as the song has it. As long as you have 2p and go on liking lollipops, whatever the transformation of cost and commodity in that sentence, you will be fine.

Technical Terms

Arbitrage. Dealing in commodities, securities or currencies to profit from the differences between two or more markets. If eggs are cheap in England and expensive in France . . . OK, that's a fairy story without a happy ending.

Asset, asset-backing, asset-stripping. Assets can consist of cash, stock, debts to the company, buildings, plant and machinery, goodwill, patented inventions and such. Asset-backing is the net assets divided by the number of issued shares. If Smith and Co. have £1 million of net assets and 200,000 shares, the asset-backing is £5 per share. Every shareholder should know exactly what the asset-backing is to compare it with the share price, but too few actually even think about it. Asset-stripping is what a company's owners or managers do when they sell off or strip the assets rather than putting them to work for the good of the company. Jim Slater was a famous stripper.

At the Back Door describes the way the Bank of England helps the money market by injecting more cash or by juggling cash needs by interfering with interest rates. At the Front Door is the term for the money market members doing things in their own way, when the Bank of England neither helps nor intervenes.

Bank Giro. A system to speed up money transfers between the British clearing banks.

Bankrupt. Unable to pay one's debts. Once a crime, though unpunishable by law, but subject to many restrictions. Still limiting, but more often the better way out, an admission of inability to pay and an expression of willingness to try, to do what one can. A bankrupt files a court petition with a full list of assets and debts with names of people and companies to whom money is owed. Once the bankrupt has paid all debts, or paid as much as any court thinks he or she can humanly manage at so much in every £1 owed, a bankrupt may apply for a discharge. The stigma, the disgrace of being a bankrupt varies in degree according to the ease with which credit can be got. In America, bankrupts tend to get sympathy (remember Mickey Rooney and George Sanders). Here, much the same is beginning to happen.

Bargains are deals on the Stock Exchange; all those prices at the back of the *Financial Times* and *Times* are the prices of bargains or deals. In the City, the word has nothing to do with cut prices so, when your stockbroker refers to bargains he has done for you,

never relate to reductions. For those, try the local grocer or electrician (see Chapter 7).

Barter. The exchange of goods instead of the exchange of goods for money. On TV, they call it 'Swap Shop'.

Bearer Bonds or **Stocks** are certificates for securities of which ownership can be instantly transferred from seller to buyer without a formal deed or re-registration.

Below the Line. Once almost entirely a Government term, used when Budgets were being presented, as it still is. Below the line payments and receipts are those concerning capital payments and loans such as to nationalized industries or for public works, etc. These items are not voted on each year but are accepted as Government costs. Below the line also includes interest paid by the Government on its own debts just as the receipts include interest received, among other things. So, when the Chancellor presents a Budget, he gives this below-the-line arithmetic as well as above-the-line items, which are mainly current commitments and contingencies. Now often used to describe the profit line.

Bradbury. The banknotes your father or grandfather knew, issued between 1914 and 1919 and signed by John Bradbury, then Secretary to the Treasury.

Break-up value is the value of a company's realizeable assets minus its liabilities and any priority charges such as preference stocks, etc. A phrase often found in comments on companies and something eagerly scanned by takeover bidders who look for companies with a break-up value that is much, much higher than the market value of the company based on the share price. The difference between the two pays for the many costs, and yields a fast profit even after offering and paying shareholders a nice, lucrative premium above the share price.

Budget. Every government's and every company's plan for the time ahead, be that a month or a year. The Budget includes forecasts of spending and income and is – or should be – flexible and adjusted as time goes on and as actual figures come in or circumstances alter forecasts up or down.

Bullion is simply gold or silver in bulk, as ingots, bars, etc., not made up as gold objects.

Busted Bond is something you ought not to have and should not consider risking, which is why you might as well know what it is. It is a loan to a Government which has ceased to pay interest; speculators buy them in case the interest is revived which, historically, it has been from time to time but only for brief time. Britain has not been guilty, though central Europe and some other areas have been.

Capital. Any asset, be it cash, bricks and mortar or a business, as long as it is saleable on an open market and negotiable for cash. Assets that cannot be disposed of, such as the raw materials needed for manufacturing, are not normally classed as capital.

Capital intensive. Production methods are capital intensive when involving equipment that is costly in proportion to the number of people employed and manhours worked. If capital charges account for more than about half the costs of production, the production is capital intensive.

Captive Markets. Markets catered for by monopolies. Before natural gas was found the gas industry was a captive market for the Coal Board. The nationalized industries enjoy captive markets – and we consumers are the captives.

Cartel. A sales ring; a central selling body of which the members have a share in the combined output. No one member can exceed his agreed output.

Cash flow. Simply the cash that goes through a business, in or out. It may be positive (more coming in than going out) or negative (vice versa).

Cheap Money. Money that is available for borrowing at low interest rates.

C.I.F. Stands for Cost, Insurance and Freight. Prices for shipped goods are quoted C.I.F., meaning the seller meets all costs up to the goods being on board ship. F.O.B. (Free on Board) is the opposite of C.I.F.

Closing prices. Prices of all stocks, shares, etc., at the close of daily dealings in London's Stock Exchange. (Provincial exchanges keep the same hours.) The prices are those given in most published lists, apart from lists that mark all bargains (or deals). After-hours dealing does take place and there can therefore be changes between closing and opening (next day) prices.

Collateral. The security put in charge or on deposit against a loan. Can be anything from a building to life assurance certificates, but is often shares. As a rule, the lender will want the securities to come to about three times the value of the loan to allow for market fluctuations (especially downwards). Our advice is to play just a little safer than the bank docs, especially if the collateral represents all your assets.

Consumer durables. Merchandise that lasts for some time, such as washing machines, furniture, etc.

Coming out price. The price at which new shares are issued.

Commodity. A product or products and/or services in demand, according to most dictionaries. But a special market in the City, where dealers handle things like tea, cocoa, coffee, rubber, sugar, copper, lead, tin and such, dealing in goods rather as the Stock Exchange deals in shares.

Consols. Government stock or other securities which, though soundly founded, do not have to be repaid until the Government is good and ready. Short for 'consolidated annuities'. Will have a percentage annuity (3 per cent giving £3 per £100 nominal and adjustable according to the rise of the nominal £100 share). Selling prices tend to be geared to the yield.

Convertibles. Stocks that carry the right or option to convert into other stocks or shares. Usually debenture or preferred stock.

Cornering. The buying of as much as possible of a certain commodity in order to build up a monopoly and then charge whatever you like for the stuff. Rarely done nowadays but was popular in the 1920s and 1930s.

Credit transfers. Transfers via a bank or similar financial institution to someone else's account so that no actual cash is passed or tranferred.

Dated securities. Otherwise Dated Stocks or Government issues. They have a stated date for the cash repayment (in jargon, 'redemption') of the face value of the stock.

Deflation. Falling prices and incomes, usually coinciding with an economic slump. Technically, what happens when money is not being spent on the available supply of goods and services.

Denarius. The old Roman coin that became our pre-decimalization penny, which was symbolized with a 'd' (in Lsd, the others being Libri and Solidi for pounds and shillings). It is interesting only because it meant 'ten asses' in Latin, which goes to show what you could buy in Britain when Julius Caesar came, saw and conquered compared with an Oxo cube when the 'd' went from our coinage in 1972 (see Inflation).

Depreciation. The fall in value of anything. From loss of funds, from wear and tear, from obsolescence, from any circumstance. In currency, not too dissimilar from devaluation.

Devaluation. The act of reducing the value of one's currency against foreign currencies, usually to make goods cheaper to tempt foreigners to buy them, to lure tourists, to increase exports. Economists like it, the Bank of England hates it and it can make a country distrusted. Sterling, almost respectable once, fell into disrepute through the 'sixties and 'seventies but is almost respectable now. In fact, whether a nation's greatness and wealth does depend on maintaining its currency rates against the once-almighty dollar is now open to doubt. For see how the mighty are fallen! The dollar lies very low now against the pound. Indeed, there are those in the money market who forecast the dollar as 'the next confetti' – like the German mark of the 1930s (see Chapter 10).

Disposable income. The total of personal income left after subtracting all tax commitments, National Insurance payments and any other payment the State might make mandatory.

Dividend cover. The degree to which the dividend is covered by a company's earnings (see Chapter 7).

Double taxation. System of two taxes calculated on the same 'base'. In America, where they have a national (Federal) and a State (local) tax system, they have double taxation. Anyone living and working in two countries may be taxed in both. However, most countries have got together to sort this out by means of double taxation relief, which prevents this punishment through agreements to absolve the individual from tax in one country.

Dow Jones averages. The index of share prices in America, the equivalent of our own *Financial Times* index.

Engels' Law is the law that the percentage of a household's spending money on food is the real measurement of the family's living standards and that the percentage lessens as income rises. In fact, this law has been changed to bring other essential items into account so that its name remains to describe modernized, adapted variations on the original theme.

Equity is the goodwill and assets of a company after all liabilities have been deducted. The equity normally belongs to the ordinary shareholders and, if any, the holders of deferred securities. You will hear the word used merely to mean a block of shares in the company.

Equities are the ordinary shares of a limited company, which give holders the rights to the company's assets after all liabilities and to a profits distribution. Loosely and frequently used as a synonym for shares – people talk of 'investing in equities' when they mean buying shares (see Chapter 7).

Ernie. Electronic random number computer that picks Premium Bond winners.

Eurodollars are American dollars held by people living outside the United States. These dollars serve a large dollar market in Europe.

Face Value is the nominal value printed or written on any document such as £1 note or a bond or some such paper money. The market value is not always the face value.

Financial or Fiscal year is the Government's accounting year. In Britain, the financial year is from April 1st to March 31st the following year but, for fiscal year, the dates are April 6th to April 5th the following year, during which the Chancellor of the Exchequer must present his Budget, his accounts.

Fiscal Policy. The Government's financial policy, the way it raises revenue and influences the level of business and financial activity by us all.

Floating Exchange Rate. An uncontrolled exchange rate, allowing the currency to find its own natural level against other currencies.

F.O.B. Free on Board, the term used to describe goods of which the price excludes freight or insurance costs. The seller therefore pays all costs up to the aircraft, ship or container only. The letters appear on quotations, invoices, etc. Opposite of C.I.F.

Forward purchase, forward exchange, etc.
Buying securities or currency for delivery at
a future date at an agreed price. Sometimes
called 'futures' (mainly in goods and commodities) or 'options'. Companies buy
forward currency when they want protection
against the possible devaluation of a currency
at or near delivery and payment time.

Fringe benefits. Payments in kind, part of
the remuneration that an employee gets on
top of normal earnings such as the company
car, medical insurance, canteens, meal
vouchers, subsidized travel, clothes hire, etc.
Must be declared on tax form (see Chapter
2).

Futures. Market for buying and selling
future deliveries (usually of commodities).

Gazumping. Mainly used in the context of
buying and selling houses, this means any
higher offer for goods which the buyer is
unprepared to accept although he has
already given his word to accept a lower
offer but uses the let-out that he has so far
put nothing in writing.

Giffen goods. Inferior goods. So-called since
Sir Robert Giffen highlighted for economists
how the staple diet of the poor included
unduly large quantities of bread and potatoes
of poor quality because they were cheap,
filling foods. Has come to mean shoddy
goods too.

Gross National Product. Usually G.N.P., the
jargon for the 'total value at current or
constant prices of the annual flow of goods
and services available to a country for consumption and maintaining or adding to its
material wealth'. Now you know.

Growth Stocks. Shares with rapid increases
in value as the companies raise earnings
and assets.

Growthmanship. President (Watergate)
Nixon's word for the pursuit of economic
growth at the expense of other national
economic objectives, intended critically.

Hard Currency. Any stable currency that is
welcomed worldwide and is readily convertible into other currencies because the under-
lying strength of the country to which it
belongs is trusted, a trust often judged by
that country's balance of payments. Gold
was probably the first hard currency that
gave us the name but the dollar became the
principal hard currency after the Second
World War and held that place, with the
German mark, the Dutch guilder and the
Swiss franc joining alongside it, until the end
of the 'seventies, when sterling hardened.
A soft currency is the Russian rouble, for
one example, which is accepted almost
nowhere except in Iron Curtain countries,
where you can sometimes get a much
higher rate for your hard coinage than is
stated in official circles.

Hot Money. The money that moves between
countries as the owners (sometimes called
investors) move in or out to take advantage
of special circumstances or to avoid them.
A 17 per cent interest rate, as announced in
November 1979 attracted a lot of hot
money into Britain because of the attractive
yields involved. As a currency looks like
hardening, hot money will move into it —

Inflation is something you feel and know even
if you have no money — or especially if you
have no money. To our grandparents it meant
a car cost £120 in 1938 instead of £100 in
1935. To us, it means everything soaring
expensively out of reach. In living memory
(for many of us, anyway) the most rampant
inflation was in Germany in the 'twenties,
when people used Deutschmarks to paper
their walls because it was cheaper than buying
wallpaper. Germany's second bout was after
the Second World War when barter took
over from those rarities, coins and banknotes,
and when a packet of tea, tin of coffee or
packet of sugar were more valuable than
coins. William Davies, well-known financial
journalist who spent his boyhood in Germany,
says he was at school when he began to
realize that chocolate bars were for eating,
not simply money or trading currency.

Instalment Credit. Hire purchase to you
and me.

Inter vivos, or gifts or money transfers
made during the life of the owner. Used by
Inland Revenue in context of CTT, etc.

Irredeemable Securities, such as a loan.
Another way of saying Undated Stocks,
on which there is no redemption date and, if
the Government never redeems, the price can
plummet. They can be bought and sold in the
Stock Market but the Government won't
honour them as they have no obligation to
do so.

Laisser faire. A French phrase used by economists to describe a specific policy of
allowing market forces to work, without
too much Government control or intervention.

Leaders and Laggards The popular way
of describing shares (and companies) that
do well or badly. The top and bottom of
their leagues.

Leak. Abhorred and loved by the City,
according to whether it makes shares go up
or down and whether such movements
accord with City tactics as a whole. Frequently used deliberately, especially by
politicians who want to fly kites to see
what everyone thinks, or who hope to force
a line of action.

Legal Tender. Money that must be accepted
in settlement of a debt. In Britain, copper
may be refused if the coins total 20p or more.
A boy who, in 1979, was fined for skate-
boarding in a prohibited area, tried to pay
with the contents of his money box and was
refused so that he had to get his small change
converted into legal tender.

Liquidity. The state of having cash or assets
readily realizeable into cash. Cash is very
liquid, Government stocks are pretty liquid,
paintings and antiques less so.

Loss Leader. A retail phrase for merchandise.
sold at a loss to attract what they call 'store
traffic' and what you and I term 'customers'.

Money Supply. Jargon again, a phrase
which refers to the liquidity of our banks
and money markets, meaning the supply
of the stuff readily available to us to spend.
The control of it by politicians, governing
their monetary policy, can be a brake or
an accelerator on our spending,

Pump Priming. A Keynesian theory, an
attempt to revive flagging economies by
Government spending even if the Government's own deficit becomes severe as it
subsidizes the nationalized and other industries to combat unemployment and slump.
Sometimes called 'deficit spending'.

Purchase Tax. Now extinct in England, the
forerunner of Value Added Tax.

Quota. In international trade a way of protecting home industries by imposing quota
restrictions on certain imports, by rationing
goods that compete with our own. Sometimes achieved by raising tariffs.

Rat Race. The blind pursuit of success,
probably called after the headlong rush of
rats after the Pied Piper of Hamelin or the
way they leave a sinking ship. Alleged to be
something everyone longs to escape, actually
something many cannot wait to join.

Real Income. Salary or wages adjusted to
changes in levels of current prices. It means,
perhaps, that the £10 per week increase is,
in real terms, only £4. You know exactly
what I mean.

Redemption. 'Payment back'. The Government does not repay but redeems gilts at
the maturing or redemption dates. No
rhyme nor reason. More jargon.

Reflation. The act or period of recovery from
slump before a country gets started once more
on inflation. Yes, known in living memory.

Scrip. Short for subscription, so you get a
scrip certificate (for shares, debentures or
government bonds). It certifies you've paid
and is eventually exchanged for the proper
share certificate once you are on the relevant
register of shareholders. Also 'scrip dividend',
a provisional certificate for dividends; and
scrip issue, slightly different, being an issue
of 'free' additional shares in proportion to
those you already hold in the issuing company.

Soft Currency. Obviously opposite of hard
currency: an unpopular currency that is
difficult to convert into acceptable currency.
Like the rouble.

Speculation. Euphemism for gambling,
buying (hopefully) cheap to sell dear.

Stale Cheque. One that is more than six
months old, out of date, useless.

Stop-Go. A persistent trait of the British
economy since about 1945, a policy that
suddenly accelerates and brakes the economy, fluctuating between measures to boost
production and cut unemployment, and
measures to cut spending which leads to
reduced production which . . . . Usually
unleashed and leashed by regulators and mini-
Budgets between standard annual Budgets.

Surplus. Wouldn't it be luvverly?

Surtax, supertax. What the wealthy used to
hate having to pay and what most wished
they could qualify to pay. Outdated by
stepping-stone system of tax and replaced by
surcharges on rates of income tax at higher
levels of unearned income (currently above
£5,000 per annum).

Tax. I pass.

Tax Avoidance. Legal avoidance of taxes. For instance, you can legally avoid to pay income tax at all if you earn too little. Or you can avoid paying tax on articles you buy entirely for business use; and so forth.

Tax Evasion. The illegal evasion of paying tax.

Tax Havens. Those places with low taxation – Channel Isles, Monte Carlo, Switzerland, California, etc. But beware. Other drawbacks may exist. In California, the property laws can bankrupt anyone in a marriage who wishes to end the marriage by divorce.

Treasury Bills. Short-term bearer securities with a maturity term of 91 days. In big denominations of £5,000, £10,000 or £50,000.

Underwriting. Literally writing a name under a guarantee to pay so much in the event of such money not being realized from the sale of shares or in the event of having to pay compensation on an insurance claim

Viability. The ability to pay all debts, to meet all financial obligations.

Zero Growth. The ultimate undesirable.

Index

'A' shares, 132
A.P.A. (additional personal allowance), 26-7, 39
Access card, 16-17
accidents, insurance against, 87-8
Account (Stock Exchange), 117
accountants, 23-5, 42
additional personal allowance (A.P.A.), 26-7, 39
'age allowance', 29-30
agricultural land, exemptions from capital transfer tax, 45
allowances, tax, *see* tax allowances
American Express Card, 16-17
animals, insurance for, 90
annuities, 83-6; deferred, 83-4; guaranteed, 83; joint survivor, 85; minimum, 85; reversionary, 85; tax on, 30, 85-6
antiques, buying, 160
Association of Scottish Life Offices, 87
assurance, *see* insurance
auction sales, 160

Balance of payments, 10-11
bank(s), 9-22; 'Big Four', 10; borrowing from, 13-18; clearing, 10-12; fringe, 21; history of, 9-10; merchant, 21; National Giro, 20; National Savings, 20-21; services of, 11, 12; Trustee Savings, *see* Trustee Savings Banks
bank accounts, 18-20; budget, 16; deposit, 19, 94; direct debits from, 19-20; drawing money from, 18-19; joint, 19; standing orders, 19-20
bank charges, 12-13
bank cheque cards, 18
Bank of England, 177-83; history of, 178; issue of banknotes, 180-82; operation of, 179-80
bank loans, *see under* loans
bank manager, choice of, 12
bank overdrafts, 14
bank service tills, 184-5
banknotes, issue of, 180-81; fiduciary, 182
Banking Act (1979), 182-3
Barclaycard, 16-17; as bank cheque card, 18
'bargains' (Stock Exchange), 119
bear (Stock Exchange), 117-18
Beveridge Plan, 97-8
BIBA (British Insurance Brokers' Association), 86
blind persons: increased supplementary

benefit rate, 102; tax allowance, 30
blue chips, 133
bonds, 95; British Savings, tax on, 46
Bondshares, building society, 154
bonus issues of shares, 130-31
book-keepers, 24-5
borrowing money (*see also* loans), 167-8
brokers, *see* stockbrokers
'bounced' cheques, 13
British Insurance Brokers' Association (BIBA), 86
British Savings Bonds, tax on, 46
budget accounts, 16
building societies (*see also* house, purchase of; mortgages); Bondshares, 154; history of, 51-5; investment in, 152-4; tax on, 154; types of, 153-4; structure of, 152-3
Building Societies' Association, 54, 152
bull (Stock Exchange), 118

Capital Gains Tax (CGT), 25, 43-4; on unit trusts, 150-51
capital transfer tax (CCT), 25-6, 44-7, 162
capitalization issue of shares, 130-31
car(s): company, 32; insurance, 165-6; purchase, 166
cheque(s): bounced, 13; stopping, 19
cheque cards, 18
child allowance, 30
child benefit, 26
children: earnings of, 156; insurance for, 89; tax allowances for, 30; child benefit, 26; covenants, 30; step-children, 26; parents abroad, 26
companies, public: conglomerates, 134; floated, 127; new shares, 127-9; prospectus, 128-9
company cars, 32
company pensions, 105-9; amounts, 107; *and* change of job, 106-7; disability provisions, 108; fixed, 107; lump sum on retirement, 107; reasons for joining, 108-9; widow's (widower's), 108
conglomerates, company, 133-5
Consumer Credit Act (1974), 17, 167
council mortgages, *see under* local authorities
Countdown discount cards, 17
covenants, tax on, 30
credit brokers, 22
credit cards, 16-17, 184
credit price and purchase price, 22

credit rating, 17-18
cumulative preference shares, 125-6
currency(ies), 174-5; early forms of, 171-3

Debentures, 126-7
Defence Bonds, tax on, 46
deferred ordinary shares, 124
Department of the Environment list of properties, 57
deposit accounts, bank, 19, 94
Diners Club card, 16-17
direct debits, 19-20
disablement, insurance against, 87-8
discount cards, 17
dividends, share, 132
divorce, 163-5; 'do-it-yourself', 163; life insurance and, 82-3; maintenance payments, 39-40, 164-5; taxation after, 39-40; additional personal allowance for children, 39
donations and capital transfer tax, 45

Earnings-related benefit, 90
elderly, tax allowances for, 28-30
emigration tax, 47
employee shares, 127
employees, insurance for, 89-90
endowment mortgages, 67-8
endowments from insurance policies, 46, 81-2
equity shares, 124
escalator mortgages, 70
estate duty, *see* capital transfer tax
Eurocheques, 185
European Monetary Agreement, 176
exchange controls, 179-80
Exchange Equalization Account, 179
executor for will, 163
extensions, home, loans for, 73-4

Family businesses and Capital Transfer Tax, 46
'Fed' (Federal Reserve Bank, New York), 174
fiduciary issue, 182
finance houses, 21-2; savings with, **94**
financial management, personal, 155-68
Financial Times: index, 133; *specimen pages*, 133, 141
fire insurance, 78
football pools, 161
foreign exchange, 169-70
'free' issues of shares, 130-31
fringe banks, 21
furniture, purchase of, 56

190